James Harrison Wilson

The Golden Fountain

Bible-truth unfolded - a book for the young

James Harrison Wilson

The Golden Fountain
Bible-truth unfolded - a book for the young

ISBN/EAN: 9783337170349

Printed in Europe, USA, Canada, Australia, Japan

Cover: Foto ©Lupo / pixelio.de

More available books at **www.hansebooks.com**

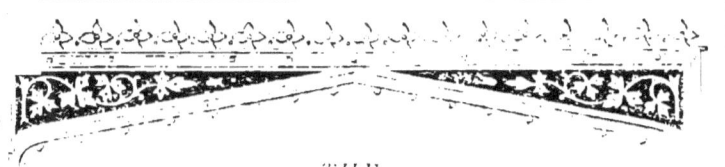

THE GOLDEN FOUNTAIN;

or,

Bible-Truth Unfolded

A BOOK FOR THE YOUNG.

By the

REV. JAMES H. WILSON, M.A.,

Fountainbridge Church, Edinburgh.

LONDON:
T. NELSON AND SONS, PATERNOSTER ROW;

1861.

Contents.

	Page
I. The Bible: The Use to be made of it,	9
II. The Bible: The Power of it,	30
III. Robbing God,	49
IV. The Great Question and Answer,	75
V. Christ our Example,	97
VI. The Holy Spirit,	121
VII. Companions,	142
VIII. Waste Not,	164
IX. Truth and Falsehood,	190
X. Prayer,	213
XI. Prayer (*continued*),	235
XII. Jesus Passing By,	259
XIII. The History of a Lost Soul,	293
XIV. The Account,	306

APPENDIX.

HYMNS AND MELODIES FOR THE YOUNG.

MY desire is, through this book, to be a drawer of water—a cup-bearer to the little ones; bringing to them, in an earthen vessel, a draught of the water of life from that truly Golden Fountain—THE BIBLE. In another form, some have already been helped by what is here provided, and these have thought that it might be helpful to others.

As accounting for occasional repetition, and the frequent use of illustrations taken from the humbler walks of life, I may state that these Addresses were originally delivered on the first Sabbath afternoon of each quarter, to the young people of my flock and district; and, amid the unceasing labours and cares connected with a young Mission-Church, there has been little time and less inclination for anything like elaboration. The one end in view has been, to come down to the understandings, to awaken the interest, and to reach the hearts of the young, in order to their being led, by the Spirit's blessing, to seek and to walk in the good way of the Lord.*

In the reading of these Addresses to children, either in the family or in larger groups, as in preaching children's sermons, I attach no small importance to the withholding of the text, till their attention has been so far excited by other thoughts bearing upon it. I therefore make no direct mention of text or subject, till the close of the introductory remarks. In such little gatherings as I have referred to, I would suggest that the evening exercise be begun and closed with prayer and the singing of the hymn at the beginning and end of each Address, to a lively and suitable tune. A psalm or hymn in the middle of the Address might also be sung to advantage, to prevent weariness; and asking for the various particulars as they occur, and at the close, would help materially to impress them on the memory.

I long to see an improvement in the singing in our families and Sabbath schools. Something more lively and attractive in this department is urgently called for, and would prove a

---

* It is long since that sentence in the "Pilgrim's Progress," describing part of the fare provided for the pilgrims at the house of Gaius, took my fancy: "The meat was *a dish of milk well crumbled;*—Gaius said, Let the boys have that, that they may grow thereby." I have taken this very much as my motto throughout.

powerful help alike to parents and teachers. I
do not see why, in juvenile gatherings, there
should not be far more of hymn-singing than
there is; and especially why, at family worship,
where there are young children, there should
not be substituted, now and then, a lively hymn,
which the little ones know and love, for the
psalm and heavy psalm-tune in which they feel
no interest. This, at least on special occasions,
as on Sabbath evenings, would make them feel
that family worship was an exercise in which
they had some concern, and might help to invest
it with a charm which, I fear, it too often lacks.
I yield to none in love and admiration of the
Psalms of David, and especially the Scotch
metrical version of them; but in our Home
Mission work, and in labouring among the
young, we have yet to learn that there is a power
in connection with good hymns and hymn tunes,
which has not been developed and taken advantage of as it might and should. I have made a
small beginning, in the way of trying to meet this
want, by adding a short Musical Appendix, containing, besides the hymns in the book, a number
of others, with melodies which will, I feel assured,
very soon commend themselves to my young
friends. Many of these are copyright; and for
the permission to use such as belong to others,

I have to express my acknowledgments to the respective composers or publishers. The harmonies of the whole have been beautifully arranged by Mr. T. L. Hately. A few—which are sufficiently indicated alike by the words and melodies—are inserted for very young children. I recommend the singing in two parts whenever this can be done. In addition to the Common Musical Notation, the Tonic Sol-fa Notation has been given, so as to make the tunes available to all classes of singers. I trust that this Appendix—unlike many others—will be frequently perused, and prove not the least valuable part of the volume.

In the preparation of the Addresses, I must own to having many a time betaken myself, especially for their tone and spirit, to the model writings for the young, of the much-loved and lamented M'Cheyne.

I commend this endeavour to guide and feed the lambs of the flock, to the prayers of those who love the little ones, and to the care of Him who was and is pre-eminently the CHILDREN'S FRIEND. May He be pleased to use it for the advancement of His own glory and the good of souls.

J. H. W.

FOUNTAIN BRIDGE MANSE,
February, 1861.

THE GOLDEN FOUNTAIN.

The Bible:
THE USE TO BE MADE OF IT.

THE HYMN.

A GLORY gilds the sacred page,
   Majestic, like the sun:
It gives a light to every age;
   It gives, but borrows none.

The Spirit breathes upon the word,
   And brings the truth to sight:
Precepts and promises afford
   A sanctifying light.

Let everlasting thanks be thine
   For such a bright display,
As makes a world of darkness shine
   With beams of heavenly day.

MY DEAR YOUNG FRIENDS,—I can fancy a very wonderful thing to have happened. I shall just tell it to you as it came into my mind. It is a great holiday in the town; thousands are assembled on the public streets in their best attire, their eyes wide awake to see whatever is to be seen; and while they are moving to and fro, something like a cloud is discovered falling from heaven; and as it comes nearer, it is seen to be a great roll, which at length alights on the ground in presence of the gathered crowds. Eagerly they rush forward to see what it is, and lo, it is written all over with bright golden letters, and when it is examined a little more closely, it is a very wonderful thing indeed. It tells how men came to be here, and what they were sent here for, and what will become of them afterwards. It tells about things that happened thousands of years ago, and what will be, thousands of years after this: how the world was made at first, and who made it, and what has befallen it since, and how it will again be destroyed. It tells how there is so much that is evil in the world, so much unhappiness, so many people weeping, and suffering, and dying; and how they may be made better, and have their hearts cheered, and their homes gladdened; how the miserable may be made happy, and the sorrowing comforted, and the poor and the sick made peaceful and contented. It tells how young and old may have true enjoyment in life, and peace in death, and something better beyond the grave. It tells each individual what he should be, and what he should do, and gives him directions how; and, in connection with these, reads his fortune to him as distinctly as if each name were separately mentioned, and shows how each may get a fortune indeed. In short, it tells all that one can need or rightly wish to know.

You can fancy what interest, what excitement there would be; how men would hurry home to tell their wives and children, who had not been there; how others would write of it to their friends; how it would be copied into the newspapers; how the telegraph would spread it over the country; how eager every one would be to have a copy for himself; how the poorest and the youngest would join together to buy it; what crowds would assemble in our churches, if it were announced that it would be read from the pulpits; how each would be asking his neighbour in the street, Have you heard the news? how you would see groups of children in the playground forgetting their play, and men in their workshops, and women at their doors, all eager to speak of it. And how those who wished well to the world, would send it off to other lands or go to tell them; because it was so good in itself, and there was no doubt where it had come from, and it was doing such good already, wherever it had been believed and acted on; and because it charged those to whom it came, to make it known everywhere. I cannot picture to you all that would be.

Has there never been anything like this? Has no such flying roll come down from heaven to earth—to *us*—as worthy to be believed as if we and thousands besides had seen it come; as really good tidings as we have described, telling all we have told, and doing all we have said, and infinitely more? Is it a mere fancy to be no more thought of, or is it not a blessed reality for which we do well to give thanks to God? Yes, beloved, it is all true; and if any one still does not see it, and asks, "When, where, how, did it come?" my text will throw some light upon it. I might have given you a text to-day without opening the Bible at all. I might for once have asked you to read the text, not from the *inside*, but from the *outside* of our Book of texts. I might hold it up to you, and say, "Read it there." Will you read what is on the back of your own books—"The Bible,"—"The Holy Bible,"—"The Holy Scriptures?" I feel as if that were too large, too wide a text for me to take up; and so now I call your attention more particularly to,—

2 Tim. iii. 15.—" From a child thou hast known the Holy Scriptures, which are able to make thee wise unto salvation, through faith which is in Christ Jesus."

Hundreds of years ago there lived an old Jewish lady, a godly woman, who loved her Bible, and knew it well, and taught it to her household—a kindly, gentle, winning, happy-looking old woman, as some grandmothers are still. She had a grown-up daughter, like herself, a lover of God and of her Bible—like herself, the anxious praying mother of one sweet child. When her husband died, it is likely the aged widow came to reside with her daughter; and you might have seen now the one, and now the other, taking the little boy on her knee, and telling him old Hebrew stories, even before he could read for himself, making him well acquainted with the only Scriptures they had then—the books of the Old Testament—so that even then he knew and loved the Bible. And as time wore on, how eagerly he read it to himself and to those who had first taught him; and when the first preachers of the gospel came to the town where he lived, and explained the Old Testament Scriptures in the light of New Testament events, how eagerly that boy listened, and drank in the truth, and was saved by it, and afterwards became himself a preacher, and one of the most loved and loving friends of the great Apostle Paul. Would you like to know their names? The grandmother was *Lois;* the mother *Eunice;* the godly youth *Timothy.* In the passage we have read, he is reminded, when grown-up to be a man and a minister, of all that we have been saying, and is set forth as a model for other young people to copy, especially in becoming early and savingly acquainted with the word of God.

Our text speaks of four things : I. The *use* to be made of Scripture — it is to be *known.* II. The *excellency* of Scripture — it is able to make wise unto salvation. III. The *means* by which it becomes efficacious—through faith which is in Christ Jesus. And, IV. The *time* when it may be thus used and blessed—from childhood onwards. I can only hope to overtake the first of these now.

The USE to be made of Scripture — it is to be *known.* "Thou hast known the Holy Scriptures." The

Bible is *God's* blessed book; it comes from him. He wrote it. It tells of him; it reveals his will, it describes his character, his holiness, his justice, his power, his wisdom, his love. The Bible is *our* blessed book; it comes to us—it tells us about ourselves, it describes our characters; it is a looking-glass in which we may see our own hearts; it sets forth the way of salvation; and while it warns of hell, it invites to heaven. It is, therefore, to be *known* by us; God meant it should. Now, as I desire your good, and would like to be helpful to you in this matter, I shall give you five directions that may aid you in "knowing" the Bible.

1. READ it! It certainly cannot be known without being *read*. Some one says, You need scarcely have told us that; everybody knows that. And yet I am not so sure but somebody needs the counsel, Read the Bible. It is much *to have* a Bible—a Bible of your own, with your own name on it, so that if you were leaving home you could take it with you, without asking any one's leave. I thank God for every young person among you who has a Bible, and to all such I earnestly say, because it needs to be said, *Read* it! Some keep their Bible as an ornament; some let it lie on the shelf so covered with dust that I could write upon it with my finger what I am now saying; some leave it in the church all the week, without having another at home; some lay it past in the pocket of their Sabbath-day jacket or Sabbath-day dress till the next Sabbath comes

round; some wrap it up carefully, and keep it under lock and key in their drawer or trunk; and some allow it to be knocked about till it is soiled and tattered, and eventually lost. I ask you if *such* are in the habit of *reading the Bible.* I have seen some of you, even boys and girls, reading the newspapers, to learn what news there was from India formerly, as from China now; what sufferings were endured, how our brave soldiers fought, and our helpless women and unoffending little ones fell by the hands of savage men, and I do not wonder at your being interested; and yet you don't read the Bible. Some of you, even boys and girls, read weekly journals and miscellanies, and pore over them till your young eyes are dim and your feelings are excited; and yet you don't read the Bible. Some of you, even boys and girls, will read any interesting book, any novel, any foolish tale that comes in your way, and lend them to each other, and weep over them; and yet you never read the Bible. My dear children, is this right? is this safe? can you expect to get the approval which Timothy got for "*knowing the Scriptures?*" It fills us with deepest alarm to see it—it fills our hearts with grief.

When first the Bible was introduced into this country, old grey-headed people, not content with hearing it read, learned to read for no other purpose than that they might be able to read it for themselves; and many a one in our own and in other lands has done the same since. They were willing to go to school, to sit on the same benches with their grandchildren, laboriously to learn their A, B, C, just that they might read the Bible; and will you be so unwise as to neglect it? Read it *often*—not only on Sabbath, but on week days—not only at school, but at home—not only to prepare your lessons, but for your soul's good. It is God's letter— it is your guide; it tells about eternal things, and if you would know it, you will often take a glance at it, and so spend a passing moment. Read it *through!* Why are these Bibles of yours so small that you can carry them in your pocket? why are they not so large as the family Bible, which you see read at worship, or the pulpit Bible, which the minister uses on Sabbath? why did they not extend over scores of volumes, and thousands of pages? why were they made so plentiful that you do not need merely to get the loan of one for a night, and that with great difficulty and by paying a high price, but have them in your own possession —left in your own hands? Was not all this in order that you might read them *through*, and know them *thoroughly?* Do you leave any part of your fathers' and brothers' letters unread, when they are far away from you? Do you think they would write as they do, if they had any notion of such treatment? Do they not fancy,—some of them away at the seat of war, as, on bended knee, they write with such difficulty, with no chair, or table, or desk but their soldier's kit, and with the noise of battle all around them, worn out after their day or night's hard work,—do they not fancy they see you, thousands of miles away, watching for the postman and hurrying in with the letter, and reading it over again and again, through and through, day after day, till the next letter comes? Is not that what you do? and will you not treat God's letter as you treat your soldier-brother's? Will you leave it unread, or leave the reading of it unfinished, putting off till you have more time, like many leaving an unread, unknown Bible behind you when you die? Will not He take it amiss? What if he should take his letter back again, or take away your power of reading it, by depriving you of that precious eye-sight which you have misimproved? Would you not have to say, "Lord, thou art just, for we have sinned?" Oh, find time, from your work, from your play, from your sleep, to *read* the Bible. And yet I must not stop here; it is not enough to read it; I must go deeper, and say—

2. SEARCH it! The full and thorough knowledge of anything is only got by searching. There is a ship at sea; a heavy fog has come on; there is nothing to be seen all round about, the very stars are shut out of view, and no longer serve to guide the vessel's course; and as the man at the mast-head hoarsely cries out, "Breakers ahead!" and the crew furl the sails, and the helmsman turns the wheel,—what is the captain about, old sailor as he is, now poring over his charts, and now glancing at the compass, and now loudly giving his orders? What can he mean by looking so often and so eagerly at that map-looking thing of his? That is his *chart* by which his course is guided, and he is *searching* it, to find out

where he is, and how he may steer his ship in safety,—to keep clear of a rock here and a shallow there, and make a good passage through the channel, and save his crew and his cargo, and at length gain the harbour. So says the great Teacher, "Search the Scriptures." Or a miser has died, leaving millions of money to hundreds of people; each relative is eager to know if he has any share in it, and what. See that man—he has got the will into his hand—how, first, his eye runs over the whole, and then his finger carefully traces word after word, and line after line; he does not observe the people coming into the room, he does not see them looking at him, and he does not care, he is so intent. What is he doing? *Searching* the will, in the hope of getting a fortune. So says Jesus, "Search the Scriptures." Or the mail has arrived from India; there is a rumour that some who were long ago reported as killed, have been concealed and protected by the natives in some distant Indian village, and here is the list. See that young woman, her hand trembling as it holds the paper, her countenance flushed, her heart beating quick, her eye as if it would start from its socket, as it comes nearer and nearer the end of the long catalogue. What is she doing? She is *searching* that precious list, in the hope of finding that she has still a living, loving father. So says the blessed Saviour, "Search the Scriptures."

Search them, know them thoroughly, get into their meaning, labour to understand them. They are worth more to you than the chart to the sailor, or the will to the pauper, or that list to her who fears she has lost her all. Many of you are in danger; there are rocks on which you may strike at any moment, gulfs into which you may sink, wrecking and losing your soul for eternity, past all remedy. You are poor, in the saddest sense of all, and you have none to help you, for you have not God as your Father, the only one who can give the help you need; you do not know anything about him, and unless he come to your rescue and give you his help, like poor uncared for orphans, you must miserably perish. But when I bring the Scripture to you, O what a guide, O what riches it sets forth, O what a Father it offers— will you not *search* it? Search it as you would a list of royal pardons if you were lying under sentence of death; search it as you would the doctor's prescription if you were sinking under some terrible disease; search it as you would for a door of escape, if you had belonged to one of those besieged, famished, slaughtered garrisons in India. Search there for life; search there for Christ, for such is his own word: " Search the Scriptures, for in them ye think ye have eternal *life*, and they are they which testify of *me*."

3. Love it! It is worthy of your love; it is the *holy* Scripture, so pure, so blessed, so like the God who sent it. Some one says, "What connection has *loving* the Bible with *knowing* it? I know these lessonbooks of mine well enough, but I am far enough from loving them, and I can know them without loving them." Not so fast, my friend; I am not quite sure of

that. At least I am sure of this, that the book you love, you will know best; and still more sure am I of this, that the Bible cannot be rightly known without being really loved. "O how *love I thy law!*" says David; and then what follows as the effect of this? "*It is my study all the day!*" You cannot know the Bible without taking some trouble with it: it is not just so easy to be understood that you scarcely need to think of it, or put yourself at all about. It needs pains, diligence, earnestness, perseverance; and to master the difficulties in your way, you must *love* it. I have got two letters by post; the first I open is ill-written, I cannot even make out from whom it comes, it seems to be of little consequence to me, or to anybody else, and after trying for a little, I lose my temper with it, and throw it aside. The next I open is not very plain, it is written in a small hand, some of the words are contracted, it will require much pains and much patience, but I know the hand without even looking at the signature, and my heart leaps when I see it, for I am far away from home, living among strangers, and the letter is from MY MOTHER. How I clasp it to my bosom; how the tears fall as I read it; how I forget everything but her who sent it; how I get over all the difficulties, and only think how kind she was to take the trouble, with that dim eye and trembling hand of hers; how I kiss that dear name over and over; how I say to it, "My mother's letter! how I love you, **next** best to my mother herself!" and I would sit up at night to read it when others were off to bed, and I would carry it with me in my walks, and I would have it read to me if I were sick and sad! Oh, would I not know and love my mother's letter?

Children, children! do you love the book of God—your heavenly Father's letter—written with his own hand, sent by his most trusty messengers, telling of all his love to you, of all his compassion for you, of all his sympathy with you; of all he has *done* for you, and *given* for you, and *promised* to you, and *prepared* for you: how he has already given his best beloved and only-begotten, Jesus, that in and with him he might freely give you all things; how, after having foolishly and wickedly forsaken him, he is willing, waiting, wearying to receive you to his heart and to his home? Oh, can you but read it, and love it as you read it, and weep, and stop, and read again, and as you go on, love it the more, till at length you clasp it to your bosom and say—

> " Holy Bible! book divine,
> Precious treasure thou art mine!"
> How I love thee!

That is the way rightly to know it—the only way!

I will tell you of a sight—a sad sight, I have sometimes seen. I have seen young people going to read this blessed book against their will, and with sulky, angry look. When they had been reading some interesting book, which they did not wish to lay aside, and their parents kindly asked them, after they had had a good spell at their own book, to take up God's, I have seen them take it up irreverently and open it carelessly, and as it lay on their knee or on their table, they scarcely saw what was before them, or if they did, it was as a hated taskbook, which they thought it cruel to have put into their hands at all. I fear that is a feeling to which some of you are no strangers. Did my ear deceive me when I thought I heard such words as these? "O that Bible, that hateful Bible! I cannot bear to be bored with it in this way; I wish I might never see it again, or never till I should be old, and sick, and dying; it might serve some purpose then." Father, forgive them for they know not what they do. They cannot "know" the Scriptures.

What stories I could tell of the Bible being loved. I wish you had seen the people of this country when the Bible was first introduced. I might show you even on week-days, a crowded church, and a Bible chained to the pulpit or to a pillar, which one read, others eagerly drinking it in, and aloud thanking God for it, while they sang, "The lines have fallen to us in pleasant places." I might show you the first load of Bibles taken to Wales just fifty years ago, the people going out to meet the cart that carried them, as if it had been Israel's ark, drawing it in triumph into the town, bearing away the blessed volume with overflowing heart, young people sitting up all night to read it, and labourers taking it with them to the fields and loving it as I cannot describe. I might show you the Tahitians, when France took possession of their island not many years ago, hurrying to the mountains and leaving their Bibles with the missionaries till they should come back, to save them carrying them so far; and ere long they were back in the face of all danger, to say they *could not live without their Bibles*, and must have them whatever should befall. " A few hundred years ago," I read the other day, " a labouring man would have required to give all his earnings for eight or ten years to buy a Bible." A little further down, they were still very costly, and yet I find two young apprentice lads joining their earnings together for many a long day to buy a Bible. Oh, how they prized it! A Hindoo is dying, and under his head lies his treasure. What is it? Some dirty scraps of paper, worn and tattered, which he had got years ago,—texts of Scripture translated and written by a missionary, before Bibles in the language were to be had. There is a blind boy; he has got some volumes of the Bible for the blind, he hurries with them into his own room, and with beaming face takes up each, feels it over and over, and kisses it on both sides, as much as to say, How I do love you and wish to know you! There is an Irish peasant copying with his own hand the entire Scriptures. There is a poor widow in an English town. The looms have stopped, and the people are in deepest distress. A few pence are all her living. She has gone to lay out her money; a penny for bread, a penny for tea and sugar, and a half-penny for some other thing: she would only have one luxury, and rather want a meal than be without *it;* and her last penny goes for *oil,* "that I may see to read my Bible in the long dark nights, for it is my only comfort now when every other comfort has gone away." There is a soldier hiding it in his bosom as he goes to the wars, and a sailor tying it round his waist as the most precious thing on board, ere the vessel goes down. There is one calling it his best earthly friend; and another, his book of bank notes; and another, sweeter than honey, better than gold. Oh how they knew it, because they loved it!

"Did ye ask me if I had a Bible?" said a poor old widow in London,—"did ye ask me if I had a Bible? Thank God, I have a Bible. What should I do without my Bible? It was the guide of my youth, and it is the staff of my age. It wounded me, and it healed me; it condemned me, and it acquitted me; it showed me I was a sinner, and it led me to the Saviour; it has given me comfort through life, and I trust it will give me hope in death." Oh, how I love thy law! Can you but love it? will you not love it? Then, indeed, you will know it.

4. REMEMBER it. It must be remembered if it is to be really known; it will surely be remembered if it is loved. How the little Jews remembered their Scripture long ago, so that even had the parchment-rolls been lost on which the Scriptures were written, they could almost have replaced them from memory! How Jesus remembered the Scripture; how often he refers to it; how familiar he shows himself with it, leaving us an example to copy! How the godly in all ages, in all

countries, at all times of life, have loved to remember it! There is nothing in all the world so worthy of being remembered; nothing so good for storing the memory with. Some one says, "But I am not good at learning off things." There is a boy who learned off a whole book of songs, and he did not take long to it either, and *he* had not a very good memory. How was it? He just took verse by verse, and *his heart went along with it.* Another boy knows, I cannot tell you how much of Scripture,—verses, chapters, books. How? Just as in the other case. He took it verse by verse, and his heart was in it. That is just what I would have you to do. I would not burden you with chapters: just one verse to-day, and another to-morrow, and another next day, and soon, with God's help and blessing, you would know the Scriptures. I would like if you would begin that at once, and make the experiment. I have heard of a little boy who *put his books into his head.* Have you done that with this Book? have you put it into your *memory?*—still more, into your *heart?* "Thy word have I hid in my heart." You should not put it into your memory as "into a *coffin,*" to lie buried there, dead, useless; but as "into *a cradle,*" as one says, "to be cherished, to gather life and power." *

My dear children, do not forget the Bible. It is a

---

* See Dr. Eadie's "Lectures on the Bible to the Young," a most interesting and instructive volume.

sad loss, when people grow old or become palsy-stricken, to have the memory fail; but it is sadder still, to have a place in the memory for everything but the word of God. See that old woman, as she is getting blind, going from one shop to another, as if on the most urgent business. Let us look in and see what she is doing. I see now; she is in search of a pair of glasses. Anxiously she tries pair after pair. She would give almost all she has to get them. I feel interested in her, and when I inquire, I find she has come to know something of God's truth. She had neglected it in her early days, and so has nothing to fall back on now. She feels it a terrible want, and would fain make up for it yet, so far as she can. She wants the spectacles to help her to read her Bible, for she can knit her stockings without them. She has begun to learn it; and often she tells her young friends, not to lose the precious season of youth for laying up in the heart the knowledge of the Book of life.

5, and lastly. PRAY over it. All will not do without this. You will never come to know the Scriptures without prayer. If your teacher were to give you a paper of great importance to you, but written in a foreign language,—in Latin or Greek—and were to say, "Now, take this and make yourself acquainted with it: if you should ever be at a loss to make it out, or to understand it, just come to me and ask me, and I'll explain it to you;"—wouldn't it be very strange if you were never to apply to so kind a teacher,—if you were to work away at it yourself; when you failed, getting discouraged, and beginning to cry, and at length laying it aside altogether? Now, we cannot understand the Bible of ourselves. God himself tells us that: but he tells us also that the Holy Spirit will explain it—will open it up to men—will throw light on what is dark in it, and that he will give the Holy Spirit to them that ask him. Dear children, have you ever asked the Holy Spirit's teaching? Do you ever pray before you begin to read your Bible, and while you are reading it, and after you have done with it? Do you ever send up some little prayer like this, "Lord, teach me to understand thy word. Lord, give me thy Holy Spirit to open up the Scriptures?" Oh, pray when you read. Be like one of our great Scottish worthies, who, when about to speak in an important case in the General Assembly, kept writing busily on a piece of paper, and when one looked over his shoulder thinking he was taking notes,—he had been *praying*, and his paper was all written over with, " Lord, give light! Lord, give light!" Be that your prayer when you read the Bible. Be like little Samuel, when God spoke to him : "Speak, Lord, for thy servant heareth!" I have heard of one who never read the Bible but on his knees, that is, never without prayer. Go you and do likewise. " Open thou mine eyes that I may behold wondrous things out of thy law."

Now, all these five particulars were true of Timothy, otherwise Paul would not have spoken to him as he did.

You have better opportunities in many respects than ever Timothy had. You have a better Bible—more full and complete than he had. Oh, will you not use yours as he used his—read it, search it, love it, remember it, pray over it? If you do not "know" the Scriptures thus, what shall I say? Nothing will make up for it. You are like a traveller on a trackless moor with neither light nor guide. You are like a blind man on the verge of a precipice, unaware of his danger or how to escape. You are in danger of being lost—lost—lost for ever! Oh, it will be a terrible thing if *you* neglect, if *you* live and die without the saving knowledge of the Scriptures! Your Bibles will rise up against you at the day of judgment, and your Sabbath-school teachers, and your churches, and your ministers; ay, this address, in which I would fain commend the Bible to you, will only add to your guilt, and increase your condemnation. And, just a word for those who have no Bibles like you. Will you not pity them—will you not pray for them—will you not seek to send to them the book which tells the most blessed tidings men ever heard, " Glory to God in the highest, and on earth peace, good-will to men;" "Unto you is born A SAVIOUR, which is CHRIST THE LORD?"

THE HYMN.

FATHER of mercies, in thy word
    What endless glory shines!
For ever be thy name adored,
    For these celestial lines.

  Here the Redeemer's welcome voice
   Spreads heavenly peace around ;
  And life and everlasting joys
   Attend the blissful sound.

  O may these heavenly pages be
   My ever dear delight ;
  And still new beauties may I see,
   And still increasing light !

  Divine Instructor, gracious Lord,
   Be thou for ever near ;
  Teach me to love thy sacred word,
   And view my Saviour there.

NOTE.—Let me suggest the use of your pencil in reading the Bible. When any verse seems specially interesting or applicable to you, mark it neatly on the margin, and underline any particular words, thus :—

  | Those that seek me <u>early,</u> shall find me.

It is pleasant in after-life to come back on these marks made in early days.

The Bible:

THE POWER OF IT.

THE HYMN.

HOLY Bible, book divine,
 Precious treasure thou art mine!
Mine, to tell me whence I came;
Mine, to teach me what I am;

Mine, to chide me when I rove;
Mine, to show a Saviour's love;
Mine art thou, to guide my feet;
Mine, to judge, condemn, acquit;

Mine, to comfort in distress,
If the Holy Spirit bless;
Mine, to show by living faith,
How to triumph over death;

Mine, to tell of joys to come,
Mine, to show the sinner's doom:
Holy Bible, book divine,
Precious treasure, thou art mine!

Y DEAR YOUNG FRIENDS,—I wonder what you would say, if I were to put the question to you, "What do you think is *the principal thing*—the principal thing in the world?" I would get many answers, some strange enough, some foolish enough—perhaps not one giving me exactly the answer I want. I suppose each one would just name the thing he likes best—the thing he would be most delighted to get. One child would say, money; another,

learning; another, fine clothing; another, good living; and some, I daresay—and these would not be the furthest wrong—a kind mother and a happy home! Each would say, "*That* seems to me the principal thing." Now, the answer I am going to give you is the correct one. I am quite sure of it, because God says it, and he knows best; and I would have you to receive his word as true: "WISDOM *is the principal thing.*" This question was once virtually put to Solomon, the young king of Israel, and put in this particular way, that he was left to choose whatever he liked, by Him who was able to grant his request, whatever it might be—by *God*. For God said, "Ask what I shall give thee." And what think you was his choice? Not long life, nor riches, nor power and grandeur, nor the life of his enemies,—none of all these; but *wisdom*. And Solomon never rued his choice, and God approved it, for we are told, "The speech pleased the Lord, that Solomon had asked this thing." And so, long after, when he had tried it, and could speak from experience, we find the wise man saying, "Wisdom is the principal thing; therefore, get wisdom, and with all thy wisdom, get understanding." I could scarcely resist the temptation to take that for my text to-day.

But another question comes up, "What kind of wisdom is it that is the principal thing?" for there are many kinds. There is wisdom in making money; wisdom in keeping out or getting out of difficulties; wisdom in knowing a great deal about men and things—

about the stars and the earth, and the sea, and the atmosphere—about plants, and animals, and stones, and other substances—about steam and electricity—about the world's past history and the ways of the world as it is now, and I don't know how many things besides. Some people have a natural turn for these things. Of some men we say, "Such a one is born a genius;" and by hard study, and long and close application, they make great progress, and become famous men—astronomers, or geologists, or botanists, or zoologists, or chemists, or such-like names. My dear children, the wisdom of which I speak is different from all these, is higher than all these, and better far. These are the wisdoms of earth—this is the wisdom of heaven; these are the wisdoms of men—this is the wisdom of God; these are very useful, and important, and good for time—this is all-important and needful for eternity. Without it you cannot live a good life; without it you cannot die a happy death; without it you cannot spend a blessed eternity. This is a wisdom which we have not naturally, and have no natural taste or turn for. We do not need to go to college, and to study many "text-books," as they are called, in order to get it. It is only to be got in one way—in one quarter. Of what kind can it be? *Wisdom unto salvation.* These others, however good and useful, cannot tell me *how I am to be saved*, and that is my great concern. They tell me nothing of salvation; they will not lead me back to God; they will not guide me to heaven; and, however they may impress me with God's wisdom, and power, and goodness, they are all silent about a Saviour for lost sinners. And so I say there is something better than to be a *philosopher;* and that is, *to be a Christian,*—a man, or woman, or child, *wise unto salvation.* And where is this kind of wisdom to be got,—this which is now the "principal thing?" for we have come to it at last. Where shall we hear of it? Turn to —

2 Tim. iii. 15.—" From a child THOU HAST KNOWN THE HOLY SCRIPTURES, which are able to make thee wise unto salvation, through faith which is in Christ Jesus."

In my last address I called your attention to the *use* to be made of Scripture. It is *to be "known;"* and, in order to knowing it rightly, I gave you these five counsels: 1. *Read* it—read it *all*—read it *often*. 2. *Search* it. 3. *Remember* it. 4. *Love* it. 5. *Pray over* it. I promised next to speak of the *excellency* of Scripture—to answer the question, "*Why* should we seek to know it?" Or I might thus express it—*the power of Scripture;* it is "able to make wise unto salvation."

Now, in thinking over this subject—*the* POWER *of the Bible,* I have felt somewhat in difficulty as to how I should take it up. Perhaps I should, first of all, call your attention to some of the *figures* under which the word of God is spoken of in Scripture. For instance, it is called a LAMP—a LIGHT; and it is such in more ways than one. There is a midnight thief prowling about that house, and after having looked round and round, and satisfied himself that he is unobserved by any one, he sets to work, as he thinks, in safety in the dark. But just as he is effecting an entrance, the watchman turns the corner, and suddenly flashes his lantern full on the offender. There he is, caught in the very act; so thoroughly taken by surprise, that he can neither deny his guilt nor attempt to escape: terror-stricken and self-condemned, he at once yields himself up. Such is the Word; one is engaged in a sinful course, as if no eye saw him, as if he were sinning in the dark, when of a sudden the word flashes forth; some passage of it stands written before him as if in characters of flame; and as it lays bare his sin, and lifts up the hand of vengeance, it makes the sinner tremble, as it says, "Thou art the man!" Or again, there is a traveller who has lost his road, and been overtaken by night and darkness. He knows not whither he is going, and is wandering about in utter despair, when a guide overtakes him, lamp in hand, sending forth a strong and steady light, and on he marches with glad heart. So, to me, a benighted traveller in a dark world, in danger of losing myself for eternity, the light of the word has come, and I sing as I go, "Thy word is a lamp unto my feet, and a light unto my path!" What a blessed power it has!

It is compared to a FIRE. Do you see that ugly-looking mass of earth? It is said to be precious, for there are bright golden particles to be seen here and there; and yet, as it is, it is useless. But the fire is applied, and the mass begins to dissolve, the dross separates from the precious metal, and at length you get the pure gold. And there is a precious soul, embedded in worldliness and sin, and in danger of being cast away as bad metal; but the word of God is brought to bear upon it, and, like a strong heat, it cannot be resisted—what is evil is thrown off, and at length you have a soul reflecting the image of its God. Hence the prayer of Jesus : " Sanctify them *through thy truth;* thy word is truth." " Is not my word like as a fire ?" See the power of Scripture.

It is compared to a HAMMER. You have seen a man breaking stones by the road-side. He has taken up a large piece of hard whinstone, and again, and again, and again, he strikes, and each time he seems to make no impression; but he perseveres, and at length it yields to repeated strokes, and is broken to pieces like the rest. Your heart, dear children, is like that whinstone, so that the Bible calls it a stony heart ; it seems as if nothing could make an impression on it. But the word is tried ; sometimes there is the heavy blow of a threatening, and sometimes the gentle stroke of love, and at length you see, as the result, a *broken heart*—a humble, contrite spirit. " Is not my word as the hammer, that breaketh the rock in pieces ?" What so powerful as this ?

It is compared to a SWORD. There is a diseased man, gradually sinking under his distemper, till a skilful physician comes in, who draws his lancet and rips up the diseased part, and probes it to the bottom; and from that moment he begins to recover, even though the pain is greater than ever it was before. Such is the disease of sin in a man—producing drowsiness, insensibility, deadness, so that no effort is made with a view to recovery. But the Lord sends his word. The Spirit takes his sword, and pierces the sinner's heart, so that under the smarting pain he cries out, "What shall I do?" and again and again it is repeated, till the same word that wounded, heals. "The word of God is quick and powerful, sharper than any two-edged sword." Oh, the power of Scripture! Beloved children, let it be our prayer, that the Bible may be all this to us—a lamp and light to convince and guide us, a fire to purify us, a hammer to break our hearts, a sword to pierce them, that so it may prove itself, in a blessed way to us, *the power of God.*

Again, I might show the power of the Bible, *by what it has done.* And here I could say very much. An American whaler founders in a storm; the sailors take to the boats, two of which, after drifting for days to and fro, come in sight of an island in the Pacific. One of them pulls to land, and when the natives see it, instead of helping the men, they rush upon them and devour them. A sight like that drives off the other, and after terrible sufferings, its crew are at length picked up by a friendly ship. Years pass on, and another vessel is wrecked on these same shores. One of the old crew is there, and as he tells the sad tale to his comrades, as they stand shivering on the beech, they know not what to do. Stealthily they creep among the bushes, till they reach the brow of a hill, fearing every moment lest they should be discovered, when the whole party is startled, as one of their number springs up, clapping his hands and shouting aloud, " SAFE ! SAFE ! SAFE !" They thought he was mad, till they too looked where he pointed, and saw in the midst of a native village a *village church*, as in their own loved land, telling that protection and help were sure. And so it was. And how the change ? It was the Bible—the blessed Bible that had done it. That native village, that native church, these cannibals changed into civilized, into Christian men, proclaim the power of the Bible !

Or let us look nearer home. There is a man of whom you would have been afraid—an idler, a gambler, a drunkard, and a terror to all about him. Hitherto a stranger to the Bible, he now begins to read it. What is the effect of it ? " Sir," says his sister to the priest who would have them to lay aside that bad book, " since he began to read that book he is another man; he works with industry, no longer goes to the tavern, no longer touches cards, brings home his money to his poor old mother, and now our life at home is quiet and delightful." *That* has been oftener than once or twice ; and many a mother, and sister, and daughter, has had cause with overflowing heart to speak of the blessed power of the Bible. Now, perhaps, you would like me just to go on in this way throughout the sermon, and do my best *to entertain* you. My dear children, that is not my purpose or desire. I would like rather to *profit* you,—to come closer home, and try to get the power of the word brought to bear upon *you*. Let us, then, return to our text and look at these words, "The Holy Scriptures, which are able to make thee wise unto salvation." Let me be like the chemist, who separates bodies into their various component parts, and tells you about each of these. What are the elements of *wisdom unto salvation?* I think they are two, and Scripture furnishes them both,—*the knowledge of ourselves*, and *the knowledge of God;* so that I ask this wisdom when I offer the twofold prayer, "Lord, show me *myself!* Lord, show me *thyself!*"

1. THE KNOWLEDGE OF OURSELVES. That is the first part of this heavenly wisdom which the Scriptures are able to give. Perhaps, my dear child, you think you know yourself very well; it is the oldest acquaintanceship you have, and the most intimate and unbroken, so that if you know anybody, it is *yourself*. If you are right in this thought of yours, you have begun to be wise. But I am afraid you are wrong. I fear you are still a stranger to yourself—you don't know your own heart—you don't know what you really are. You know what like your face is, you know what like your personal appearance is, so that if you saw your portrait you could not mistake it. But the same is not true of your heart and of your life, so that when the likeness of these is held up before you, you don't recognise it;

you say that it represents some other person. Do you know yourself *as a sinner*,—Have you ever seen yourself in that light? Do you know yourself *to be lost*,—Have you ever seen yourself in that light? I fear not; and I'll tell you why.

There is a block of houses on fire. Every house has been cleared of its inmates without delay, glad to leave their furniture behind, if they may have their lives. But yonder, far up, as the partition is laid open, I see a sleeping boy, lying in his comfortable bed, smiling perhaps in his sleep, dreaming, fancying that he is the son of a lord, that he has got what he so often wished, and oh, he is proud and he is happy! Poor boy, he does not know his danger. And you shout, and shout, and shout, till at length he awakes, and listens, and looks about him; and then the truth flashes upon him, and he springs from his bed, and never thinks of going back to it. See him, now at one window, and now at another, trying door after door, and passage after passage; hear him crying for help with cries that go to the very heart. He cannot sleep now, and it is well he is awake. My dear young friend, *that is you*. You are sleeping, you are dreaming, and yet you are lost,—the fire of God's wrath is burning around you, the fire of hell is burning beneath you, and any moment you may be enveloped in the flames; and, poor boy! poor girl! you don't know it. For if you did, you would be up, you would be in deep distress, you would be crying out, "What shall I do? How shall I be saved? Oh, save me, or I perish!"

And you would never rest till you had found salvation. And so the Word comes and knocks at your door, and says, "Awake! get up! flee for your life! You are sinners against God, children though you be; and you are lost, children though you be; and you are in danger of being lost for ever, children though you be. Up! get you out of this place, for the Lord will destroy it!" And if you listen to the Word when it speaks to you thus, and if you bestir yourselves, and if you look about you, and see that what it says is true, and seek help,—oh, it has done you a good turn indeed,—it has *begun* to make you wise unto salvation.

The plague has broken out: unless it be taken in time there is no chance of escape. And on that man beside me, I see the marks of it; I see it on his brow, I read it in his eye, and as I put my finger on his pulse, doubt there can be none. But he will not stir. He says it is a mere fancy. He feels no pain, he sees no danger, and as I almost force him to that looking-glass and say to him, "Look there!" how his colour changes!—another instant and he is off to where the best of help is to be had. Dear child, *that is you!* You have got the plague, the plague of sin, the worst and most terrible of all; the marks of it are unmistakably on your soul, and if *you* could only look into a faithful mirror, you would see as clearly as if the letters were stamped upon your forehead, L-O-S-T—*Lost!* But you don't know it—you don't believe it, or you could get no rest. You would be off to the one Physician—you would be pleading for the one remedy that can recover you from it—you could not do otherwise. And the Bible is such a glass, in which you may see yourself, and get a knowledge of yourself; and as you turn over leaf after leaf, you will know more of yourself; and if only you will not look at it *in the dark*, as so many people do, and so see nothing, but will seek light from heaven, and cry, "O send thy light forth and thy truth," you will get such a sight as you will never forget while you live—a sight of *yourself!* And when the Word gives that, it has at last begun to make you wise unto salvation,—you have taken the first step to it. Make this, then, your prayer, "Lord, make me to know *myself!*" for we must all begin there.

The power of the Bible in this way is wonderful. People have often thought the Bible must have been written just for them. When it has been read or preached, they have thought that the preacher must have known about them, and had them in view; for the word tells just what they have been thinking; it sets before them what they have been doing,—it shows them themselves. So it was with a youth who lived long ago, whose name was Augustine. He had a godly, praying mother; but, unlike her, he neither feared God nor regarded man, till he seemed hardened in ungodliness. One day he thought he heard a voice saying to him in Latin, again and again, "*Tolle lege! tolle lege!*" —" Take and read! take and read!" He took his Bible, he opened, he read; it was the thirteenth chapter of Romans, "Let us walk honestly as in the day, not in rioting and drunkenness," &c. "But put ye on the Lord Jesus Christ and make no provision for the flesh," &c. And even then that Scripture began to make him wise unto salvation. Dear children, hear a voice saying to you to-day, "Take and read! take and read!" Who knows but it may be the beginning of salvation to you? For He is faithful who hath promised.

2. THE KNOWLEDGE OF GOD. That is the second ingredient in this wisdom unto salvation, and we have it too in the Scriptures. When we have got the other, we have begun to be wise, we are on the way to wisdom; and yet we have but *begun*, and if we stop short there, we must perish after all. Having come to know ourselves, we must now pray that other prayer, "Lord, show me thyself!" Yes, beloved, we must get a sight of ourselves,—and that is a strange sight; but more, we must get *a sight of God*,—and that is more wonderful still. I cannot be saved without a sight of God. And where shall I get the sight? In the Bible. Blessed be God, he has given us a likeness of himself there. Did you ever search the Scriptures for that? I spoke of the Bible being a *light*; and so it is, not only setting myself before myself, but shedding light, if I may so speak, on the God who formerly was hidden from my view, giving me the "light of the knowledge of the glory of God." I spoke of the Bible being a *glass*; and so it is, in which I may behold, not only my own face, my own heart, my own history, but also the reflection of God,—ay, and

the one as answering to the other—the very God for such a being as I am.

And what do I learn about God? His holiness, hating sin; his wisdom, all-knowing; his power, all-mighty; his justice, doing right. And is there any comfort in all this? None. Taking this with what we saw before, it only makes my case more hopeless; it shows me more plainly than ever that I am lost; it makes me feel like that drowning man whom the now back-going tide is carrying out to sea—the very thought of salvation is vain. Ah, but our text says, "Which are able to make thee wise unto salvation," and so we must go further. In a certain district in Russia, there is to be seen, in a solitary place, a pillar with this inscription, "Greater love hath no man than this, that a man lay down his life for his friend." That pillar tells a touching tale, which many of you must have heard. It was a wild region, infested with wild beasts, and as a little party travelled along, it soon became too plain that these were on their track. The pistols were fired, one horse after another was left to the ravenous wolves, till, as they came nearer and nearer, and nothing else remained to be tried, the faithful servant, in spite of the expostulations of his master, threw himself into the midst of them, and by his own death saved his master! That pillar marks the spot where his bones were found; that inscription records the noble instance of attachment. But there is another nobler still. There is another pillar, and on it I read, "Herein is love, not that we loved

God, but that he loved us, and sent his Son to be the propitiation for our sins." That pillar is the Bible—the noble pillar of Scripture, written all over with loving words, and telling of salvation. As I walk round it, I read such sayings as these: "God so loved the world that he gave his only-begotten Son" to save it.* "God was in Christ reconciling the world to himself, not imputing to men their trespasses."† Now, I read of *God in Christ* as a God of *grace*, loving sinners, saving sinners, delighting in saving them—able to save *me*, willing to save *me*, waiting to save *me*, and such as me, the worst of sinners; and now I begin to get a glimpse of what that means, "wise unto salvation."

During the time of the persecutions, it was customary to cast God's people into bottle-shaped dungeons, letting them down by a narrow opening into a wide and deep cavern below, so that escape seemed impossible, unless, like flies, they could creep along the roof. If you could have gone to them at midnight, and told them of one expedient, which you yourself had found effectual, by which they could escape from that living grave,—might not your words, in a temporal sense, have been said to make them wise unto salvation, to be the means of saving them? I was once told by an old man, a native of the town, of a strange room in the High Street of Edinburgh. In the troublous times that are not so long gone by, a man was often a prisoner ere ever he was aware, and, however, brave, he could not have fought his

---

* John iii. 16.   † 2 Cor. v. 19.

way to freedom. But had he been a prisoner there,—if I have been rightly informed,—he might, in seeking to while away his time, have come upon an old book containing good tidings. It would have told him of an invisible door in the room where he was,—known but to few, the panelling was so contrived,—opening into a passage that led underground until one got without the city wall; and such tidings to such a one, had been, in a temporal sense, able to make him wise unto salvation.

Children! we are in the dungeon, not for serving God, but for *sin;* and it is like to be imprisonment for life— that is, for ever, for the soul lives for ever; and I have tried to climb these walls in vain, and am now in dark despair. But lo! a letter comes flying down to me, sent by some good hand; ay, it is from heaven. God's hand sent it, telling me of one way of escape,— that one way sure to lead to safety,—that one way, CHRIST! Children! we are in the house that is intended to be for us a house of death, and there are enemies all round about,—not armed men, but wicked devils, rejoicing to keep us in hopeless captivity; but lo! I have come upon an old book, covered with dust, long neglected, which tells of an invisible door and of a secret passage by which I may get my life for a prey, and baffle my foes,—that door, that passage, CHRIST! And that letter, that old book, is THE BIBLE, in which I read such words as these: "I am the door; by me if any man enter in he shall be saved"—"I am the way, and the truth, and the life: no man cometh unto the

Father, but by me." And when I read it, and believe it; when I enter in at the door and press along the way; when, by God's grace, I take Christ to be my Saviour, only and complete, freely and for ever; when, on the strength of his bare word, and with it as my alone warrant, I lay claim to Christ as my Lord and my God; —then, then, beloved, these Scriptures have been blessed of God to make me "wise unto salvation."

Then, indeed, I can call the Bible the *Book of Salvation*, for it has guided me to it; or, with John Newton, my Book of Bank-notes, all others but as silver and copper; or, with another, "my only one book, but that book the best." I can sing with David, "The law of thy mouth is better unto me than thousands of gold and silver. The law of the Lord is perfect, converting the soul; the testimony of the Lord is sure, making wise the simple." And if you ask me now, how I know that the Bible is the word of God, I reply like an old negro, upwards of seventy, who could neither read nor write, when argued with on infidel grounds, "Though I cannot even read it, I know it by *its effects upon my own heart.*" Oh, how the saints in heaven will praise God for the Bible through all eternity—and shall we not praise him for it now? It is the language of heaven, which we cannot learn too well beforehand; and which, even if we be already among the saved, will, the better we know it, fit us the more for the society and converse of heaven.

And now, dear children, the question is, Will you be made thus wise? It will not come to you and force you; you must go to it and ask to be taught. You must go to the Bible *on purpose*. Have you ever done so? If not, go this day. It will be sad to have had that which makes wise unto salvation, and after all to perish. "It might have made *me* thus wise, but I would not!" It is not the Bible's fault,—it is *your own;* and better you had never had a Bible than be unsaved by it. It is not enough *to have a Bible:* the mere *having* of it will never make you savingly wise. Many are now among the lost who had their Bibles, like you. It is not enough to read and learn the Bible: the mere reading and learning of it will never make you wise unto salvation. Many are now among the lost who read it and learned it, like you. What more, then, is needed? There is an Ethiopian noble driving along in his chariot, reading the Scriptures, and the servant of the Lord draws near, and stops his chariot, and asks him, "*Understandest* thou what thou readest?" That is my one question to you. The other is, "*Believest* thou what thou readest?" for without faith there can be no blessing. Our text says, "By faith, which is in Christ Jesus."

And can you be content to keep all the blessing to yourselves? Will you not be like that fisherman who, when overtaken by the blast, and past all hope of making to land, was guided at last by the light in his cottage window; will you not be like him, when, again restored to his family and home, he resolved that from that night forward, his little lamp should never be taken from his window, but should ever send forth its cheering light, if perchance some other hard-pressed mariner might be blessed by it as he had been—thanking God for having been helped by it himself, and now for the privilege of helping others? Will you not be like that African woman, who, as she watches over her sick child in a far off land, weeps,—not for her child, but for her mother? See her holding up her Bible, wet with tears; and hear her words: "My mother will never see this book; she'll never hear its glad tidings. She'll never hear that glad sound that I have heard. The light that shone on me will never shine on her. She'll never taste the love of the Saviour that I have tasted. O my mother! my mother!"

THE HYMN.

CAN we, whose souls are lighted
    With wisdom from on high;
Can we to men benighted
    The lamp of life deny?
Salvation! O salvation!
    The joyful sound proclaim,
Till each remotest nation,
    Has learned Messiah's name.

Waft, waft, ye winds, his story,
    And you, ye waters, roll,
Till like a sea of glory,
    It spreads from pole to pole:
Till, o'er our ransom'd nature,
    The Lamb for sinners slain,
Redeemer, King, Creator,
    In bliss returns to reign.

Robbing God.

THE HYMN.

AMONG the deepest shades of night,
    Can there be one that sees my way?
Yes; God is like a shining light,
    That turns the darkness into day.

When every eye around me sleeps,
    May I not sin without control?
No; for a constant watch he keeps
    On every thought of every soul.

If I could find some cave unknown,
    Where human foot had never trod,
Yet there I could not be alone,—
    On every side there would be God.

He smiles in heaven, he frowns in hell;
    He fills the air, the earth, the sea;
I must within his presence dwell—
    I cannot from his anger flee.

Yes!—I may flee—he shows me where;
    Tells me to Jesus Christ to fly;
And when he sees me weeping there,
    There's mercy beaming in his eye.

MY DEAR YOUNG FRIENDS,—I know you are very fond of *stories*, and I never saw young people listen so eagerly to any stories as to those about *robbers*;—even though they got frightened, they still liked to hear them. Now, I am going to tell you about *robbers*, and, what may interest you still more, about *young robbers*,—

some of them *very little robbers;* and, in one sense, I wish I could make you *afraid,* so afraid that you would be like Noah, when, being warned of God, he was moved with fear, and prepared an ark to save him from the coming flood. I would like to be as faithful to you as Noah was to the men that perished; and as successful with *you* as Noah was with *his* children in getting them into the ark,—in getting them saved. That is what has led me to speak to you now,—the hope that some of you may be *saved;* and if that be not done, I may say with Isaiah, "I have spent my strength for naught and in vain." So, dear children, keep this steadily before you—that the grand object I have in view is your salvation—from sin, from wrath, from hell; and let each say, "That must be my object too."

I do not come to you, then, as a mere *story-teller.* I come like one of the old prophets of God. Like which of them do you think? Not Isaiah, the evangelical prophet; nor Jeremiah, the weeping prophet; nor Ezekiel, though you could not name better;—not to prophesy of *the future* merely, but to speak of *the past;* not to tell of what *will be* merely, but of what *has been* and *is*. I want to be like Nathan, when he came to David and said, King David, I have somewhat to say unto thee; but read the passage, it is so touchingly told:—

2 Samuel xii. 1-7.—"And the Lord sent Nathan unto David: and he came unto him, and said unto him, There were two men in one city; the one rich, and the other poor. The rich man had exceeding many flocks and herds; But the poor man had nothing, save one little ewe-lamb, which he had bought, and nourished up;

and it grew up together with him, and with his children: it did eat of his own meat, and drank of his own cup, and lay in his bosom, and was unto him as a daughter. And there came a traveller unto the rich man; and he spared to take of his own flock, and of his own herd, to dress for the wayfaring man that was come unto him; but took the poor man's lamb, and dressed it for the man that was come to him. And David's anger was greatly kindled against the man; and he said to Nathan, As the Lord liveth, the man that hath done this thing shall surely die: and he shall restore the lamb fourfold, because he did this thing, and because he had no pity. And Nathan said to David, Thou art the man."

So I come to you. You will find the name of the prophet I have referred to, if you will turn to the last book in the Old Testament:—

Malachi iii. 8.—" WILL A MAN ROB GOD? YET YE HAVE ROBBED ME."

Some of you will see at once why I said I would be like Nathan. The first part of the text answers to the story, and the second, to the application of it,—"Thou art the man."

In connection with the text there are three things to be spoken of,—three great things,—the *Sin*, the *Punishment*, the *Pardon*. The text speaks only of the first of these, but the chapter speaks of the other two, and I could not take up the one without the others.

I. The SIN: *Robbing God.* The sin, you see, is the breaking of one of the ten commandments—the eighth, "*Thou shalt not steal.*" But you never thought of that being one of its meanings, and perhaps you say, "Rob God! How can that be? Who can do that? Could a man ascend to heaven and take away anything that belongs to God? Could he enter in by stealth at those ever open gates, and snatch away one of those glorious crowns,—one of those golden harps?" No, my children, that is not the idea. And you are not wrong in thinking it strange: that is implied in the question, "*Will a man rob God?*" "Could such a thing ever be thought of? Could it once enter into a man's mind?— a *man to rob God!* Never speak of such a thing— monstrous—impossible!" "*Yet ye*"—*men, women, children*—"*have robbed* ME," says *God*. The strange, monstrous thing has been actually done! Perhaps you say, like the Jews in the text, "Wherein have we robbed thee?" I shall answer that question in four particulars: You have robbed God of your *hearts*, of your *time*, of your *talents*, of your *money*, which are all *his*, given to you to use them for *him*, to give them back to *him*. You have often seen men's names stamped on what belonged to them. You may have seen their name engraved on their silver-plate, or written on their books. Well, it is so with those things about which we are to speak; it is as if the word "GOD," were stamped in large characters on your heart, your time, your talents, your money, telling that they are all his. And so,—

1. I charge you with robbing God of your HEART, for that lies at the root of all. The heart is the first thing on which God sets his seal,—the first thing to which he lays claim,—the first thing which he demands. You have it in that word, "Ye are not your own," ye

are God's. You have it in that word, "Give me thine heart." Satan asked you for it, the world asked you for it, and you gave it to them, and they have written their name upon it, as claiming it for their own; but if you will look narrowly into it, and go down a little beneath the surface, you will still see traces of the old mark. There are times when the old and rightful name may still be seen shining through, just as you may have noticed on the sign-board above the door of a tradesman's shop, the name and occupation of its old master still appearing through the gaudily painted letters that tell who is its owner now. Deep down, out of sight, the original stamp is still there—"G-o-d's." And so in the hands of its present owners, it is stolen property. You had no right to give it to them. God has not given up his claim to it, and still regards it as his. You have robbed him of your heart's *love*—your heart's *service*—your heart's *fear*. "The ox knoweth his owner, and the ass his master's crib: but Israel doth not know, my people doth not consider. I have nourished and brought up children, and they have rebelled against me. If I be a father, where is mine honour? and if I be a master, where is my fear?" You have set other gods before you, and given your heart to them, and you have cast off the living God, and the true. You know what it is to give your heart to another. I ask, Have you ever given it to God? Is there none of you whose heart God touched, a year, or eighteen months, or two years ago, or more; and it seemed as if then the heart was about to surrender to God? As the demand was made in God's name, "Give me thine heart," you *seemed likely* to give it—you *resolved* to give it—*promised* to give it, but have never given it yet? Ah, that boy or girl has all the while been *robbing God!* What a wonder that such a one is still alive this day, to be told of his sin again! What a wonder that he has not been cut down—so like he has been to the barren fig-tree, growing in the best part of God's garden, and yet yielding him no fruit!—

> How many years hast thou, my heart,
> Acted the barren fig-tree's part,
>   Leafy, and fresh, and fair;
> Enjoying heavenly dews of grace,
> And sunny smiles from God's own face—
>   But where the fruit? ah! where?
>
> How often must the Lord have prayed
> That still my day might be delayed,
>   Till all due means were tried!
> Afflictions, mercies, health, and pain,
> How long shall these be all in vain,
>   To teach this heart of pride?

2. You have robbed God of your TIME. It too bears God's stamp. He gave it to you to improve it diligently—to spend it in his service, in preparing for eternity. And especially is this true of *Sabbath*-time. It bears God's name on the very face of it—the *Lord's day;* and yet you have given God's precious day to God's enemies. You have wasted it away, as a worthless thing. You have given hour after hour, that belonged to and was claimed by God, to this and the other sin,—

to the indulgence of some evil habit—to some godless companion—to some bad book—to unholy conversation,—and all the time you were robbing God. The time that should have been spent in fitting you for life and in preparing for death; the time that should have been spent in the house of God, or in the Sabbath school, or in reading the Bible at your own fireside, to yourself or to those about you, has been given to sin— I say again, to God's enemy. And all these mis-spent, stolen hours have been taken account of. Many years ago, in our churches, instead of using clocks to tell the time, as they do now, there stood beside the pulpit, at the minister's hand, an hour-glass or sand-glass, containing as much sand as would run through in an hour, the little particles hurrying after each other as fast as possible through the small opening, as if they could not get through fast enough. That measured the time. And it is as if each of us had his great Life-glass, running while life lasted, and stopping when it ceased; like the other, ever as if in haste to have its work done: and that heap of golden particles—where you have not lived for God—is the measure,—keeps account of your robbery. What shall we say of this waste and abuse of God's time—these moments, and minutes, and hours, and days, and weeks, and months, and years,—so precious—so impossible to be called back—so valuable, that we may one day cry, like one of England's queens, "Oh, for an inch of time!—a whole world for an inch of time!" Ah, in this respect, what robbing of God has there been!

3. You have robbed God of your TALENTS. By that I mean the powers of your mind and of your body, by which you can think, and speak, and act. What was the chief end of God in giving them? To glorify God. Some have as it were buried them in the earth —turned them to no account, so idle and indolent; and some have turned them to ill account. Some clever boy has only been clever in mischief, and turned out expert in sin, leading others astray. Some clever girl has turned out proud and vain, putting on airs because of her good scholarship or good looks, and has taken to herself the glory that should have been given to God. God has not been in all their thoughts. They have, as it were, said, "Our lips are our own; who is Lord over us?"

4. You have robbed God of your MONEY. "Ah," you say, "for once you are wrong! You forget now that you are speaking to young people, for as to money, we have not much of *that*." And yet, if it had been much, it would have been the same. Such as it was, God gave it to you; but *you* never thought of giving any of it to *God*. There was some poor disciple of Christ for whom he claimed it; but you would not give it. There was an appeal made to you on behalf of poor children in heathen lands; you were told of them perishing for lack of knowledge, never hearing of Jesus, or only asking, "Who is Jesus? Who is this Jesus?" And as they cried to you across the sea with a piteous voice, "Come over and help us!" you refused to give them help. Nay, but you spent your money on yourself, on

what did you no good, but harm; and just as the Jews did, to whom God speaks in our text, you *robbed* God.

The heathen do not rob their gods; they give them all they fancy them to ask or like. Parents sacrifice their children to them, and children give up their parents, their blood, their very life. Their false gods,—so vile, so cruel and bloody, they will not rob *them;* but our God, who is in the heavens, who is the God of purity, the God of love, the God who gave up the best he had for us,—his dearest treasure, the very Son of his bosom,—who made, who preserves, who redeems —you rob *him*. The little heathen children of other lands may be seen, ere they take their food, or go on a journey, praying to their gods,—and *our* children will not do the like to *our* God. There are not many like Amelia Geddie, a little girl of whom we are told, that seeing some children playing on a Sabbath, she reproved them and said, " It were better for you to be praying." " We are but bairns," they said. Hear her answer : " Though we be but bairns, yet we must die." And then she went away and prayed for them; and when they mocked her, her only answer was, " Know ye not that the word of God saith, Remember the Sabbath-day, to keep it holy ? " There are few like that same girl, who, just before she died, exclaimed, " Give me thine heart ! O reasonable demand ! If I had a thousand hearts, thou art worthy of them all, who art the Lord my God ; and none hath right but thy great self."

You rob God when you will not take God's way of

being saved—coming to Jesus, believing in Jesus; when you think to save yourself by your prayers, and Bible reading, and good behaviour, and the like, instead of just casting yourself as a helpless sinner on the Great Saviour. You rob him of his glory, the praise of the glory of his grace.

You would say the man who passes false, counterfeit money—a bad penny, or a bad shilling—is a *robber*. He robs the man to whom he gives it. And when you put on a false appearance and pretend to pray, and to serve and to love God, while it is not real; when you come to his house and seem attentive, while the heart is far away, you are trying to pass bad money upon God—*to rob God*.

You may rob a man of something more precious than gold—of his *character*. If you say, "That man is a liar," and spread it abroad, you rob him of the best thing he has. Thus you rob God. "*He that believeth not, hath made God a liar.*" God himself says that; and thus, as far as in you lies, you rob God of one of the most precious things he has.

If the Queen makes a law, or sends a letter written by herself, and signed by her own hand, and you take it and trample it under foot, you rob her of her *honour*. So you do with God, when you despise his word, and break his law, and neglect his invitations, and are heedless of his reproofs.

You say it is a terrible thing for a Banker to rob those who deposit money with him. Ah, my dear child, you are, as it were, a banker for those around you, and as we have seen, for the heathen far away, who have no Bibles, no schools, no missionaries like you. Every boy and girl among us is a steward or banker, intrusted by God with certain things for the good of others,—for "none of us liveth to himself;" and if you keep them all to yourself, you are guilty of robbery of the worst kind. If a servant is trusted by his master, and, though he does not actually steal, yet *wastes his master's property*, or applies it to an improper purpose, he *robs* him. So do you rob God.

You say, when one makes a bargain with another, enters into a solemn agreement, and then breaks it, does not fulfil his part of the bargain, he robs the other of his right; he is a dishonest, bargain-breaking man. And so you rob God. When you were lying ill, and feared you were going to die; when a little brother or sister was taken away; when cholera or fever was raging round about, and many children were dying; when you had heard a solemn sermon, or had read an arousing passage of Scripture, or some touching story,—you promised to be another child, to give yourself up to God, to live to him, to love him, to serve him. But you have got better; the danger has disappeared;—you have forgot your promise; you have drowned all your better thoughts; you have broken your engagements, and are now as careless as ever: you have *robbed God*. *You* know this, and *God* knows it!

You say, What a thing to *rob* a *mother!* and you

may well say it. See that boy; his father dies when he is yet an infant, and his mother has to work hard for his bread. She will not be helped by the parish; she thinks she would like to earn her boy's bread herself, and she washes, or works out, or keeps a mangle, or opens a little shop; and far on at night, when every other light is put out, you may see the light shining in her window. She is up late and early; nothing but work! work! work! from Monday morning to Saturday night. And when she comes home one night, after a hard day's washing, just before the term, she goes to add her day's wage to what she has laid past to pay the rent; and when she pulls out the drawer, lo! it's all gone!—all her hard-won money. And can you think of that mother's grief; how her heart is like to break, when she finds that the thief has been her own boy? *He* took it; he spent it on trifles, on toys and sweetmeats, on worthless, profitless things. And the mother is at her wit's end. She knows not what to do. "What a hard-hearted, wicked boy," you say! "he deserves no common punishment; he should be banished beyond the seas. To rob such a mother—such a kind, loving, generous, self-denying mother!" Ah, I might single out one and another of you, and say, like Nathan, Thou art the boy! Thou art the girl! Will a boy rob his mother? yet ye have robbed *Me!*—worse than the robbery even of a mother, the robbery of God. Satan *tempts* you to do it; Satan *likes* you to do it; Satan *gets* you to do it.

You may have been robbing God without knowing it; without thinking of it. "Father, forgive them, for they know not what they do." You would not rob a man; you would not associate with a thief; you look down upon a dishonest person; and yet I say again, "Thou art the man, the girl, the boy,—far worse than that—one that *robs God!*" You may be attending the church and the Sabbath school, and yet be robbing God; you may be sending the gospel even to others past yourselves; you may be obedient to your parents, and good scholars, and well thought of by men; you may read your Bibles daily, and bow the knee in prayer morning and evening; you may be very young, and yet be robbing God: robbing a God of *omniscience;* robbing a God of *justice;* robbing a God of *power;* robbing a God of *mercy;* robbing a God of *love;*—a God of omniscience, who cannot but see and know; a God of justice, who cannot let it pass; a God of power, who is able to punish it; a God of mercy and love, who has deserved so much otherwise at your hand. "Ye have robbed ME." Oh, that ME! not merely servant and master; not merely child and mother; but a man—a child robbing God! It is like that word of Jesus to Paul, "Why persecutest thou *me?*" Dear children, think of this, "God so loved the world that he gave his only-begotten Son,"—to save it; and *yet, ye* have robbed *Me!*

II. The PUNISHMENT—death. We have the first

example of it in the sin of our first parents. They directly robbed God—took of God's tree; and what was the punishment? "In the day thou eatest thereof, thou shalt surely die." "The wages of sin" —that which it deserves and must have—" is *death*" —*eternal death!* Repeat the question, "What doth every sin deserve?" "*God's wrath and curse, both in this life and that which is to come.*" *That* is the punishment; and that, dear children, will be the punishment of this terrible sin of yours if unrepented of, if unforgiven. So was it in the case of Achan. Achan had literally robbed God. Everything in Jericho was devoted to God, and so was God's property. Achan took part of it; and the punishment was, that he was *stoned to death.* Now, with God there are no *small sins;* they are all "*capital*" offences. Capital offences are those for which a man loses his head—loses his life; and every sin is a capital offence against God; and robbery of God, like murder among men, demands death. And so you are in the condition of men condemned to die. Oh, what a state to be in! What a spectacle it is when the judge puts on the black cap, after the man has been proved *guilty*, and, amid the intensest and most solemn silence, all sitting with drawn breath, pronounces the terrible sentence; sometimes, the poor man, when he hears it, fainting away, and his friends shrieking out with grief and terror! Ah, this has already taken place with you! God the Judge has brought you in guilty, and pronounced the sentence on every sinner whom I address, young and old. He not only *will do* it, but he *has done it:* "He that believeth not *is condemned already.* . . . the wrath of God *abideth on him.*"

You may have read of one who thought it would be a fine thing to be a king, and who got trial of it for a while, lying on a gilded couch, surrounded with everything he could desire, saying to himself, It's worth while to be a king. But see above his head;—a *sword* suspended by a thread! it may at any moment come down, and how can he be happy? Would it not be strange to see him laughing and making merry, when every moment may be his last? and would it not be terrible, if when he is thus engaged, the thread should give way, and the sword come down and kill him instantaneously, so that even when dead there should be the expression of merriment on his face? Beloved children, it is so with many of you. The sword—God's wrath because of sin,—is hanging over your head! hanging by a thread! and as you go on sinning, God may any moment cut it asunder, and the sword may come down and go to your very heart. When you lie down, while you sleep, when you rise, when you are at meals, when you are at school, when you work, when you play, the sword is there—above your head! Solemn thought! Oh, can you be happy with *that there?* Can you make merry, and eat, and sleep, and play, and never ask God to take that sword away—to put it into its scabbard, and to hide you in the only safe refuge,—Jesus Christ?

"But what difference does it make to the great God, our robbing him?" I cannot tell you that, beyond this, that he commands and deserves the reverse. But I can tell what difference it makes to *you*. *There* it is that the difference lies; who shall tell it?—a difference that only eternity shall open up and fully show. What difference is there between your having God, and happiness, and heaven on the one hand, and wrath and hell on the other, for your portion? You may think you can do without God now—not then. You may relish the company of the ungodly now—not then. One of the worst things about a prison is, that there the company is so terrible,—the vilest of men and women, there for all sorts of crimes, so that it is sometimes worse than to be beside wild beasts. There is sometimes a softness of nature in the beast that is not in the man. I have visited the prison, and as the heavy doors closed after I had entered, and were carefully locked,—as for a while I was left alone, waiting for a young prisoner whom I had gone to see; with the long rows of cells before me, I could not but think, How dreadful to be shut up here, away from the happy and the good, with none but criminals all around! Well, dear children, we may suppose that to be one of the most awful things about the prison-house of the lost,—the *company*, and no way of getting out of it; no end of it; nothing else to all eternity,—for the Bible says, "The unbelieving, and murderers, and idolaters, and all liars, shall have their part in the lake which burns with fire and brimstone." *That* is the punishment. I saw a picture yesterday of a policeman and a prisoner. The prisoner was suspected of murder, and as the policeman sat with him in his cell, chained to him through the long night, the young man suddenly said, " Well, I did it; I know I did it; but it's hard I should die for it, and I only twenty!" The policeman was startled; he was miserable; he was almost overpowered; he wearied for morning light to come; never did night seem so long before. Oh, the thought of being chained to a murderer for a whole night! Then what must it be to be with such eternally? I tell you the truth in this matter; the very truth of God. I would warn you about the prison, if I thought there was any risk of your going there; and so, as a friend and brother, I now tenderly warn you of the prison of eternity, for some of you seem to be hurrying on to it. Will none be warned?

"But may I not hope to escape—to escape in the crowd?" No; be sure your sin will find you out. Remember Achan: how the lot came nearer and nearer, till it pointed out the very man! Remember Nathan's word to David, " Thou art the man!" Remember Gehazi, the prophet's servant : " Went not mine eye with thee?" Remember Hagar, Sarah's maid: "Thou God seest me!" You would never think of robbing a man to his face, when his eye was right upon you; yet this is what you do with God. There are places in London where young people learn to steal, to pick pockets and the like, so skilfully that you would almost think they did it by magic; we might call them *training schools for hell!* But the most expert among them all, who could empty your pocket or mine without being noticed by us, *cannot* without being observed by *God;* and cannot rob God but with his bright eye glancing broad upon them. That is one reason why you rob God; you forget that his eye is on you,—on tongue, and hand, and heart. Did you ever see a sailor belonging to the British navy? If you had looked at the back of his hand you would have seen there *an anchor,*—a blue mark made on the hand that can never be taken out, so that if he should desert from his ship, he can be found out, do what he will. Let him change his dress as much as he likes, and alter his appearance, and speak a different language; whenever those in search of him come upon him, they just turn up his coat, and *there* they see the anchor, and he cannot say a word, for *that* is evidence that cannot be denied. It is so with you. You have God's mark on you; and you may sell yourself to sin, to Satan, to the world; you may enter their service and disown God; you may speak their language, and wear their livery, and call yourself by their name;—but the mark is still there; you cannot wash it off, you cannot alter it; of itself it condemns you; escape there is none!

"But may not God forget?" Nay: not only does God *know*, but he also *remembers;* he never forgets what he sees. Every act of robbery is written down—page after page, as it were, is filled up with your sins, not one passed over,—the exact truth told in every case. There it stands written against you. Oh, if I could read off from one page after another of that book of remembrance, what terrible things I would have to mention! One page would be more than enough! And all these are written as with an iron pen on the rock; they cannot be rubbed out. And conscience will at length awake, and when it hears the charge, it will say, "It's all true; they have done all that is alleged. I warned them. I told them it was wrong; but none believed me; none heeded me. I was silenced and trodden under foot." And Satan will rise as an accuser, and say, "It's all true; I tempted them, and they did it." And again I say, there is no denying it. There are *the stolen goods* found in possession!—the strongest of all proofs. There is the *stolen heart!* "He will keep that which I have committed unto *Him*," said Paul. But my heart is found, with my full consent, in the world's possession; in Satan's—not in Christ's, and I cannot deny it. And then, all will be read aloud before an assembled world. Then, children, then, where will you look; what will you do; where will you hide your face; what will you get to say? Alas! you will be speechless, and you will have none to speak a good word for you; for Jesus, the only Advocate, you have despised. And as you stand trembling and terrified, the Judge shall say to you,—yes, to *you*, "Depart from me, ye cursed." Oh, what a day will *that* be! What weeping and wailing will be then; and then ye shall go away into everlasting punishment. Children! dear children! some of you may be there; yes, some of you Sabbath scholars: some of you who are reading these words in which I warn you of it beforehand, may hear these very words spoken *to* YOU. I cannot bear to think of it. What shall we do to prevent it? Will you not be warned? Must we mourn over you as David did over his Absalom,—" O my son Absalom! my son! my son!"

Thus, you see, *robbing God* is *robbing yourselves.* Men forget that, and children forget it. If I rob God, I am robbing myself—of happiness, of peace, of heaven; and to think of a man, of a child, robbing himself! What regrets will be uttered at last! "I thought I was only robbing others. I thought I was robbing God; but I have been robbing myself, and now I have nothing left. I am a beggar for eternity; I am undone; I am *lost!*" "The wicked shall be turned into hell, and all the nations that *forget* God." Stop, dear children, stop and think, before you further go!

> "O children, children, seek His face,
> Whose wrath you cannot bear;
> Fly to the shelter of his cross,
> And seek salvation there."

III. and briefly, The PARDON. I would not have spoken to you as I have done of the sin and the punishment, unless I could tell you now of the *pardon*—pardon in Jesus Christ. I have spoken of even children being *great sinners,* but I can also speak of Christ as a *great Saviour,* and so the very Saviour for you. I have spoken of your sins being all written down in God's book, standing there against you, like so many debts which you can never pay. Ah, but I can also tell of Jesus, who is ready, if you will come to him, to take his pen and dip it in his own blood, and write across it in bold letters, like a merchant in his book,—PAID! Nay, he will *blot out* your sin, so as no more to be remembered.

> "There is a fountain filled with blood,
>   Drawn from Immanuel's veins;
> And sinners plunged beneath that flood,
>   Lose all their guilty stains.
>
> The dying thief rejoiced to see
>   That fountain in his day;
> And there may I, as vile as he,
>   Wash all my sins away."

There is a missionary travelling in India; he sees a man apparently asleep, and when he comes up to him, he finds him in the agonies of death. He would like to whisper into his ear, some sweet word about Jesus, before he dies; and kneeling down, he says to him, "Brother, what is your hope for eternity?" He is not a heathen, as you might have expected, for as he opens his eyes and faintly whispers, it is to say, "The blood of Jesus Christ, his Son, cleanseth us from all sin;" and when he dies, there is found firmly grasped in his hand, a single leaf of a Bengalee Bible, with that text upon it. That is enough to save the soul. "Yes," said another Emily, when asked, "What do you believe?" "I believe that the Father sent his Son into this world to die for sinners, and *I am a sinner.*" Beloved children, what is your hope for eternity? is it *that?*

There is a little boy, poor, haggard, ragged, brought up and tried for stealing. His crime is proved, but the judge says, "I cannot send that poor boy back to prison; we must pity his youth;" and he admonishes, and warns, and pardons him. But no one will speak to him; everybody says, "That is the boy who stole—who was in prison;" so that it is almost as if he were another Cain,—as if he had a mark on his forehead, telling what he has done. Every one avoids him, and in his misery I hear him saying, "What good has my pardon done me, when I am a poor outcast? It were better to die than to live thus." It is not so with God when he pardons. "How shall I put thee among the children?" Look at the story of the prodigal: "Bring forth the best robe and put it on him." "Thou shalt call me, 'My Father,' and shalt not depart from me any more." The poor robber is made a *son of God;* and that is better than to be a *prince*, better than to be a *king*. "Behold, what manner of love the Father hath bestowed upon us, that we should be called the sons of God!" Oh, what rejoicing: "This my son was dead, and is alive again; he was lost, and is found!" No wonder that I hear the pardoned sinner singing out, "*I'm forgiven! I'm forgiven!*" "Bless the Lord, O my soul;— who forgiveth all thine iniquities, who crowneth thee with loving-kindness and tender mercies." Will you not cry, as did one like yourselves, "O Jesus, save me, save me!" till Jesus saved him; and then say as he said, "I am not afraid to die now, for Jesus has died for me?" Was it strange that that Scotch boy added, in his own simple way, "What a pity it is they do not a' come to Christ—they would be sic happy?"

Dear children, there is everything to induce you, and to induce you *now*. During the French Revolution, we are told, there were many shut up in the prisons. A certain number of these prisoners were led out to execution every day, no one knowing whose turn it would be next, till the executioner appeared. What a state they must have been in, as they heard that well-known footfall that was bringing death to one or other of them, they knew not which! So every unconverted child is this day in the prison; and every year some are thus being led forth to execution—sent into eternity. Who may be next? Oh, my dear young friends, there is no time to put off! I have seen many little coffins of late. I have stood by many death-beds, and beside many little graves. I know few families where there are little children, in which —as in Egypt—there has not been one dead. I have seen five fathers in church in one day, each clothed in deep mourning, after the death of a beloved child. Who may be next? What place may be vacant next year? What little boy or girl may be away? And *where*, O where, the precious, the immortal soul? Will you not offer the prayer of a young boy, "Lord! make me quite, quite ready to die, in case Jesus comes for me in a hurry?" It was well to have prayed that prayer, and to have got it answered, for Jesus *did* come for him in a hurry. When the train was rushing along at fearful speed, an accident occurred, and in an instant soul and body were parted,—and absent from the body, he was, so far as man could judge, present with the Lord. He had been repeating to his mamma that morning the verse, "Boast not thyself of to-morrow." I do not know what may happen to-morrow; to-morrow is not yours, only to-day. God says, *Now—this day.* He is ready to pardon; will no one come and say, " O God, pardon mine iniquity, for it is great, for Jesus' sake. God be merciful to me a sinner?"

You may come afterwards, and then find it *too late.* Remember the foolish virgins,—"And *the door was shut."* There is a boy sent by his dying father for some medicine to relieve his suffering; the boy does not get it, and, to save himself a little trouble, tells his father a lie, and in a little that kind father dies. Just before he breathes his last, his boy seizes his cap, runs to the druggist, brings the medicine, but—he is *too late,—his father is dead!* Oh, if he had lived but one minute longer, that I might have confessed my sin, and got him to lay his hand on my head, and say he forgave me, —but now it can never be!* Oh, bitter, bitter thought! There are two young omnibus-men in London, who have written to their employer, promising never to repeat the fault for which they have been turned off; but see their sad, sad look as the letter comes back, with these words written in large letters across it, "NEVER APPLY AGAIN!" Sometimes God says that: " Then shall they call upon

* Todd.

me, but I will not answer; they shall seek me early, but they shall not find me" (Prov. i. 24-31).

And then might you not as well have been born, and lived, and died in some heathen land—in Africa, where the face of a missionary was never seen, or in the heart of China, where the name of Jesus was never heard,— as to have had your Bibles, and your churches, and your schools, and so many other privileges, and after all to have robbed God, and to be cast away for ever because of it? Think of this, dear children; and remember that if you persist in it, the little heathen children in these distant lands will rise up against you in the day of judgment and condemn you. Will they not point to the children of Britain and say, "*We* have robbed God, but no warning voice ever spoke to us, except the voice of our own conscience;* we never read the Bible like them; we never had sermons preached to *us*, telling us of our sin and danger, and of the way of salvation by Jesus Christ; we never had kind teachers to help us to understand these things; we never knew, like them, that the great God who made the earth was the true God, who alone ought to be feared, and served, and worshipped, and loved; we never heard of a Saviour, or heaven, or hell?" None of you can say *that*. It will be an awful day if you shall have to say, "Oh, that I had been a poor heathen! Oh, that I had never been born!" Take care lest it should be so. Most that are pardoned at

---

* Rom. ii. 14, 15.

all are pardoned in early life. That is both an encouragement and a warning—an encouragement to come *now*, a warning not to delay another day.

THE HYMN.

HEAR, O sinner! mercy hails you,
 Now with sweetest voice she calls;
Bids you haste to seek the Saviour,
 Ere the hand of justice falls;
  Trust in Jesus—
'Tis the voice of mercy calls.

Haste, O sinner! to the Saviour,
 Seek his mercy while you may;
Soon the day of grace is over—
 Soon your life will pass away!
  Haste to Jesus—
You must perish if you stay.

The Great Question and Answer.

THE HYMN.

NOT all the blood of beasts,
   On Jewish altars slain,
Could give the guilty conscience peace,
   Or wash away the stain.

But Christ, the heavenly Lamb,
   Takes all our guilt away;
A sacrifice of nobler name,
   And richer blood than they.

My faith would lay her hand
   On that dear head of thine,
While as a penitent I stand,
   And there confess my sin.

Believing, we rejoice
   To see the curse remove;
We bless the Lamb with cheerful voice,
   And sing his bleeding love.

MY DEAR YOUNG FRIENDS,—You must often have noticed what a way children have of asking *questions;*—some of them very amusing, some very trifling, some very foolish, and yet all useful in their way, as one of the means by which they get information about all sorts of things. Now, in trying to answer children's questions that are really worthy of being answered, you need to be very simple and very direct;— as short as possible, and as plain as possible, for their memories are not able to remember long things, nor their

minds to understand difficult things. Hence it is, that when God answers important questions in the Bible, he does it both shortly and simply, so that the youngest and the simplest may understand what he says. Well, I wish to call your attention to the most important question that can possibly be asked; and though it is for old people too, it is yet quite a child's question; so much so, that after we have looked at it, I trust many of you will make it yours, and ask it for yourselves. If all the questions that ever were put, were arranged in a long, long list, in the order of their importance, though there would be thousands upon thousands,—though the list, I daresay, would reach for miles from where we are,—I am sure this question, to which I have referred, would be at the very top,—the first on the whole list. Or, if I were to say of *questions*, what a good man has said of *books*, There are a great many very little worth, some of them of copper like our pennies and half-pennies, and some of them of silver like our shillings, and some of them of gold like our sovereigns,—then I would call this a *golden question*. I might almost compare it to Moses' rod, which, when cast down before the King of Egypt, became a serpent, and swallowed up all the rods of the magicians and wise men who tried to do the same with theirs. This question of mine—of yours—swallows up, or should swallow up, multitudes of other questions, which have too often stood in its way, and prevented it getting the attention which it deserves. Ay, and its answer, too, is no less important;—so important that God has spoken it from heaven, and written it with his own finger, that there may be no mistake about it. None could have answered it but himself, and there is no answer to it but *one*,—at least there is only *one right answer*,—so that if we may speak of a *golden question*, we may still more speak of the *golden answer*. What can it be? You will find both in—

Acts xvi. 30, 31 : "WHAT MUST I DO TO BE SAVED? BELIEVE ON THE LORD JESUS CHRIST, and thou shalt be saved."

"Is that all?" somebody asks Yes ; and a good "all" it is. "That's nothing new." True; and it is none the worse for being old, but all the better. You are going off to America with two or three hundred others,—men, women, and children,—taking with you everything that belongs to you. When you see so many passengers and such quantities of luggage, you wonder that any ship can safely carry such a load. Well, here is a fine-looking vessel, strong and well-built, painted with bright colours, the rigging and everything about it quite new. When you are off to bed at night, you hear your father talking of it to a neighbour who is going along with him; and as they consult about what should be done, you hear him say, "She's a fine ship, but she has never been tried,—this is her first voyage. She may be all right, better than any other, but somehow I have not confidence in her; the first storm that comes may break her up, and send us all to the bottom, and only, when too late, we may discover our mistake. No; we must have one that has crossed the sea before, that has come safely through the storm, that has proved herself a good ship; and then with confidence we shall set sail." So say I of this old text of mine. It has been tried and found trustworthy. It has carried many to heaven, and will carry thither many more, old and young. It is better than anything newer that has been found out since. Will you not say, "The old—the old for us! We shall try it too!"

A word as to the story. Once upon a time, God directed two of his servants to set out for a far off land, to tell the people who lived there, how they were to be saved. One night in a dream or vision, one of them saw a man of that country stretching out his hands, and pitifully crying across the sea, "Come over and help us! Come over and help us!" They lost no time, but pressed forward over land and sea with all speed, and soon reached the place. The first Sabbath after they arrived, they went to a little prayer-meeting on the bank of a river, and there God opened one woman's heart. Then they healed a poor girl who was possessed of an evil spirit; which so enraged her masters, that they raised a tumult, and the end of it was, that the strangers were brought before the magistrates, stripped naked, beaten with rods, and all sore and bleeding, were cast into a dark and filthy dungeon. In the middle of the night, as they were praying to God and praising him, there was an earthquake; the prison was shaken to its very foundations, the doors flew open, the prisoners' chains fell off, and when the jailer, a careless, hard-hearted man, awoke, and saw what had happened—fancying that his prisoners had all made their escape, and that he would have to answer for their lives with his own, he thought it better just at once to kill himself, drew his sword, and was about to plunge it into his body, when a loud voice from the prison was heard, "Do thyself no harm, for we are all here!" It was one of God's servants who thus stopped him; and the next moment, as the good Spirit of God began to deal with him, the jailer—coming to himself, seeing himself as a lost sinner, all but cast into hell, full of horror and grief, careless about his body and everything else, and only concerned about his soul, —ran as fast as his trembling limbs would carry him to those who could tell him, and put to them the question we have now read, "Sirs, what must I do to be saved?"

Let us look at two things in our text—I. The sinner's GREAT QUESTION; II. God's ONE ANSWER.

I. *The sinner's* GREAT QUESTION: "What must I do to be saved?" It was not strange that the man, about whom we have been speaking, put this question. He did not say, "I wonder how all this has happened!" He did not say to Paul and Silas—for it was to them he spoke—"How do you think these doors have been so strangely opened, and every man's chains loosed? What am I to do to secure my prisoners, to prevent them killing me; for we have some of the most desperate men in the town here, who would not scruple to do anything, and would be but too glad to be revenged on me? What am I to say to the magistrates to-morrow? They may not believe my story, and it may cost me my situation, perhaps my life. Oh, what shall I do?" No, he never thought about anything of the kind,—he did not care about all that. "Oh, my sin, my sin! My precious, precious soul! What shall I do for my *soul*? Can there be salvation for me? How,—where shall I get it? Tell me—tell me what I must do to be saved." I say it was not strange that he should speak thus.

What a noise there is on the street! What screaming —what a gathering of people, and especially of young people! Two policemen are dragging along a little boy who has been stealing, and it is neither the first nor the second offence, so that he *must* be punished. He has been struggling with all his might to get free, but the more he struggles the firmer they hold him; and as they come nearer and nearer the police-office, what should you expect him to be doing and saying? Why, what but weeping and crying out more and more bitterly, "Oh, what shall I do? what shall I do to be saved?" Wouldn't it be strange if he were saying anything else? Or there are three little girls; they are spending their holidays at the seaside, and as they walk along the shore, gathering shells and pebbles, they are so intent on their work, that they never look about them. At length they are aroused by hearing some one calling to them, and when they turn to see what is the matter, lo! the tide has come in, the sea has surrounded them; already the water is too deep for them to wade through it, and unless they get help soon, they must all be drowned. What should we expect to find them doing? "Sitting down on the gravel, comparing what each has gathered; quarrelling about who has got the prettiest and most uncommon pebble; discussing some matter of dress, and making up their mind as to what their next dress should be; talking about the pleasant tea party to which they have been invited that night, and wondering who will be there, and how this one and the other one will be dressed!" Never speak of it; that is all just as unlikely as could be. They were doing that a little ago; but I fancy I see them now, stretching out their hands to the shore, the treasures they have spent the day in gathering thrown away and forgotten, their light seaside dresses all dripping with the water, and their shrieks such as I shall never forget: "Oh, what shall I do—what shall I do to be saved?" That is not strange, is it? In such a case wouldn't that be their great question?

But what have we to do with all this? I have just been trying, my dear children, to draw a picture of you. Underneath these two pictures I might write the names of many, many young people to-day. That boy is *you*. Like him you have been stealing—robbing God—sinning, ay, sinning all your days; breaking God's good and holy law, in your hearts and in your lives; every day offending God by your sinful thoughts, and sinful looks, and sinful tempers, and sinful words and actions. And though you don't see it, though you don't feel it, though you little think of it, though nobody speaks to you about it—already you are *a prisoner*—already the officers of justice have laid hold of you. They will not let go—they dare not—they cannot. They are dragging you on to the judgment-seat. Every day you are getting nearer. They will soon have you there; and if grace prevent not now, from the judgment-seat they will drag you down to the dark prison-house of hell. If that be true, and the God of truth says it, then what should be your great question, which every boy and girl should be asking, losing sight of all else? Isn't it this: "What must I do to be saved?" These three girls are *you*. You have been walking on dangerous ground, mere shell-gatherers, taken up about trifles,—your dress, your play, your food, your companions, what people said about you or thought about you;—and all the while, the flood of God's wrath has been gathering round you, so that now, it has completely enclosed you and shut you in. Already it is so deep, that to wade through it would be impossible; and it is rising higher and higher, and coming nearer and nearer, ready any moment to sweep you away—away to endless ruin. If that be true, and God says it, what then? Why, there is no time to be lost; you cannot too soon be asking—and it is your great question, the only one really worth attending to till something be done,—"What must I do to be saved?" If there be a question in all the world that befits you, it is *that*.

Beloved children, have you ever made that question yours? I have no doubt many other questions have been coming up to you. Some of you who are poor, have been asking, What shall I do to be *rich?*—some of you who have been ill, asking, What shall I do to get *well?*—some of you who have early known what sorrow is, asking, What shall I do to be *happy?* Never—"What must I do *to be saved?*" The strange thing is, that you have never asked that question—have never thought of asking it. You need not wonder when you hear of children weeping for sin, being concerned about their souls, asking their teachers, and ministers, and friends, "How shall we be saved?" For though you should get no food for days, it would not so much matter; if you had to go about in rags, if you were suffering severest pain, it would not so much matter. At most, it would only be for a little while; and even were you to die, if your soul were safe, all would be well; but if you do not attend to *this*—if you neglect *this*—if you continue to do as you have been doing all your days, just letting this matter alone, then you are ruined,—undone for eternity.

Oh, that the Holy Spirit may open *your* eyes as he opened the jailer's, that you may see and feel the truth of all I have been saying,—that it is all true of *you;* that you may be awakened out of your sleep, so that not another day may pass, without your cry being heard by God, if not by man,—your one great cry,— "What must I do to be saved?"

II. *God's* ONE ANSWER. Others have often tried to

answer the question, and they have answered it wrong —differently from God; and how dreadful to make a mistake here! It is as when your little brother has turned ill, and you run for help; the druggist's lad not being up to his business, not understanding the prescription, takes down the wrong bottle, gives you poison instead of medicine, or gives you a wrong medicine, and your brother takes it and dies. The mistake has killed him. It is as when in a dark and stormy night a light is hung out in a wrong place, and the hard-pressed vessel, mistaking it for some place of refuge, runs ashore, and is dashed on the rocks into a thousand pieces. Just so with the answers to this question. Some will say to you: "Be good children; mind your prayers; don't forget to read your Bible every day; be obedient and truthful, and honest and kind; try to keep the Ten Commandments; do your best to get your mind well stored with Bible knowledge." Have not some of you been told that?—have not some of you been trying that? Well, these counsels are all good, and right, and necessary; but there is something *besides* all these, there is something *before* all these. None of these are God's one way, they all come *after* it; of themselves, they will as little save you, and bring you to heaven, as if you were to go on a pilgrimage to Rome, or to trust to a wooden cross, which you could carry in your pocket. What, then, is it? You have heard of Martin Luther, the great German reformer. He was putting this question, and how, think you, was he answering it? At Rome there is a flight of steps called Pilate's Staircase; the pardon of sin was to be given to those who should climb up these steps on their knees; which Luther was slowly and laboriously doing, when the word rang in his ear, as if a voice had proclaimed it from heaven, "The just shall live BY FAITH." He started up, ashamed of himself, and grieved that he should so dishonour God. It was the same answer that our text gives, that thus came to him. He tried it and was saved. So now, if you are trying any other way, God says to you, You are wrong; you have begun at the wrong place; you must live by *faith;* you must be saved by *believing in Jesus.*

Some of these things I have mentioned, would take a long time to do, even if they could be done at all; and if you had no long time to do them, what then? Some of them are very hard to do, and you only hear of them with despair. What you need is something *simple*—something *immediate*—something that will certainly be successful. If I am dying, don't speak to me of a course of medicine that in a fortnight's time will remove my disease, for I cannot hope to live so long; give me something, if such there be, that will begin to check the disease at once, and keep me from dying. And here am I, a perishing sinner; by to-morrow I may be lost—by to-morrow I may be in hell: I must have immediate help; I cannot wait; I am afraid to put off even till night. Is there no remedy for my soul, that can be applied at once, so that I may even at this hour be saved? Yes, says God; our text tells how: and, by his Spirit, he *applies* the remedy as well as *reveals* it. In this, God's answer, there are two things—a *command*, and *a promise*.

1. A COMMAND: "Believe on the Lord Jesus Christ." Now, the first thing to be done in such a case is to *understand* the answer—to find out *what it means*. That is just what I am anxious to help you in. What is meant by *believing* on Jesus Christ? I cannot hope to make it plainer than God has made it; therefore, as the best thing I can do, I shall give you some of the other expressions, by which God himself explains it. And may the Holy Spirit incline your hearts to give earnest heed to it now, and teach you savingly, as he only can; for a better time than the present there never will be! One of the kings of Sweden, when dying, was anxious to know the meaning of *faith*—of *believing*. They sent for an archbishop to explain it to him; for a whole hour he talked to him, but king as he was, educated man as he was, he could not comprehend it, could not take it in. Don't you put off till then.

(1). Believing on Jesus is LOOKING to him—looking to him for salvation. The children of Israel have been sinning against God, murmuring against him as they often did, in the midst of all his goodness; and God is angry with them, and sends fiery flying serpents among them, which destroy many of the people. On every hand they are dying,—men, and women, and children,—a terrible sight it is! What is to be done? What remedy can be devised? Is there any medicine that will heal their wounds, and restore them to health?

None. What then? By God's command, Moses makes a brazen serpent, just like those that are flying about, sets it up on a pole, in the sight of the people, saying to them, "LOOK!" and as many as look are healed— are saved. I think I see them straining their eyes to get a sight of this, that is their only hope, dying men casting what seems a last look, and little children held up in their parents' arms, turning their eyes to the serpent of brass, and immediately, in every case—

> "The wounded look, and straight are cured,
> The people cease to die."

Our paraphrase supplies the application,—

> "So, from the Saviour on the Cross,
> A healing virtue flows;
> Who looks to him with lively faith
> Is saved from endless woes.

And that is Christ's very word; "Look unto Me." You say, "I can understand them looking to the serpent, but I don't understand how we can look to *Jesus*, when he is not to be seen." But you can look with your *mind*, can't you, as well as with your eye? For instance, I hear one girl trying to persuade another, to accompany her into the country for a Saturday walk, instead of sitting in the house; and when she makes some excuse for declining, the other says, "But look at this—how delightful it will be, with the fine dry roads and the bracing air, and the trees putting on their autumn dress, and by next Saturday it may be too late. Do you see that?" That is looking with the *mind*. *That is not the kind of looking I mean. But see that* poor widow with a young family, weeping as if her heart would break. When I ask her what ails her, she tells me she is behind with her rent, and her landlord threatens to turn her to the door, unless she can pay her debt, and find security for the next six months. So I tell her to dry her tears, and do her best to work for her children, and just look to me for her rent. How full of joy she is, all at once! How cheerfully she works; and though she has not a penny laid past for the term, she has no fear; and when asked, Why? she says, "I am looking to him, for he bade me, and I know he will not fail me. What he promised, is just as sure as if I had it in my hand." Now, believing on Jesus is something like this. If I might so speak, it is the *heart's look* to Jesus—a single glance, indeed, at first, and yet a *constant looking* to him ever after. Jesus has died for lost sinners, he has purchased pardon and life with his blood; he has these to give—to give freely, and so he calls to us, "Look—look to me and I'll save you! Look away from yourselves—away from your friends—away from all that you can do; for you are lost, and these cannot save you. I am the only Saviour—look to me!" Hence it is, that the gospel is preached, the way of salvation is set forth in these very words, "*Look* unto me, and be ye saved, all the ends of the earth." You ask, "What warrant have I to look to him?" *His own word.* Just what the dying Israelites had for looking to the serpent. "Oh," you say, "that is simple." So it is; for it is intended for little children, as well as for men and women. I find one saying, "Mark how simple the way of salvation is. It is Look, look, look! Four letters, and two of them alike!" It is the turn of *the eye of your heart* to Jesus, and that may be in a moment—immediately—here ; to Jesus as the Saviour—the only Saviour—the Saviour for *you*. "Believe on the Lord Jesus Christ." "Looking unto Jesus." "Behold the Lamb of God who taketh away the sin of the world."

(2). Believing in Jesus is TRUSTING him. Here is a boy whose father was buried yesterday. To-day he is wearing his father's gold watch. Some wicked lads are trying to take it from him. He is struggling to keep it, but they are too strong for him ; he is just about to lose it, when I come up and say, "Give it to me, my boy, and I'll keep it safe for you." For a moment he looks at me with doubtful eye, but as I say to him, Trust me! and he sees that I am earnest and sincere, he hands it over to me, and I prevent him from being robbed. That is just what the apostle Paul says of himself. He had, as you have, something far more precious than a gold watch—an immortal soul, and he was afraid of losing it—he could not keep it himself. Jesus said, "Give it to me," and he gave it to him, and then you hear him saying rejoicingly, " I know whom I have believed,"—which is the same thing as, whom I have *trusted*,—" and am persuaded that he will keep that which I have committed to him, against that day." Dear children, you have souls too, and they are in danger of being lost ; there is only one way of getting them saved, giving them into the keeping of Jesus,—"trusting" him with them. What warrant have you for trusting him? Just what Paul had—*his own word;* and that is always enough.

Some time ago, when in another part of the country, in the house of a minister, his little daughter mounted the dining-room table; and as he said, "Come!" standing at some distance from the table, ere ever I was aware, she sprang off right into his arms. I thought to myself, There is faith; at her father's word, trusting herself to him, trusting at once his power and his love! Or there is a young slater-boy on the roof a house. He has lost his hold, and comes rolling down. You would think it next to impossible that he should not be killed on the spot. But just as he is falling over, he gets hold of a cord, which, though it bears him for the moment, is rubbing against the slates, and in an instant may snap. "Let go your hold, my man," says a voice from below, "and I'll catch you in my strong arms,—trust to me!" and instantly he quits the cord, and is safe in his deliverer's arms. That was faith. That is just another picture of you and of Jesus. You, dear children, are hanging over the very mouth of hell,—hanging by a thread,—by a hair. You say you have godly, praying parents. You think yourselves good,—you pray, you read your Bible, you sometimes weep for sin. Well, that is just a thread; in a moment it may snap and you are lost! And Jesus, who has purchased the right to save sinners by his death, comes to you, stands underneath, and says,—" Let go your hold, poor child ; let go, or you'll perish ; drop into my arms. I am *waiting* to receive you. I am strong enough, and loving enough, to bear you and to save you—trust me !" Believe on the Lord Jesus Christ.

(3). Believing on Jesus is LAYING HOLD *of him*, and RESTING *on him*. A vessel is wrecked ; one after another of her crew is swept away and disappears. As she heaves to and fro, it seems as if every moment she would break up, and send her shivering passengers down into the deep. There is the cabin-boy, thinking of his mother and his home, and praying, though scarcely hoping to be saved, when a plank floats past. Eagerly he lays hold of it, rests his whole weight upon it, and while others perish, he is safe. That describes you again. As you are just about to go down, the plank floats along, comes near you,—within reach,—within arm's length. That plank is Christ. Lay hold of him,—rest yourself upon him. He can bear your whole weight— the whole weight of your sins, which would have sunk you to perdition—the whole weight of your soul. Try him ; and, like a sailor-boy who tried him, you'll be able joyfully to say, even in dying, " The plank bears ! the plank bears !" Oh, lay your sins on Jesus—lay your soul on Jesus—the spotless Lamb of God ! Leaving all else, and resting on him alone for salvation, is believing.

(4). Believing on Jesus is COMING to him. Long ago, you might have seen two men going out together to cut wood. As they are going on busily and merrily with their work, the axe-head of one of them flies off, and, striking the other, kills him on the spot. What is to be done? If he remains where he is, his own life may have to go for that of the dead man; and if he should go to his home, the avengers of blood may follow him thither. Here is what he does. God has appointed so many towns in various parts of the country as places to which, in such cases, men may flee for safety. They are called "Cities of Refuge." If the man should be overtaken by the way, he may be put to death; but once within the gates, none dares to touch him. Now, these cities of refuge were meant as a picture of Jesus Christ, as the Refuge of sinners. "The wages of sin is death; the soul that sinneth, it shall die." What shall be done? Flee. Whither? To Jesus. Seek shelter there; and once in him, you are safe. Hence you so often find him using this very word, "Come unto me;" and complaining, "Ye will not come to me that ye may have life." Coming to Jesus, then, is believing.

(5). Believing on Jesus is RECEIVING him. This is another of his own expressions. He comes to your door. He wants to get in. He knocks. He waits. Isn't that wonderful? I was lately visiting that part of the country where our beloved Queen stays, when she comes to Scotland. She visits among the poor. I saw some of the cottages to which she is in the habit of going. In the house of one of her servants I saw her own likeness, and the likenesses of several of her family,—all gifts from themselves. You say, What kindness! what condescension! And so it is. But what would you think, if I told you,—what I am glad I cannot tell you, for it would not be true,—that when they saw the Queen coming, they locked their doors, and pretended to be out, and kept her standing knocking at the door, refusing to let her in, though she came to speak kindly to them, and to do them good? You would say, Surely the people must not be in their right mind. And yet that is just what King Jesus does—Queen Victoria's King. He comes to your door to bless you, to save you. He says, "Behold, I stand at the door and knock." Most people keep him out, and won't have anything to do with him. They say,—ay, children say it,—"Depart from us, for we desire not the knowledge of thy ways." Opening the door to him, saying, "Come in, Lord Jesus; come in,"—taking him to our heart, and only fearing lest he should ever go away again,—is believing. The believing heart is the heart that has let in Jesus, and in which he dwells (Eph. iii. 17). I might call it the *palace of Jesus*. The wonder is, there are so few to make him welcome.

(6). Believing on Jesus is TAKING HIM AT HIS WORD. This is one of the plainest and directest meanings which it has, and is one that all can understand. You don't like your word to be distrusted. I think, even when I go the length of saying, "Are you sure you are speaking the truth?" that I see the tear start in your eye; you cannot bear to have your word doubted. And yet, how many among us listen to the words of Jesus, as if he did not mean what he says,—as if he were not worthy to be trusted! When he speaks to us of our sin and danger, it gives us no concern. When he offers to bless us, we behave to him as we dare not do, even to a neighbour who should offer us help. A few take Jesus at his word—a happy few,—they believe him; the others make him a liar. When he offers to save us, and to save us freely, he means it, and they give him credit for what he says. There was one lately who saw herself to be lost; who, when told that Jesus' own word was, that he came to seek and to save the lost, and that he was there—willing to save her, *because he had said it*, exclaimed, " Then I take him at his word. He is mine!" Is there no one of you, who will take him at his word to-day? Oh, believe him!

"Oh," you say, "that is the way for the jailer, who was such a wicked man, who could not do anything better; but we are not like him, so that that is not the way for us." You may either be like him or not; but there is only one way of being saved, for good and bad alike,—the way of which our text speaks,—Believing on the Lord Jesus Christ. There may be some of you— the children of the rich, the educated, the good—who have never done anything outwardly very bad in your life; and some the children of the poor, the ignorant, the careless, who, though young, have already fallen into open sin. Well, it is all one as regards the way of being saved. I have the same message to both—all must stand on the same level—there is no respect of persons with God. If you are to be saved at all, here is the way of it, "Believe on the Lord Jesus Christ." This, then, is God's command; what do you say to it? "We will think about it." What! *think* about it,— when God *commands!* What would a father say when he commanded, if your reply was, that you would "think about it?" Would it not be a grievous offence to *him?* how much more to *God?* The jailer believed *that night*—did not even wait till morning. So it should be with you now. Don't wait till you come to die; then you may not be able even to "think." Don't wait till you are sick or old; youth and health are the time for believing. *Look now, to-day,* and be saved!

2. A word as to the PROMISE: "Thou shalt be saved." Oh, that word SAVED! it will take all eternity to understand it. It is to have all sin forgiven. It is to "stand accepted in the Beloved." It is to be holy and happy. It is to have all real blessing, present and to come. There is a young man walking along the street; you would not notice anything particular about him, but one says to you, "That is the heir to the British crown; one day he'll be king of the country." You say, "What a happy youth!" There is a poor boy, who has just become heir to a great estate; he gets as much as keeps him meanwhile, and soon will have all. "Oh, I wish I were he!" Well, come to-day and get something better far. Come and be heir to a *crown*,—not of *gold*, but of *glory*, —gold will tarnish, glory never. Come and get all you need meanwhile, and heaven very, very soon. "Saved!" what is so important about that? I think I see you, when

you lie down on a dying bed; and you say, "I am so happy." Why? "Because, through grace, I am *saved.*" I fancy the end of all things has come; many are calling to the rocks and mountains to fall on them, but you are rejoicing. Why? "Because I am *saved.*" Hundreds of years have passed away, and lost sinners are getting no relief, no rest, but you are getting happier and happier. Your cup of joy is ever getting more full—nothing but blessing —no curse, no sorrow, no death! Why? "Because I am *saved.*" Is not all this worth while,—a present, an eternal salvation—from sin, from hell? Believe on the Lord Jesus Christ, and this blessedness shall all be yours; you shall be saved. Many young people have of late been finding it true, and are now rejoicing in Christ as their Saviour. Make haste, make haste to join their ranks, as they march on to glory, a company of happy young believers,—called by the Father, saved by the Son, guided and sanctified by the Spirit, ascribing all the praise of their salvation to GOD (Eph. ii. 8).

THE HYMN.

NOT the labour of my hands
    Can fulfil the law's demands;
Could my zeal no respite know,
Could my tears for ever flow,
All for sin could not atone—
Thou must save, and thou alone.

Nothing in my hands I bring,
Simply to thy Cross I cling;
Naked—come to thee for dress;
Helpless—look to thee for grace;
Vile—I to the fountain fly;
Wash me, Saviour, or I die!

Christ our Example.

THE HYMN.

OH, for a heart to praise my God,
   A heart from sin set free,
A heart that's sprinkled with the blood
   So freely shed for me!

A heart resigned, submissive, meek,
   My great Redeemer's throne:
Where only Christ is heard to speak,
   Where Jesus reigns alone.

A humble, lowly, contrite heart,
   Believing, true, and clean!
Which neither life nor death can part,
   From Him that dwells within.

A heart in every thought renewed,
   And filled with love divine;
Perfect and right, and pure and good,—
   A copy, Lord, of thine.

MY DEAR YOUNG FRIENDS,—I suppose all of you are, or have been—*scholars;* all of you have, or have had — *teachers.* You were not able to read and write all at once; you were not master of your trade the moment you put your hand to it: in both cases you had to *learn*— you had to *be taught.* We hear, indeed, of some as having been self-educated;—they never had a master, they never went to school, and yet they became wise and great men. One, perhaps, was a shepherd boy, who, as soon as he could do anything, was sent out to the moor or the hill-side, to herd the sheep or the cattle ; starting early in the morning with his wallet on his back, spending the whole day alone, and only returning to his home when the sun began to set at night. Another was a weaver, who, whenever he could use his hands, became his father's little helper; till, as he grew up, he got a loom of his own, working hard from morning till night. But though they never were at school, still they were *taught;* they had at least *books* as their teachers, and made such good use of them, that they got far ahead of those who had every advantage, and became distinguished as scholars or inventors, and were benefactors to their country and to the world. Even in their case they had to *learn*—they had to *be taught*. Now, I wish you to-day to be introduced to a new teacher; one whom some of you at least don't know—whose school you have never attended—who will not prescribe hard tasks to you, which you think no one ever did or could overtake—who will not give you long, dry, wearisome lessons to learn—who, while like other masters he teaches you by what he *says*, especially teaches by what he *does*—whose word is not so much, "Do as I bid you," but, "Do as you see me do,—do like me,—be like me !" If I were going to teach you boys to write, I would not be content with telling you all about the making of strokes and the forming of letters, but I would take the pen in my hand and show you how to hold it ; then I would make the strokes and letters myself,—I would set *a copy* for you, and show you how I did it, saying, "Now, just do what I have done." Had I to teach you girls to make any article of clothing, I would not leave you with written instructions, but I would give you *a pattern*, and show you all the outs and ins of it, and leave it with you for your guidance. If I had to train a body of young soldiers out of your ranks, I would not, if I knew my business, give you books to study ; as your sergeant, I would have you out on drill, and go through all the exercises with you, always keeping your eye fixed on me to see how I did, till, at the word of command, you were able to do exactly as you should. Can any one tell me what we call that kind of teaching? Teaching *by copy*,—teaching *by pattern*,—teaching *by example*. This is especially the kind of teaching I wish you to get to-day, from the Teacher of whom I have spoken.

There are many who might teach you, in this way, very profitably and well. For instance the apostle Paul, who says, "Be ye followers of me"—take me as your example. Others, whom I might mention, are very good examples for you to follow, such as Abijah, in whom there was found some good thing toward the Lord God of Israel, in the house of Jeroboam ; Mary, who chose that good part, which could not be taken away from her ; Timothy, who from a child knew the Scriptures. I wish, however, something better and more perfect than even these. Turn to—

Matthew xi. 29: "LEARN OF ME."

The subject of this sermon is *Christ our teacher;* but in this particular way,—*Christ our pattern, Christ our example.* There is much to be learned from what he *said*—from the words of Jesus; but no less from what he *did*, and from what he *was;* and Jesus intended that we should learn of him in this way, as well as in the other. Thus you find him expressly saying, "I have given you *an example*, that ye should do as I have done to you." You find Peter saying of him, "Leaving us *an example,* that *ye should follow his steps.*" And in Eph. iv. 20, you have the expression, "But ye have not so learned Christ;"—*learned Christ,* as if he were both the Teacher and the Lesson—both the Guide and the Way, as he is. And, perhaps, we may be best helped, in seeking to "learn Christ," by looking at him, or, as the apostle expresses it,—"considering" him. That is one of the ways of becoming like him: "We all, with open face, beholding as in a glass the glory of the Lord, are changed into the same image." I cannot pretend to set before you a *portrait* of Jesus. I can only select a very few features of his likeness, and ask you to consider them. In so doing I have two ends in view. I trust there are some among you, who have given themselves to the Lord, who have taken Christ as their Saviour, and whose desire it is, so to walk as to please him. To such I would present Christ as a pattern for them to copy—to frame their life by it—to use it for their guidance. There are others who are still careless, content to be without God, finding their delight in sin, or perhaps deceiving themselves with the hope that they are Christ's, when, in truth, they have never experienced a change of heart, have never come out of the world, and are still walking in the world's ways. I would fain startle these, by showing them the *contrast* there is between Christ and them—the *un*likeness, in the hope of awakening them to a sense of their sin and of their danger, as still out of Christ.

Let us then look at the likeness of Christ, as so wonderfully set forth in Scripture. I shall try to set before you six particulars in his example, in which we may learn of him: 1. *Gentleness.* 2. *Guilelessness.* 3. *Holiness.* 4. *Humility.* 5. *Obedience.* 6. *Usefulness.* I have arranged them alphabetically, that you may remember them in their proper order,—two under the letter G, two under H, one under O, and one under U.

1. GENTLENESS. This is very often pressed upon our notice in Scripture, and urged upon us for our imitation. At a certain season of the year, you often see lambs passing along our streets—on their way to the slaughter-houses. How innocent-looking, how unresisting they are! However ill-treated by dogs, or drivers, or mischievous boys, you never see them turn upon man, or boy, or dog, as some other animals would do. They meekly submit to it all, and harm no one. Such was Jesus. The people did everything they could think of,

to provoke him. They called him by all kinds of bad names; they gave him all kinds of bad treatment; they said he had a devil, that he had connection with Satan, that he was a friend of the worst of men, that he was a glutton and a drunkard; they rudely interrupted him when speaking, they falsely accused him, they unjustly condemned him, they dressed him up in mockery as a king, they spat on him, they laughed at him, they crucified him. And what did he say or do? "He was *led as a lamb* to the slaughter; and as a sheep before her shearers is dumb, so he opened not his mouth." That describes him all his life long,—a gentle lamb. That is one of the reasons why he is so often spoken of as a Lamb. No wonder that Paul in writing to some who professed to be Christ's people, said, "I beseech you by the *meekness and gentleness of Christ.*" No wonder that he is so often spoken of, as in our text, as the *meek* Jesus. And *could* he not have resisted? had he not the *power?* could he not have punished and taken vengeance on them at once? was he not the Lion of the tribe of Judah, as well as the Lamb of God? was not one of his names "the Mighty God?" And yet he *did* not,—he *would* not. And why? For this, among other reasons, that he might leave us an example of meekness and gentleness. Peter in his first Epistle thus sets forth Christ: "Who, when he was reviled, reviled not again; when he suffered, he threatened not." And to us Christ himself says, in special connection with this feature of his character,—"Learn of me."

See that Sabbath scholar, who if you were to ask him the first question in the Shorter Catechism, "What is man's chief end?" would unhesitatingly answer, "To glorify God;" who could repeat to you without a mistake the paraphrase on Isaiah's words—

> "Wronged and oppressed, how meekly he
> In patient silence stood!
> Mute, as the peaceful harmless lamb,
> When brought to shed its blood:"

or this other—

> "Gentle and still shall be his voice,
> No threats from him proceed."

Well, he has been, as he thinks, ill used;—he has been called by some hard name; he has been laughed at; he has been interrupted in his play; he has had something that belonged to him taken away; he has got a stroke from some bigger, stronger boy, or he has been provoked by a brother, or sister, or companion at home. Or, see that other, a little servant-girl, with as much knowledge of the Bible as the boy, and as ready to answer any question you may put, and to answer it well: she has been doing something amiss, and her mistress finds fault with her; or she has been doing her best, and she gets no credit for it,—not a word to encourage her, perhaps only a scolding; or she has asked to get out, of an evening, and because it is not convenient, or is thought not to be safe, she is refused; or the children have been fretful, and troublesome, and trying to one's patience. And what then? In either case, do you see that scowl upon the brow, that sullen look, that significant shake of the head, that quivering lip,—telling of a heart full of angry, passionate feelings, and a desire for vengeance,—followed (when it can be) by the sharp, angry word, or the angry blow—slamming the doors, —wearing the look of a very ill-used person,—doing everything with the worst possible grace,—doggedly. silent and sulky,—making every one around uncomfortable? What do you think of that? And yet that, or something like it, is not uncommon in Sabbath-scholars and church-going young people—ay, in some who profess to be God's children; explaining how, when such tempers are unbroken, when such feelings are unsubdued, we have men and women who say and do such ungentle, unloving things, causing great discomfort alike to themselves and others. When I see such, I often wish I could hold up a looking-glass in which they might see, and so be ashamed of—*themselves.* I wish rather they would look into that best of all looking glasses—the Bible, and at the example of Jesus; that they might be startled, as they could not but see—amid all their provocation, and all their ill-usage—how different Christ was from them, how there is no resemblance whatever between them; that the question might cross their minds, "Can I be one of Christ's people, and yet be so unlike to him?" Surely, dear children, there is room for misgiving here, and great room for improvement, even in the best of us. Will you not look to the gentle Saviour, and hear him saying to you,

"Learn of me?" This is one of the things that is so attractive about Christ, and one of the reasons why we should come under his teaching,—he is so gentle, and considerate, and tender-hearted; we need not be afraid of him—"*For* I am meek." It would make *you* attractive too.

2. GUILELESSNESS. You sometimes meet with people who have always a smile on their face, and seem always glad to see you, but who, if you could see their hearts, or if you could overhear them when your back is turned, would be found to have no very friendly feeling towards you. They are not *real* people—they are not truthful. We speak of them as being *double*—acting two parts. Jesus was not like such. He was every way real. He was just what he seemed to be. There was nothing "put on"—nothing "made." Had there been a window through which men might have seen his heart, they would have found it agree exactly with his words, and his looks, and his actions. He never said one thing and thought another. He never said one thing and wished another. He was perfectly *true*. No outside gilding,—the same through and through. This is another of the things specially mentioned, when Christ is set before us as our example: "Neither was guile found in his mouth." And it was no less true, that "in his *spirit* there was no guile." This is another most important respect in which we should "learn of him."

My dear children, let me press this upon you. Guile

is a very common, and yet a very evil and dangerous thing. Without exactly telling a lie, it is untruthfulness. Without exactly robbing any one, it is yet dishonesty. Perhaps, I may best describe it by the word *hypocrisy*, that is—*seeming to be*—*pretending to be* what you are not. For instance, if you were to make a great ado about some young companion, seeming to be his particular friend, and all the while were trying to hurt his character—to ruin him; that would be guile. Now, how often are your words guileful; how often are your actions guileful! It is so in your dealings with those about you. It is so in your dealings with God. How do you feel when you read of Judas betraying his Master? How you hate the man, how you despise him, as you see him walking up to Jesus, saluting him, kissing him,—when you know that he does not love him,—nay, that this is just the way in which he points him out to the soldiers, that they may take him! Oh, how you hate guile in Judas!—what a vile and wicked thing it seems in him; and yet how you practise it yourselves! Is there no guile in your *prayers*—when you confess your sin and profess to be sorry for it, and ask the Lord to forgive it; when you say your heart is very wicked, and you would like a new heart; when you repeat that petition, " Lead me not into temptation, but deliver me from evil?" Some of you don't *believe* in your prayer, you don't *feel* what you say, you don't *wish* it. You would not *like* to get what you have been asking; it is a guileful prayer. That is one reason why our prayers are not answered. Or you begin to think about your soul and about salvation; you ask what you must do to be saved; you seem to be seeking Jesus—sometimes reading, sometimes praying, sometimes weeping; and we say to ourselves, "Surely that girl will find Christ, and be saved, she seems so earnest." But no. And why? There is *guile* in her seeking. There is something she will not give up—will not part with for Christ; she is keeping something back. Her *heart* is what the Lord asks and requires; but like Ananias and Sapphira, she keeps back part of the price, will not make an entire surrender of herself; and so she never finds Christ, and after a while goes quite back, and becomes careless as ever.

This was often the way with Israel long ago. They seemed very sorry and very earnest, and their words were very good; they did not intend to deceive Him either, but their heart was not *sincere,* was not *right* with God, and whenever his judgments were removed, they fell away again. I fear this very thing is keeping back some among ourselves. There may be much earnestness, but there is some guile; and of the double-minded man,—the double-hearted man,—him in whose spirit there is guile, the Lord says, "Let not that man think that he shall receive anything of the Lord." Let us, dear children, pray for a simple mind—an honest and sincere heart. And let us not be *pretenders* in our religion, putting on long faces, and setting up ourselves for something very good, when it is not real. Let us seek to be like the pure gold —such that our goodness will *wear*, will *last*,—standing in no danger of having the glitter rubbed off; such that we may be thoroughly depended on. Alas, how many there are, who, as young people, once promised well, but who, by putting on and keeping up false appearances, lost even what they had gained, and either became self-deceived and died deluded, or lived to throw off the very form of religion, and laugh at everything good!

This is another feature in the character of Jesus, that makes him so worthy to be believed and trusted—there is no guile in him. When he asks us to come to him, when he promises to give us rest and salvation, when he says he will cast out none, it is all true ; there is no doubt about it. There is no room for asking, " Does he mean it ? is he sincere ? may I have confidence in him? will he not, after all, shut his door against me ?" Never, never! For these eighteen hundred years he has been tried and trusted, and his truthfulness has never failed. Make you the trial, and you will be among the first to tell how true and guileless Jesus is.

3. HOLINESS. By this I mean hating and shrinking back from all that is evil, and loving all that is good. Holiness is just the opposite of sin. Now, if there was one thing more than another that Jesus was remarkable for, it was this. Hence you have that beautiful name given to him, " Thy Holy Child Jesus." Hence you

read of him, that "he did no sin,"—that "he knew no sin,"—that he "was holy, harmless, undefiled." This, too, is specially mentioned in connection with Christ as our example. Here he says most earnestly, "Learn of me"—"Be ye holy, for I am holy." Satan tempted him to sin, as he tempts us, but he signally failed. Men tried to find sin in him, but they could find none. Pilate, the Roman governor, though he would gladly have found some evil in him, said, "I find no fault in him;" and though himself a regardless, wicked man, he was afraid to condemn him, and took water and washed his hands before the multitude, saying, "I am innocent of the blood of *this just person;*" so that we have the testimony of his greatest enemies, that Jesus was a holy man. And even the all-seeing eye of God could not see in him one stain of sin.

Dear children, what shall we say about you in this matter? Are not you sinning every day, and all day long,—in your thoughts, and desires, and looks, and words, and actions? And the worst of it is, that you *like* it. So far from being sorry for sin, you find your delight in it, and will not part with it. Your heart is unholy, and your life is unholy. And what then? Why, unless you learn of Christ—unless you ask and get from him a clean heart, and then lead a holy life,— he and you can have nothing to do with each other. If I wished to visit at your house, and were to bring with me your bitterest enemy, whom you hated so that you could not bear the sight of him, could not be in the same room with him—one who was always vexing you, doing everything he could to hinder and annoy you, willing, if only he had the ability and the opportunity, even to take your life,—would you make me welcome? Would you not say to me, "If you come alone, I'll be glad to see you; but if you bring him with you, I'll be obliged to shut my door and keep you both out. If you will keep by him, there can be no friendship—no dealings between you and me?" Now, that is just what Jesus says. If you would be friends with him, you must be like him, you must put away his greatest enemy—sin; for they cannot do together. He died that sin might be taken out of the way; he shed his blood to open up a fountain where sinners might be washed from their sins; he offers us the Holy Spirit that he may make us holy; and if, after all this, we will still keep by our sins, then we must have done with Christ.

And if we have done with Christ, then we must have done with heaven too, for Christ and heaven are alike—neither of them can bear the presence of sin. It is as if above heaven's door, the inscription were written in large letters, so that you may see and read it from earth, "Herein entereth nothing that defileth, neither whatsoever worketh abomination or maketh a lie"—that is, "No sin *admitted here!*" "The wicked"—those who love and practise sin—"shall be cast into hell." The question was once asked at a gathering of children, "Have we anything that we did not get from God?" What would *you* have said? A little Hottentot girl, five years old, answered, "Yes, sir;—SIN!" And as we did not get it from God, and it is the only bad thing in the world which he made, God will have nothing to do with it. Children! will *you?* Will you rather give up Christ than give up sin? Will you rather lose heaven than lay aside sin? Will you rather have your soul to be cast into hell than part with sin? "Blessed are the pure in heart, for they shall see God." That implies that those who are *not* pure in heart, shall *not* see God.

But how am I to be made holy? Jesus says, "Learn of me"—come to me, and I will make you holy. I will give you the Holy Spirit. "A new heart also will I give you, and a right spirit will I put within you." Will you not ask the Holy Spirit? Will you not ask Jesus to make you holy? Will you not offer up that prayer, "Create in me a clean heart, and renew a right spirit within me?" Remember that to be holy is to be Christ-like—ay, and to be holy is to be happy; and always the more holy the more happy: so that it is not only good in the end, because it leads to heaven and prepares for it, but it is very good and very blessed all the way through. The best wish I could wish for you, is that you may be like a good man of whom I have read, who said there was nothing in all the world he feared so much as sin, and that he would rather be torn in pieces by wild beasts, than knowingly or willingly commit any sin against God. And you who have reason to believe that you are Christ's, let it be your daily effort and your daily prayer, that you may strive more against sin, and follow after holiness, without which no man shall see the Lord.

4. HUMILITY. This is a very beautiful feature of character, and it appeared in all its perfection and beauty in Jesus. He was compared to a lamb for his gentleness; can you tell me, to what he was compared —to what he compares himself, for his *humility?* A flower. He says, "I am the Rose of Sharon, and the Lily of the Valleys." He is compared to the rose for beauty and fragrance; and regarding this, I give you a sentence from Samuel Rutherford, a good minister who wrote very tenderly and sweetly of Christ: "There's not a rose but hath a brier growing out of it, except the rose of Sharon, that flower of the field not made with hands, a smell whereof were worth a world." There is a saying, "There's no rose without its thorn;" but here is one—Christ! But he is not only the rose; he is also the lily of the valley,— the emblem of simplicity and humility; not raising up its showy head in the most public and frequented places, but away down in the lowly valleys, as if shrinking from public view; and when you come to it, there it is in simple beauty, with bended head, looking towards the ground. Such was Jesus. Everything we read of him, as a child or as a man, is the furthest possible from pride. Let us look at two pictures. For once, Jesus is to make a public entry into the Holy City, and to be acknowledged by the people as king. And how does he come? He might have had a royal chariot, and sent his heralds before to proclaim his coming, saying, "Lift up your

heads, O ye gates, and be ye lift up, ye everlasting doors; and the King of glory shall come in!" What a crowd!— the people spreading their garments in the way, and strewing branches of palm-trees, as when conquerors returned from the wars, and were thus honoured. At length the multitude comes up, and where is Jesus? Yonder,—as was prophesied of him hundreds of years before: " Behold, thy King cometh unto thee, lowly and riding upon an ass, and upon a colt, the foal of an ass." Even then he would teach the lesson of humility. Again, it is the night before his crucifixion—the last night he is to spend with his beloved disciples. As they are sitting at table after supper, Jesus rises, takes a towel and ties it about him, as if he were a servant; gets a basin of water, and goes round, washing the feet of his disciples, though he is their Master. Surprised, they would like to know the meaning of it, and Jesus tells them, it is to teach them humility: " For I have given you an example, that ye should do, as I have done to you." " Learn of me, for I am meek and lowly in heart."

Dear children, if you are proud, haughty, highminded, thinking this and the other thing beneath you, —you are not like Christ. If you look down upon and despise those who are a little poorer than yourselves, whose clothes are a little coarser, whose dwelling is a little humbler, whose parents are not so well off as yours, who have not got so good an education as you, who are not so clever as you,— you are not like Christ. If you pride yourselves on your knowledge, on being able to repeat so many passages of Scripture, on being so well up with your Catechism; if you think yourselves vastly better than most who are around you; if you have grown proud of your very religion, and take credit for being so good;—you are not like Christ. This is a great hindrance in the way of our coming to Christ at first; we are so proud—we think so much of ourselves, that we will not stoop low enough to get in at his door—we will not take low enough views of ourselves, and high enough views of Christ; and rather than come down to his terms—that is, rather than be admitted as poor beggars, as helpless sinners—we will not come in at all. And so it is a hindrance to after-progress. A humble Christian will always make the greatest progress, and have the greatest happiness. The greatest and best men, you will find to be the humblest, and to think least of themselves. We have a beautiful instance of it in the case of Dr. Carey, one of the earliest and best missionaries who ever went to India. He had made great sacrifices and undergone great labours for the cause of Christ; he had become a great scholar, and translated the Bible into many languages, so as to render it accessible to about three hundred millions of people. Well, when asked about a text for his funeral sermon, what do you think he fixed on? He said he was unworthy to have anything said of him, but if there was a funeral sermon, it was to be on that verse in the fifty-first Psalm: " Have mercy upon me, O God, according to thy loving-kindness; according unto the multitude of thy tender mercies, blot out my transgressions." And he left behind him this inscription for his tombstone:—

"WILLIAM CAREY, born Aug. 17, 1761, died ———.
> A wretched, poor, and helpless worm,
> On thy kind arms I fall."

"God resisteth the proud, but giveth grace unto the humble."

5. OBEDIENCE. I might speak of the obedience of Christ to his Heavenly Father, as furnishing a fine example for you and me: "I came not to do mine own will, but the will of him that sent me. My meat and my drink is to do the will of my heavenly Father." And even when his burden was so heavy, and his cup of suffering so bitter, that he was almost overwhelmed, we hear him submissively saying, "Not as I will, but as thou wilt." Oh, to be like him in this—doing whatever God gives us to do, and bearing whatever he lays upon us, patiently and cheerfully! When you get some difficult and disagreeable work to do—when sickness comes, or poverty, and you have much to try you—when you are apt to feel like Jonah, "It is better for me to die than to live,"—think of Jesus; and if you cannot get at it at once, seek to learn of him, pray for help, make that hymn yours:—

> " My God, my Father, while I stray,
> Far from my home, on life's rough way,
> Oh, teach me from my heart to say,—
> Thy will be done!"

But I mean especially now, *obedience to earthly parents;* for Jesus sets an example to us even in that.

Though he was so wise and so good, and his parents were poor and in humble life, he did not leave them, he did not despise them. I like that verse: "And he went down with them, and came to Nazareth, and *was subject unto them.*" I give you that, as a reason annexed to the fifth commandment: Why should I honour and obey my father and mother? Because Jesus did it, and did it as an example, saying, "Learn of me." I fear many of our children are unlike Christ in this. Disrespectful words and disobedient conduct are too common. Even when a thing is done, it is not done cheerfully, and certainly not gracefully—done, perhaps, for fear of the rod. I grieve over this—that children in many cases seem to stand so little in awe of their parents—that parents seem to have so little authority over their children. That is one reason why many of our young people turn out so ill. Undutiful children cannot expect God's blessing. Such are not like Joseph,—not like Samuel, —not like Jesus. It is a religious duty which God has laid upon you, which if you neglect, you dishonour God. Dear children, your parents may, sooner than you expect, be taken away from you; and you may one day, when it is too late, weep as you remember how you grieved and vexed,—ay, perhaps broke the hearts of those who loved you so well.

6. Usefulness. Christ's whole life was spent in seeking to serve God, and to benefit others. How unselfish he was! what a kind heart and helpful hand were his! As regards God, we hear him saying, "Wist

ye not that I must. "it must have been very business?" As regards men, we read, "He went about continually doing good." Even when he was on his trial, he thought of his backsliding disciple Peter, and with a look of love won him back. Even when on the cross, he could think of the poor malefactor, who was dying beside him. His whole life here says, "Learn of me." That applies even to you. My young friends, are you doing any good? Are you *trying* to do any good? or are you selfish, only thinking of and seeking what will please yourselves,—"*I* would like this and the other thing?" Children have often done much good. Remember the little Hebrew maid. I like to hear of children being kind and attentive to the sick and the old,—putting themselves in the way of helping them, and always being ready to do what they can. Could none of you read to the sick, or the blind, or the old? could you not help some poor neighbour—carrying a pitcher of water, going to the druggist or the dispensary for medicine, running on any little errand without expecting to be paid for it? Could you not sometimes speak a word of comfort, and help to dry the tears of the sorrowful?

"A little word in kindness spoken,
 A motion or a tear,
Has often healed the heart that's broken,
 And made a friend sincere.

Then deem it not an idle thing
 A pleasant word to speak;
The face you wear, the thought you bring,
 The heart may heal or break."

And can you, so wise and so good, souls of others? can you not try to keep some young friend out of evil—Sabbath-breaking, bad books, bad company? can you not try to bring some one to Christ? I read somewhere lately, that it is no good sign when one is content to go to heaven *alone*. Are *you* content to think of going to heaven alone? Would you like to have a "starless crown"? Can you not *pray* for others? *Do* you? I read a few days ago of two little Sabbath-scholars, who were such blessings to their fathers. One of them, as she lay a-dying, asked her father to pray; and when he said he could not, she began to teach him. As she prayed, he repeated after her, and soon began to pray for himself, so as to forget everything but his sin and his God. "When he came to himself, he raised his head from the bed on which he had rested it; there lay the little speaker, a lovely smile was upon her face, her little hand was in that of her father,—but she had gone to be among the angels." Happy girl! to be a blessing to her own father! Oh, be like Jesus in this!

I must stop here, though many other things might have been said about Christ as our example. And now, dear children, have you learned of Christ? Are you learning of Christ? Are you following his steps? Are you taking him as your example? Do you even *wish* to be like Jesus? Is it true, as you sometimes sing,—"I long to be like Jesus?" I have heard of a man painting a horse, and writing under it, "This is a horse!"

"Surely," you say, "it must have been very unlike, that he needed to do that." And yet I fear that would need to be done in the case of many who set themselves up as Christians,—both old and young. There is so little likeness to Christ, that one would need to tell, "This is meant to be a Christian!" I saw two people lately whom I had never seen before, and yet I knew at once who they were. How? They were so like their brother whom I knew. I saw the resemblance at once. Is it so with you and Christ? "They took knowledge of them, that they had been with Jesus." "*Living epistles of the Lord Jesus,* known and read of all men." You cannot learn of Christ in the way we have been describing, until you COME to him—*believe* on him—give up yourselves to him. *That* must be your first step, and it should be taken *now—to-day*. You must be like Christ, or perish! There is no possibility of getting to heaven, without being like Christ. You would not be fit for heaven otherwise; you could not enjoy Christ's company. It is not enough to have the way to heaven opened up; you must be made *fit* for it,— that is, you must be like Christ: so that if you are not *like him* on earth, you can never be *with him* in heaven. And as you cannot be *like Christ* until you have *believed* on him, it must be,—"Christ your Saviour" first; "Christ your example" next.

Believing children! *strive* to be like Christ; *pray* to be like Christ. Often put the question, Would Christ have done as I am doing,—spoken as I am speaking,

—felt as I am feeling? Am I like Christ in this? And though often discouraged, still persevere; day by day seek to make some progress. "Learn of him;" and "*when he shall appear, you shall be like him,* for you shall see him as he is."

THE HYMN.

I WANT to be like Jesus,—
  So lowly and so meek;
For no one marked an angry word
  That ever heard him speak.

I want to be like Jesus,—
  So frequently in prayer:
Alone upon the mountain-top,
  He met his Father there.

I want to be like Jesus,—
  I never, never find
That he, though persecuted, was
  To any one unkind.

I want to be like Jesus,—
  Engaged in doing good;
So that of me it may be said,
  "She hath done what she could."

Alas! I'm not like Jesus,
  As any one may see:
O gentle Saviour, send thy grace
  And make me like to thee!

The Holy Spirit.

THE HYMN.

COME, Holy Spirit, come,
  Let thy bright beams arise;
Dispel the sorrow from our minds,
  The darkness from our eyes.

Convince us of our sin;
  Then lead to Jesus' blood;
And to our wondering view reveal
  The secret love of God.

Revive our drooping faith;
  Our doubts and fears remove;
And kindle in our breasts the flame
  Of never-dying love.

'Tis thine to cleanse the heart,
  To sanctify the soul,
To pour fresh life in every part,
  And new-create the whole.

Dwell, Spirit, in our hearts;
  Our minds from bondage free;—
Then shall we know, and praise, and love
  The Father, Son, and Thee.

Y DEAR YOUNG FRIENDS,—Wouldn't you like very much to have a Friend, who should never leave your side from this hour till your dying day; who should watch over you like a father, and love you like a mother, and sympathize with you like a sister or brother; gentle, and kind, and forbearing; telling you when you did wrong, encouraging you in

what was right, explaining to you what you could not understand, directing you when you did not know what to do or where to go, keeping you out of the way of evil; not—like most people—taking offence on the slightest occasion, and tiring, and changing, and at last dying,—but untiring, unchanging, undying, so that wherever you might be, with temptation, or danger, or death before you, *there* you might have your Friend, and Brother, and Guide ever by your side,—wouldn't you like that?

Do you never wish that you had been one of the disciples of Jesus, listening to his sermons in public, and to his kind words at home; with liberty to go to him at all hours of the day, his ear always open to hear you, and his hand ever ready to help you; when he had to rebuke, doing it so quietly; and when he could encourage, doing it so heartily; not turning his back upon you when other people did it, not despising you when you despised yourself; a "Friend that sticketh closer than a brother,"—so closely, that he could say, "Lo, I am with you *alway*, even unto the end of the world?" I am sure you sometimes—especially those who have few real friends, or none—wish *that*. And that is just what I am going to tell you about to-day— that such a friend is to be had, and how you may get him for *your* friend. Can any one tell me who that friend is? My text will tell you:—

Luke xi. 13: "How much more shall your heavenly Father give THE HOLY SPIRIT to them that ask him?"

In order to find out who it is that is spoken of here, I shall ask and answer a question: "How many persons are there in the Godhead?" "There are three persons in the Godhead, the Father, the Son, and *the Holy Ghost*, and these three are one God, the same in substance, equal in power and glory." Now, you have often heard of God *the Father* as the sinner's friend; and of God *the Son* as the sinner's friend; I am not sure that you have heard or thought much of God *the Holy Spirit* as the sinner's—as the children's friend; and yet so it is, as I shall try to show you. I am anxious that you should know and love the Holy Spirit, for many reasons. I find a good man saying, "If you are strangers to the work of *the Spirit*, you are strangers to the work of *the Saviour*." If you look into the Bible, or into a book called a "Concordance," where all the words of the same kind that occur in the Bible are arranged together, you will see how often mention is made of the Holy Spirit. So, if you look into that remarkable summary of Bible doctrine, the Shorter Catechism, you will see the same thing. Were I to ask you five of the most important questions which it contains: "How are we made partakers of the redemption purchased by Christ?" "How doth the Spirit apply to us the redemption purchased by Christ?" &c.,*—your answers to these would show, how important it is that we should know and love the Holy Spirit. I would not wish you to have

* Questions 29, 30, 31, 89, and 91.

to say what those said, of whom we read in the New Testament; who, when they were asked if they had received the Holy Ghost, replied, "We have not so much as heard whether there be any Holy Ghost."

I. GOD'S BEST GIFT TO MEN: "He will *give the Holy Spirit.*" II. HOW IT IS TO BE GOT: "To them *that ask him.*"

I need scarcely explain to you what is meant by a *gift.* At a certain time of the year, almost every shop window is filled with nicely-bound books, or beautiful pictures, or toys of various kinds, or other things; many of which find their way into your hands, or into your homes, as *Christmas* or *New-Year's gifts.* They are *given* to you by your friends, *with* or *without* the asking. Now, though Christmas and New Year—the time for giving and getting such gifts—may have quite passed away, before you read what I am writing, I can recommend another gift, which it is not yet too late to get; a gift better far than any you can possibly have got; which your parents and friends cannot give you; which is more worth the having than anything else in all the world,—as I have called it, *God's best gift;* and which, precious as it is, is to be got for the asking—even the Friend I have spoken of,—the Holy Spirit. Your fathers and mothers have been giving you many good things; and Jesus says in the text, "If they, being evil, know how to give good gifts to their children, how much more shall your heavenly Father give the Holy

Spirit to them that ask him?" Dear children, I would like you to get this as your *better than New-year's* gift—this "good thing"—the right to bestow which, Jesus purchased with his blood, and which the Father is willing to give to the youngest of you all.

I. The Gift: "the Holy Spirit"—a good, loving, blessed Guide and Friend, whom you all need, and without whom you never can be truly happy on earth, and never can get to heaven. I wish I knew what it were best to say to you about him, that I might get you to ask him—to take him, to be your Divine Friend from this day forward. I can now only mention a few things about him,—some of the names given to him in Scripture—some of the things which he is represented as doing.

1. The Spirit *convinces us of sin*. The name I give him here, is—the Reprover. "Stop!" says some boy; "you have surely made a mistake. Surely you don't think that is the way to get us to seek this Friend, by telling us at the very outset that the first thing he'll do will be to *reprove us*,—to find fault with us,—to tell us we have been doing wrong; and perhaps even to threaten to punish us, and make us afraid?" Just wait a little. Here is a boy wandering about the streets,—a friendless, stranger-boy. He is in sailor's dress—broad-brimmed hat and blue jacket—all new; but homeless and penniless. I find he has left as happy a country-home as ever boy had. He opened his

father's desk, and took his father's money, and at dead of night, slipshod, he passed the room where his unsuspecting parents slept, and with his bundle in his hand, heartlessly stole away, bound for the sea. A pretended friend deceived him,—promised to get him a ship, purchased the necessary clothing, and having gotten his money, left him to find out that he had been duped. I pity the youth, I wish to be his friend; and as his friend, having gained his confidence and taken him under my care, my very first effort is to convince him that he has done wrong,—to set his sin in its proper light before him,—to show him how ungrateful, undutiful, cruel a part he has acted; and till he sees, and feels, and acknowledges his fault, however anxious to befriend him, my way is shut up. I can have no hope of him till that end is gained. Only when he has "come to himself," like the prodigal, and got a sense of his sin, and at length is ashamed of himself, and grieved that he should have so wronged those who have only deserved his love, do I feel that I have won the boy, and immediately take steps for his restoration to his home. Or here is a blind man, wandering along a dangerous road, having refused to let any one accompany him. He has taken a wrong turn, and missed his way, and a few steps more will be the death of him. What, as his friend, shall be my first word? Shall it not be, "Stop, sir! stop! Not another step! It is a wonder you are not killed already. Every step here endangers your life. You are out of your way, and unless you would find a grave,—turn, and give yourself up to my charge?" I can do nothing for him—I cannot save the man—till I have persuaded him that he is wrong. If I cannot do that, he will go on and perish.

That, my dear children, is just what this Friend would begin with,—*must* begin with, in your case. He must act the part of a *Reprover*—he must convince you of your sin in breaking God's holy law; in forsaking and forgetting God; in walking in the world's ways, and doing the devil's bidding; and, above all, in neglecting and refusing to come to Christ, when he would save you, at once from sin and from hell. Surely he is a friend in setting your sin before you, showing you what a dreadful thing it is, and what the end of it must be; that you may be ashamed of it, and grieve for it, and, as a poor, perishing sinner, cry for mercy. Children! have you ever got a sight of your sin? have you ever been convinced of sin—awakened to a sense of sin? If not, then it is full time that some friendly hand were knocking at your door, and arousing you out of your sleep, and making you rub up your heavy eyes, to see yourself—your sin, —your danger. If there is one in all the world that needs such a friend, it is *you*. Such a friend will be indeed a good gift—ay, as people say, a *God-send* to *you*.

2. The Spirit *renews the heart*. His name here is— the REGENERATOR—the *Quickener*. Some bad things can be improved; some broken things can be mended.

I have seen a beautiful vase,—a most elegant piece of workmanship,—that was once shattered into I don't know how many pieces, and seemed hopelessly gone; but a skilful hand put them together again, and now it looks as perfect and beautiful as when first it was made. But there are other things which, if once injured,—if once broken, can never be patched up or mended, so as to be of any use. You have seen a cracked bell; what a useless, unmendable thing it is! If that church-bell that rings us in to the house of God on Sabbath, were to get cracked or broken; notwithstanding all the money that it cost, nothing could be done for it,—we could not get it mended,—it would have to be renewed—to be made new—to be melted down and made over again, so as to be really a *new bell*. Now, it is just so with your heart. It is so bad, that there is no improving of it; it is so vile and filthy, that there is no making it cleaner; it is so much injured, that it cannot be mended. You have sometimes tried it, and have failed. Others have tried it, and have failed. One day, after having got a sight of your sin, you thought it would never do to go on at this rate, with such a wicked heart; for you yourself felt that the only fit place for such a heart was hell. And you set about cleaning it, and mending it, and making it better. You tried to give up some of your sins, and said your prayers regularly, and left off some of your bad habits, and seemed getting on tolerably well; and people said you were becoming a good child, and you became somewhat proud of yourself; but, after all, it would not do, and with the feeling that a negro might as well try to wash himself white, or a leopard to rub off its spots, you gave up in despair. And your mother, much as she loved you, could not make your wicked heart better; nor your Sabbath-school teacher, nor your minister; and it has come to be a serious question, "What is to be done?" Your heart is *dead*, you want it *made alive;* it is hopelessly *bad*, you want it *made new;* it is unspeakably *vile*, you want it *cleansed*. Is there any hope for you?

Yes! my young friend; yes! there is hope. If you have seen your heart in its true colours, you will not think so much of it as once you did. It is like a cage full of unclean birds—the smell so bad that you cannot bear to go near it. It is a wonder that Christ should ask, or be willing to receive, such a filthy heart as yours. There is only One in all the world who can cleanse it; and that One is the Holy Spirit. It is like a dead body, a mass of corruption; so that you say, it cannot too soon be buried out of sight. It cannot help itself, and no one else can help it. There is only One in all the world who can make that dead, corrupt heart of yours to live; and that One is the Holy Spirit. That is the second thing this blessed Friend does. He takes the old heart away—breaks it—melts it—washes it—*renews* it; and then in the place of the old heart he puts a *new* heart; in place of the filthy heart, a *clean* heart; in place of the sin-loving heart, a *God-loving* heart.

What a wonderful change now! what a blessed change now! surely this is a Friend worth having indeed, for he has given me the gift of a *new heart!* Now I can understand what is set forth in Scripture, as "the washing of regeneration and the renewing of the Holy Ghost." Now I can understand the meaning of that Scripture prayer, "Come from the four winds, O breath, and breathe upon the slain—upon the dead, that they may live." Now I can enter into the spirit of that hymn :—

> " Come, Holy Spirit, from above,
>   With all thy quickening powers;
> Kindle a flame of sacred love
> In these cold hearts of ours."

3. The Spirit *teaches us to pray,—how* to pray, and *what to pray for.* His name here is—the ADVOCATE—the *Intercessor.* A young man of twenty has got into bad company, and the end of it is, that he now occupies the murderer's cell. He would fain make an effort to obtain pardon, and get his young life spared; but he knows not what should be done,—what to say for himself,—what ground to take up; and everything depends on the way in which the matter is gone about. Were he to draw up the memorial himself, he might make a mistake that would be fatal to him; he might leave out the strongest and best plea of all;—he might send it through a wrong channel, so that it might never reach its destination, or reach it only to be thrown aside. So he has recourse to his counsel,—his advocate, who knows all about these things, and is accustomed

to manage them. *He* draws up the memorial, puts in and keeps out what he sees fit, and forwards it through the proper channel, so that if the application can be successful at all, it must be in his hands.

Children! that is just your position. Some of you have had no mother to teach you to lisp your infant prayers, as soon as you could speak, and, as you grew up, to get you to kneel beside her morning and night to repeat your prayer from day to day; some—because your mother was dead, and some—because she did not pray for herself, and far less thought of teaching you. But even those whose mothers taught them to *say* their prayers, have come to feel that somehow that was not *praying*, and how to pray aright they did not know. Even God's people, and Paul among the rest, say, "We know not what things we should pray for as we ought." And who shall help us? We cannot now go like the disciples to Jesus, and say, "Lord, teach us to pray." We may ask wrong things, or ask in a wrong way. Is there no Advocate—none to draw up our petitions for us, ay, and present them for us too? Yes! "the Spirit also helpeth our infirmities" in prayer; the Spirit "maketh intercession for us with groanings which cannot be uttered;" and *He* maketh intercession—*according to the will of God*. Sometimes he makes the petition very short—a single line; but it is always to the point, and serves the purpose. Here is a prayer which the Spirit taught David to offer: "Pardon mine iniquity, for it is great;" and here is another which he taught the publican: "God be merciful to me a sinner;" and here is a third, which he taught to a blind beggar man: "Jesus, thou son of David, have mercy on me!"

Perhaps some of you think you can pray very well without any teaching; you would even volunteer to teach some of the younger children, as being quite up to it. My dear children, there are many ways of praying; but there is only *one right way*, which Scripture calls "praying in the Holy Ghost." Many who have prayed all their days, are puzzled at times, and feel as if they could not pray at all. They feel the need of the Holy Spirit's help, and remind God of the promise of our text, and of that other promise, that "he will pour out the Spirit of grace and of supplications;" for they cannot—*you cannot*—pray aright without the Spirit. It is a great matter this, whatever you think of it. How thankful people are sometimes, to get one to write a letter for them, when they cannot, or are afraid to write themselves. That young girl, who, through vanity and love of dress, has brought herself to misery and to the streets,—her character gone, and, though but a girl, prematurely old—how she pleads with me, now that her sin and her punishment are both pressing hard upon her, to intercede for her, to write to her former employer, or to the friends whom she has disgraced! how she regards me ever after as her friend and benefactor! Will not you be like her? Will you not apply to, and welcome the help of, the Heavenly Friend, who is so able and so willing? Yes, we have an Advocate and Intercessor *in heaven,*—Jesus Christ the righteous; but we have also an Advocate and Intercessor *on earth*—ay, *within us*—the Holy Spirit.

4. The Spirit *enables us to understand the word of God.* Here his name is—the TEACHER—the *Interpreter*—the *Enlightener.* I shall suppose a case which may explain. There is a boy whose father has long been in foreign parts. A letter has come of great importance, inasmuch as complying with or neglecting the instructions contained in it, will affect his whole future life. But the boy has lost his eyesight, and though he has the letter in his hand, he can make nothing of it; or it is written, in a foreign language, so that, while he sees the writing, he might as well have been blind, it is quite unintelligible; or he can read the words, but cannot make out the sense, cannot understand what his father means, and so is just as before. Now, what in such a case would be needed? One of three things: a skilful physician to cut the cataract that obscures his vision, and restore to him his eyesight, that he may read for himself; or an interpreter who can translate the words into his own tongue, so that he may at once comprehend their meaning; or a further and fuller explanation from the writer of the letter, clearing up what was dark and doubtful. Now, all these cases occur with regard to God's letter, which he has written to us concerning the great matter of our salvation, and all these cases the Holy Spirit meets. Like a physician, he opens and enlightens the eyes of our understanding; like an in-

terpreter, he translates God's truth into words that we can understand; like a friend, he explains and throws further light upon what we could not comprehend. "Open mine eyes," says David, "that I may behold wondrous things out of thy law." The Spirit does *that*. "Understandest thou what thou readest?" said Philip to an Ethiopian prince, as he drove along in his chariot, reading the fifty-third chapter of Isaiah, "He was led as a lamb to the slaughter," &c. "How can I," said he, "except one teach me?" The Spirit does *that*. Then, it was the Spirit who wrote the Bible at first,— who taught the writers of the different books what to write; "for holy men of old spake as they were moved by the Holy Ghost;" so that it is *His* book. He is the author of it, and he can teach us to understand what he himself has written, and write it on our hearts anew. And such was the promise: "When he, the Spirit of truth is come, he will guide you into all truth." So he is called the "Spirit of wisdom and revelation in the knowledge of Christ."

My young friends, if ever you are to understand the Bible, it must be by the teaching of the Holy Spirit along with your study of it. This is one of the great purposes for which God promises and gives the Spirit. So Nehemiah says, "Thou gavest also thy good Spirit to instruct them." Hence the need, whenever you read the Bible, of seeking the Spirit's teaching; otherwise, you will never find Christ and life and salvation in it. Every time you open God's book, send up a silent prayer, however short, "Holy Spirit! help me to understand the Scriptures. Take of the things of Christ and show them to me. Lord, open mine eyes that I may see!" No one can understand the way of salvation except as the Spirit teaches him, through the word. And so with regard to other things. You are often perplexed and don't know what to do. The Holy Spirit is willing to be your Guide, to point out the way to you, to do for you what Great-Heart, in the Pilgrim's Progress, did for Christiana and Mercy and the boys,—to conduct you all the way to heaven. So I find the Psalmist saying, "Thy Spirit is good; lead me to the land of uprightness." Never venture anywhere,—to do anything, without this blessed Teacher and Guide.

5. The Spirit *strengthens us to resist what is evil*, and *to do what is right*. His name here is—the HELPER and UPHOLDER. He not only converts the sinner to God—he not only enables him to believe on Jesus at first, but he helps him ever after. I know some of you have been trying to do well—to keep out of the way of temptation—to resist the devil. You had got accustomed to some bad habit, and strove hard to get quit of it, and though you have so far succeeded, yet you are often falling, and sometimes fear you will never get the better of it. You have seen a little child when he was beginning to walk,—how carefully his mother watched over him, and though sometimes he fell, how firmly for the most part she kept hold of him, especially when he came near

the fire, or the top of the stair, or any place of danger—how she gave help just as he needed it, till he could walk in safety alone. This is just what the Spirit does; he helps our infirmities; he leads us; he upholds us. "I will put my Spirit within you and cause you to walk in my statutes." "Uphold me with thy free Spirit!" Dear child, make that your prayer now, if you have failed before. Look to the Spirit—cry to him for help.

6. The Spirit *comforts us.* Here his name is—the COMFORTER. Some of the youngest of you have been at *a funeral.* I have sometimes observed your concerned and anxious look—now into the grave, and now at the chief mourners. You have sometimes seen a boy like yourselves, burying his widowed mother,—weeping, as the earth fell upon the coffin-lid, and reminded him that he was now an orphan. Oh, how you pitied the orphan-boy, and wished that some one would take him up and befriend him, and be a father to him, and dry his tears, and cheer his sorrowful heart; and at the thought of being one day yourselves like him, the tears flowed fast down your cheek, and your little heart heaved and fluttered as if it would burst. That was once the feeling of the disciples. Sorrow filled their hearts because their Master and Friend was about to leave them. But Jesus told them, that when he left them he would send another Comforter, who should be with them for ever. And who was that Comforter? The Holy Spirit. And he is the same now that he was then. I spoke at first of him as the *Reprover:*

what a sweet name now—the *Comforter!* So gentle is he, that he is compared to the *dove*—to the *dew;* and while we read of the "*love of the Spirit,*"—and of the "*good Spirit,*" we nowhere read of the *wrath* or *anger* of the Spirit.

I suppose there is scarcely any creature more harmless, gentle, loving, than the dove. There are two— sitting upon the cradle of a sick child, from whose hand they have got many a little meal. As the child lies suffering there, the doves' mournful cooing continues; and when at even, the little one dies, his faithful loving attendants—unable to live alone—fall down beside him—first the one, and soon after, the other— *dead!* So it is recorded in the family history of one of our old Scottish Reformers :—

> "There were two milk-white doves, my wife had nourished,
>   And I too loved, erewhile, at times to stand
> Marking how each the other fondly cherished,
>   And fed them from my baby's dimpled hand.
>
> So tame they grew, that to his cradle flying,
>   Full oft they cooed him to his noontide rest;
> And to the murmurs of his sleep replying,
>   Crept gently in, and nestled in his breast.
>
> 'Twas a fair sight—the snow pale infant sleeping,
>   So fondly guardianed by those creatures mild;
> Watch o'er his closèd eyes their bright eyes keeping—
>   Wondrous the love betwixt the birds and child!
>
> Still as he sickened, seemed the doves, too, dwining,
>   Forsook their food, and loathed their pretty play;
> And on the day he died, with sad note pining,
>   One gentle bird would not be frayed away.

> His mother found it when she rose, sad-hearted,
>   At early dawn, with sense of nearing ill;
> And when at last the little spirit parted,
>   The dove died too—as if of its heart chill!
>
> The other flew to meet my sad home-riding,
>   As with a human sorrow in its coo;
> To my dead child, and its dead mate then guiding,
>   Most pitifully plained—and parted too!" *

It is to such that the Spirit is compared. Or you have seen in the heat of summer, when everything was parched and withered, and every blade of grass seemed drooping, as evening came on, how the dew began to fall, gently, noiselessly, yet so that the effect was almost instantaneous, reviving what had seemed all but dead; and when morning came, shrub, and flower, and field, and tree were fresh and beautiful as ever. It is to such that the Spirit is compared. Even so does he come to revive, and heal, and soothe—binding up broken hearts, and filling the soul with peace and joy. There is no Comforter like him, whatever is your sorrow; and then he is so near,—always within reach, when all else are far away. He "dwelleth with you, and shall be in you," and that for ever. What a Friend is this! Well may we say, "Thy Spirit is good!"

7. The Spirit *makes us holy,—like God, and fit for heaven.* Here his name is—the SANCTIFIER. It is not enough to be pardoned,—we must be sanctified. It is not enough to be reconciled to God,—we must be made like God. It is not enough that Christ has

---

* "Lays of the Scottish Martyrs."

purchased heaven for us,—we must be made meet for heaven. Just suppose that some poor child were taken at once, without any previous training or preparation, to Windsor Castle, to live with the Queen, and associate with lords and ladies, and live in spacious rooms, and have the best of everything,—do you think such a child could be happy, or would it not rather be happiness just to get back again to his own humble home? Or, suppose one of you boys were to be carried right off to India, to get a high post in the army or in the councils of the country, with a large salary and honour to his heart's content,—do you think the change would be a happy one? I suppose not; just because he had not been trained and fitted for it. Neither the society, nor the place, nor the work would be agreeable to him. And how would it be with many of us if we were to be taken to heaven, where we say we hope to go when we die? Would such a change be likely to be a happy one—would we be *fit* for it—would we not feel, "This is no place for me; I love sin, and this is a holy place, and all who are here are holy; I have no care for God, and here God is *everything*, and His presence makes heaven to be what it is, to the rejoicing spirits around the throne?" Do you ever think of this, dear children, that *as you are*, heaven would only be a place of punishment to you? It requires training and preparation; and it is the Holy Spirit who prepares and makes fit for it, by making men holy and like God. And Jesus, in his love, has not only prepared heaven for his people, but by his Spirit he also prepares his people for heaven. If you have any thought of heaven for *your* home, it is time you were getting ready for it. People don't get ready for it in a day. In heaven God's people are all priests; in heaven God's people are all kings; in heaven they all love God, and serve him, and praise him, singing the song of Moses and of the Lamb, " Worthy is the Lamb that was slain!" Oh, seek to get the Spirit at once, to teach you—to fit you for the work and the song, the enjoyment and the glory of heaven. " Therein entereth nothing that defileth."

Such, then, is this good gift of our heavenly Father, this most precious Friend.

II. Just a word as to how *the gift is to be secured.* Not by purchase; not by our goodness; but, for Christ's sake, *by our prayers.* He will " give the Holy Spirit *to them that ask him.*" I don't know how the promise could be more free; I don't know what more anybody could wish. We have nothing like this among men—the best of all gifts *for the asking !* Ask, and ye shall receive it. Oh, my children! is there one of you this day who shall be content to want it—who shall let this day pass without seeking to get it? Other children like you have asked and got it,—why not you? " I was no better than you," I find one saying to his companions; "but the Holy Spirit opened my eyes, and I saw that I was on the very brink of hell." That was the first step, and the others followed. Make this your prayer to-day, and from this day forward, "O Lord, for Jesus' sake give me thy Holy Spirit!" Pray it this evening—alone—with all your heart. Take your Bible, open it, put your finger upon our text; and though no human ear should hear you, lift up your eyes to heaven, remind God of his promise, plead with him,—say, "I will not let thee go except thou bless me."

Love the Spirit, who so loves you; *read* more about him; *think* more about him; *pray to* him. Do not vex him; do not resist him; do not grieve him; do not quench him!

THE HYMN.

SPIRIT DIVINE! attend our prayer,
   And make this house thy home;
Descend with all thy gracious power,—
   O come, Great Spirit, come!

Come as the LIGHT—to us reveal
   Our emptiness and woe;
And lead us in those paths of life,
   Where all the righteous go.

Come as the FIRE—and purge our hearts
   Like sacrificial flame;
Let our whole souls an offering be
   To our Redeemer's name.

Come as the DEW—and sweetly bless
   This consecrated hour;
May barren minds be taught to own
   Thy fertilizing power.

Come as the DOVE—and spread thy wings,
   The wings of peaceful love;
And let the Church on earth become
   Blest as the Church above.

Companions.

HYMN.

ONE there is above all others,
 Well deserves the name of Friend!
His is love beyond a brother's,
 Costly, free, and knows no end.
  They who once his kindness prove,
  Find it everlasting love.

Which of all our friends to save us,
 Could, or would have shed his blood?
But our Jesus died to have us
 Reconciled in him to God.
  His was boundless love indeed!
  Jesus is a friend in need.

Oh! for grace our hearts to soften;
 Teach us, Lord, at length to love;
We, alas! forget too often
 What a friend we have above.
  But when home our souls are brought,
  We shall love thee as we ought.

MY DEAR YOUNG FRIENDS,—The salvation of your souls is the most important of all subjects, and the one which, most of all, I would like you never to lose sight of. To-day, however, I have chosen a subject somewhat different, yet very important too, as I daresay you will agree with me in thinking, before I close. There is a thing you children are all very fond of, about which, with all your liking for it, you have not thought much. So little are you aware of it, amid all the enjoyment you have in it, that if I were to ask you to name the things you like most, I am not sure that you would mention it first,—I am not sure that you would mention it *at all.* Now what can that be? You have it every day; the longer you have it you like it the more; and if you are not very different from most other people, you will like it to the last,—which is the very reason of my taking it up now. You have often seen crows, and sparrows, and swallows, in the country and about the outskirts of the town. Sometimes you may have noticed them flying above our houses and churches, perching on the vane of the spire, or on the roof, or on the trees in the neighbouring gardens; and if so, you must have observed that they are very fond of—*company!* They have been accustomed to it all their days, since first they came out of their shell in their warm nest, and they seem to like to fly, and feed, and twitter, not alone, but *in company*, at least so they generally do. You have seen the little lambs in spring-time: they don't always keep apart, each by itself; but usually in pairs, and often in little groups they play and frisk about, returning to their mothers when they are tired of each other—they, too, are very fond of *company.* And so are *you.* You must have companions. You would not like to live alone, to work alone, to sleep alone, to play alone, to learn your lessons alone, to eat your meals alone, to have each your own little room, however nicely furnished, all to yourselves,— never having anybody in it except yourselves,—with nobody to speak to, to share your joy or sorrow. You say, "What a lonely, miserable way of living that would be! it would be like living in a prison." You must have company. How well some of you like it, I know,—better than your books and lessons, ay, better than your meals. The moment you are up, the moment you are out of school, the moment you have got your dinner, you are off to your companions, and you stay with them till hunger, or fatigue, or the lateness or darkness of the night, sends you home. You could draw your pictures, and make your cages and little boxes, and build your houses, at home—alone; but that is not half so pleasant as when you have one or two companions with you to join you in it,—then it is a pleasure indeed. And God did not intend *you*, any more than the birds or the lambs, to live, and work, and play alone. It was he who made you to like company, and so it is a right thing and a good thing. The *wrong* does not lie *there*. But there is a question, which is worth your looking at,—as to *the kind of company* that is safe, and right, and good. What should our company be—what kind of company should we seek and keep?

I cannot tell you how much depends on your dealing rightly with this question. How you are to get on in the world; whether you are to be good or bad, useful or hurtful, as children, or as men and women; what you are to be when you die, and what is to be your dwelling-place in eternity;—all this depends very much on the company you keep—on what your companions are. Perhaps you say, "That may be all very true of grown-up people, and you may speak about this to them; but surely it can matter very little to us boys and girls, what young people we associate with." It is because you think so, that I have resolved to devote a whole sermon to the subject. I press it on you, dear children, because, so often, friendships formed in youth *last for life;* and because, still oftener, friendships formed in youth *make our after-life what it is,*—ay, AND OUR ETERNITY TOO! *Good* done thus, lasts for ever; *evil* done thus, is never undone.

Now where are we to seek advice regarding so important a matter? who shall tell us what to do? Always go with such matters to the Bible, and put your questions to it; and you cannot do better than go at once to the wisest of men, Solomon,—or rather to the Greater than Solomon, who speaks through him. Turn to—

Proverbs xiii. 20.—" He that WALKETH WITH WISE MEN shall be wise, but A COMPANION OF FOOLS shall be destroyed."

This text answers two pairs of questions: Whose company should we seek,—and why? Whose company should we avoid,—and why? What kind of company should we seek? That of *the wise.* Why? That we may be like them. What kind of company should we avoid? That of *fools.* Why? That we may escape their destruction. My first remark, therefore, is—GOOD COMPANY *to be* SOUGHT; my second,—BAD COMPANY *to be* SHUNNED.

I. Good company *to be* sought. It is as if the text said, "*Walk with wise men.*" But what is meant by "*walking*" with them? I often meet two boys walking together, sometimes in the town and sometimes in the country, so that when the one comes in my way, I am sure the other will not be far off; and I say to any one who happens to be with me, "These two lads must be companions, bosom friends; they are scarcely ever away from each other." The expression,—"*he that walketh with,*" in the first clause of the verse, is thus just the same with the expression,—"*a companion,*" in the second; it means, "he that has wise companions." But again, who are meant by "*the wise?*" Does it mean those who are good scholars; who have a great deal of learning; who are acquainted with foreign languages,—Latin, French, Greek, Hebrew, and the like; who have read a great many books; who have seen much of the world, and are very clever and far-seeing; in a word, who have much of what is generally understood by knowledge and wisdom? No, my dear children, it is not that at all; for some have all the knowledge I have mentioned, and yet they are not *wise;* and some have very little knowledge of these things, or none at all, and yet they are wise men, or wise children, beyond all question. You or I might not be able to get such learned people for our friends and companions, however anxious, so that it must mean something else than that. Come back to the Bible again, and ask your question as before. What says the Scripture? "The *fear of the Lord, that is wisdom:*" and again, "The *fear of the Lord* is the *beginning* of wisdom, and *to depart from evil* is *understanding.*

The wise, whose company Solomon says we are to seek, are thus THOSE WHO FEAR GOD. We are to have *God-fearing companions.* Such was the youthful Joseph, who, when he was tempted to sin, said, "How can I do this great wickedness, and sin against God." Such was young Abijah, in whom "was found some good thing toward the Lord God of Israel in the house of Jeroboam." Such was good Obadiah, the wicked king of Israel's godly servant, who could say, "I thy servant fear the Lord from my youth." Such were David's friends: "I am companion of all them that fear thee, and of them that keep thy precepts;" and again, "The saints on the earth and the excellent, in whom is *all my delight.*" Such were those in Malachi's time: "Then they that feared the Lord spake often one to another." Such was little Timothy, who "from a child knew the Holy Scriptures, and was wise unto salvation." *These* are the wise spoken of, who are to be found among the young as well as the old—the poor as well as the rich. It is thus—*wise friends, godly companions* you are to seek. Let us see what such ought to be—how we may find them out. Here are a few marks by which to try them: *Prayerfulness, truthfulness, obedience, faithfulness,* and to sum up all—*love to Christ.*

1. You should seek to have PRAYING companions. A prayerless boy or girl cannot be good company for

anybody. Long ago, in Rome, when the Christians were persecuted by the godless Emperor Nero, they had fearful tortures to endure. Sometimes they had inflammable materials wrapped round them, and were then set on fire. Sometimes they were covered with the skins of different animals, and infuriated dogs tore them to pieces. But there was a more lingering and terrible death than even these. A living man had a dead body chained to him, so that he could not get rid of it. It might have been the fair face of a loving man before; but now, how loathsome and sickening, and at length fatal, the companionship! Children! *that* is like companionship with a prayerless boy. He may be otherwise pleasant and agreeable, but in the sight of God he is *dead*—he has *no breath*—for prayer is the Christian's *breath;* and if you saw and felt things aright, the bad effects would be so manifest, that if he would not pray, you would be obliged to give him up. The good Dr. Morrison of China once came unexpectedly to a brother-missionary's house, late at night. The missionary had no alternative but to give up his own bed to his friend; and when his little daughter, who was sleeping in the same room, awoke early in the morning, and saw a stranger where her father used to be, she started up afraid, and said, "*Man, do you pray?*" When he said he was a praying man, she at once lay down and quietly fell asleep again. Had he said "*No*," she would not have thought it safe to be near him. It should be the same with you. It is not safe for you to keep company with a prayerless boy or girl; so that if you think of being intimate with any one, it would be well to ask, like that little girl, "Do you pray?"

It is a fine thing for young people to have as friends, those who can pray *with* each other, and *for* each other. I have sometimes heard of little friends who would kneel side by side in their closet, or underneath some tree, unseen by any eye but God's,—pleading for the new heart; or, when that had been got, on behalf of some other companion or friend. I think angels will look with joy on such a sight as that. Then perhaps one of them is taken ill, and the other is not allowed to see him—what can he do to help his sick friend—what can he do but *weep?* Ah, he can do better!—he can *pray*—pray that he may get better, or that he may be prepared for dying, and taken to glory; for the fervent prayer even of a godly child availeth much. We are told of a little boy who wished to pray for a sick brother, and was told by his father to repeat the Lord's Prayer, that he said, "O papa, that prayer will not do for making George well; it's this one, 'O God, make my little brother better.'" Young friends should thus pray for each other when they are ill,—ay, and when they are well too. Dear children, do you ever pray for your companions? Do you think they ever pray for you? Begin to-day, if you don't; and each day ask God to bless them, and to be their Father and their Friend.

2. You should seek TRUTHFUL friends,—*truth-loving, truth-speaking, truth-acting* companions. There is

a father who has promised to his son, that he shall be present at the taking down of a certain old wall. It is taken down in his absence, and the workmen are instantly ordered to rebuild it; the boy is sent for, the wall is pulled down in his presence, the workmen cannot understand it, but the father knows what a bad effect even one lie has on a boy, and he will be at any expense or trouble rather than run the risk. Or there is a boy who has done something wrong at home, or at school. To escape punishment he must either deny it, or lay the blame on others. But he would rather suffer anything than tell a lie. That's the companion for me! I have heard of a boy who had such an abhorrence of lying, that whenever a companion was guilty of it, instead of being a party to it, or laughing at it and saying it was cleverly done, he was so grieved that he had to leave him; and when his most intimate friend fell into this sin, though sorry as could be, he said he could have no dealings with him, till he had repented of it, and forsaken it. Why? Because God loves truth; and those who are like God, and love God, must do the same. A truthful, straightforward, sincere friend, is worth having.

3. You should seek THE OBEDIENT as companions. I know it is a recommendation to the friendship of some, to set a father or mother or teacher at defiance. It is thought to be bold, courageous, manly, independent, to take one's own way, to speak back,—ay, shall I say it? to *strike* back! I have heard of such

young people. They swagger about as if they were *men*, regardless of everybody. Save me from such a friend! Continuing in such a course, he can come to no good end; the less I have to do with him the better. A disobedient, undutiful son or daughter cannot but be a bad companion. But see that other, whom wicked boys cannot inveigle into sin; who will not be laughed out of what he thinks right, or into what he knows to be wrong; who is not ashamed to say he will not go to such a place, or do such a thing, because his mother forbade him; who is willing to do many things, and go many an errand, which others would think beneath them, that he may give all the help he can to one who has done so much for him; who when he goes from home, is not ashamed to take out of his trunk the Bible his mother gave him as a parting gift, and to read it unabashed, out of love to her, and to Him whose word it is, as well as for good to himself; who, without waiting to see whether prayer is the fashion there, kneels down—the only praying boy in the room, and prays on amid the whisper and the laugh, as he was wont to do in the home of his childhood; who always feels as if under a mother's eye, and always asks, "What would she think of this?"—delighting to obey that first commandment with promise, " Honour thy father and mother:"—I say, thank God for such a companion as that; make him your fast friend. He is, as people say, "one among a thousand:" He is one of *the wise* of whom our text speaks.

4. You should seek FAITHFUL friends. I do not

only mean those who are true and steadfast, not always changing about from one to another,—very intimate to-day, and very cold and distant to-morrow—your friend when you are at the head of your class, not when others have got above you—your friend when you have got a little pocket-money, not when your pocket is empty—your friend at school or out of public view, not when you are walking with a poor, and poorly-dressed mother on the street. There is much of that, I grieve to say; but that is not what I mean. I mean those who will be faithful in acting a friend's part to you; who will not go in with whatever you do, whether it be right or wrong; who, if you do what is wrong, will kindly tell you so, and try to keep you from it. There is a boy with a sore arm: the lancet should be used,—it should be sent in to the very bone, to let all the bad matter out. But the doctor says it would be very painful, and the family would perhaps take it amiss, and get another doctor; so, instead of his lancet, he takes out healing ointment which gives no pain, and the wound is healed over; and the youth regards the physician as his kind considerate friend. What would you think of that? I should say, "Cruel man! unfaithful man! to avoid giving offence, you have endangered that boy's life. Better you had cut to the quick, ay, cut the arm off, than thus to let the disease secretly go on till it ends in death." It is even so here. Faithful are the wounds of a friend. Call things by their right names; say, such and such a thing is wrong; say, God has forbidden it. You may thus keep your friend from sin;—and the day will come when he will say, it was kind in you to do it. And when he does the like to you, thank him, and love him all the more, and cling to him more firmly then ever.

5. Seek to get CHRIST-LOVING friends. You could not be intimate with one who hated, and spoke against, and injured—*your mother* or *your father ;* and can you be intimate with one who hates, and rejects, and dishonours—*your Saviour ?* Can you take into your friendship one who is crucifying your Lord,—one who, had he lived among the Jews, would have cried, "Away with him, away with him! Crucify him, crucify him!"—who would have nailed him to the tree? On the other hand, one who loves Christ will be *like* him, for here is what he sings—

> "I want to be like Jesus,
>   Meek, lowly, loving, mild;
> I want to be like Jesus,
>   The Father's holy child."

That is a safe companionship; in such a one, you are likely to have a faithful, lasting friend. You can ask and expect God to bless such a friendship. It is a friendship for heaven—for eternity. Oh, that there may be many such!

Now, *why* am I to seek the friendship of such? "He that walketh with wise men *shall be wise.*" You *will be like them.* Their company is good in itself, it is well worth having; but the best of it is, that through companionship with them, my character will become like theirs, and my conduct like theirs. We shall help and encourage each other in good. Two are better than one; as iron sharpeneth iron, so a man the countenance of his friend; and as men took knowledge of the disciples that they had been with Jesus, so will men take knowledge of us, that we have been walking with the wise, for we shall be wise too. Do not be in too great a hurry in making friends. Pray for good companions; ask God to direct you to them: "Lord, send me good companions; the poor in spirit, the mourners, the meek, the hungering and thirsting after righteousness, the merciful, the pure in heart, the peacemakers, the persecuted for righteousness' sake!" That is Christ's own list; of all such he says, "Blessed are they." In having such as companions, you will be blessed with them.

II. BAD COMPANY *to be* SHUNNED. It is as if our text said: "Don't, on any account, make companions of the foolish. Now if the *wise* are such *as fear God*, the *foolish* must be such as *don't fear God*—such as have no fear of God before their eyes,—the ungodly. Here, too, it may be well just to look at some of the *marks* of these. I give you other five: *flattery, dishonesty, idleness, evil-speaking, Sabbath-breaking.* If ever you have been at sea, you may have seen or heard of *beacons* to warn of danger. There are rocks which, when the tide is full, are covered by the water, or are otherwise in a dangerous position. Many a gallant ship has been wrecked on them; many a scene of terrible distress has been witnessed,—men, and women, and children swallowed up in the deep, or dashed against these jagged points. So many have perished there, that something must be done. And so as you sail along on a summer day, you see a tall lighthouse, catching the sailor's eye by day, and having its brilliant light sparkling amid the darkness of night. What is the meaning of it? It is as if it said, "Take care! there is danger here; here has been many a wreck,—keep off! beware!" Well, this text of ours is just such a lighthouse—a beacon—warning of danger, telling us to be on our guard. It says, "Avoid the foolish!" it cries out, "Of evil companions, beware!" Some of the particular rocks to be guarded against are those I have mentioned, which we shall now consider. It is sad to think that countless thousands like yourselves, have been wrecked upon them, and you may well be afraid.

1. Beware of FLATTERING friends. What this means, I shall try to explain. A companion wishes you to do what is wrong. He knows you would refuse, if he were bluntly and directly to propose it. So he makes great professions of friendship: he would be willing to do anything for you; he is more anxious to be friends with you than with anybody, you are such a fine fellow, —so noble, so bold, so good-hearted. Having thus paved the way, he makes his proposal: "Come, join us in this. If it had been a bad thing, you are the last I would have thought of coming to. It will do you no harm. Of all people, there is no fear of *you*. Even if

there were danger, you could stop at the right point. Come and be a safety to the rest of us." That is one of the "crooked ways"—the serpent-like ways, in which some succeed in tempting to sin, by *flattery*—praising you, and pretending to be your friend while in reality they are like Joab when he said to Amasa, " Art thou in health? my brother!"—" and he took him by the beard to kiss him; but Amasa took no heed to the sword that was in his hand, and he smote him under the fifth rib, and he died." Says Solomon, " Beware of flatterers!" He seems to have known them well, and so he counsels us, " When he speaketh fair, believe him not, for *there are seven abominations in his heart;*" and again, " *A flattering mouth worketh ruin.*" Many fall in this way, who else would stand firm. There are flatterers among children as well as among men. A companion of such shall be destroyed.

2. Beware of DISHONEST friends. I mean both plain—downright stealing, and something else. I know some are thieves whom people would little suspect. And I know that children who are dishonest themselves, like to get others to keep them company. I warn you of them. Our prisons have had more than one young thief from districts like those you live in, whether these be high or humble,—ay, from schools and churches like those which you attend. Solomon says regarding such: " My son, if sinners entice thee, *consent thou not !*" Refuse,—say *No*. I have heard of a boy, thirteen years of age, being waylaid by some older boys who would have him to be

one of a party to steal apples from a neighbouring garden. He refuses, saying, "*I cannot steal from anybody!*" They threaten to put him into the river that runs close by. He is steadfast. They plunge him in, they push him down, asking if he will not. "*No!*" is the only answer of that noble youth. "And so," we are told, "this martyr-boy was drowned. He could *die*, but he could not *steal!*" Be like him, children, and choose such for your companions. But I don't merely refer to the stealing of money, or fruit, or such things. There is a scholar copying from the slate or book of another, or gaining a place in his class by unfairness. That is *stealing*—that is *dishonesty*, whatever may be thought of it. Say, "It is wrong;" say, "God sees!" say, as did a girl to her brother, in their mother's absence, "Perhaps *God counts!*" Don't be one of them; keep out of their way. It will not be strange if such a boy should find his way one day to prison, or to banishment beyond the seas. A companion of such shall be destroyed.

3. Beware of IDLE friends. Indolence and idleness are little thought of, yet are they very sinful and very hurtful. Some one has said, that the devil tempts the busy, but the idle tempt the devil. And certainly it is true that—

> "Satan finds some mischief still,
> For idle hands to do."

Now you must have noticed, that idlers try to keep other people from working. You see it in our streets,—you see it at school. No good ever comes of an idle scholar, and he is a dangerous person to have to do with. He wastes his own precious time (I should rather say, God's time); his opportunities, his abilities, are worse than thrown away, and he is a perpetual hindrance to others. If I were asked to point out one of the most dangerous people in the town, I should fix on the idlest. The idle man, or woman, or child, is one of Satan's busiest and most successful servants,—for lack of better work, ready for anything he gives them to do. Beware of idlers, for a companion of such shall be destroyed.

4. Beware of EVIL-SPEAKING friends. I refer to talebearing, which is ever a mean, low, vile thing; but I also refer to all kinds of improper language—low, trifling, unholy, wicked words. Like bad books, such words pollute the minds of those who hear them, and leave marks which perhaps will never be wiped out. The coarse, vulgar jest, which some think clever, and which makes people laugh, is very offensive to God, and very hurtful, especially to the young. It is like the spotted serpent, which stings while it is admired. It is one of Satan's poisoned arrows,—it does Satan's work, though he who shoots it says all the while, "Am not I in sport?" Those who use low, bad language, must have a bad heart; and it is sure, sooner or later, to end in a bad life. Don't laugh at such, don't go in their way; put your finger in your ears, and run out of sight. And what shall I say of swearing, which also is too common, even among the young? Flee from the

presence of a swearer, be he young or old. It is not manly—it is not gentlemanly; it is base—it is devilish—it is the language of hell. I grieve to think there should be so much of it about our very doors,—that one hears it so often on the street, so that I fear, the children cannot but be familiar with it. Be like the little girl who would not sit on the knee of a swearer, or go near him, as if afraid lest they should both be swallowed up like Korah and his company. A swearing companion *must* be bad; a companion of such shall be destroyed.

> " When I hear them telling lies,
>   Talking foolish, cursing, swearing;
> First I'll try to make them wise,
>   Or I'll soon go out of hearing."

5. Beware of SABBATH-BREAKING companions. This is a very common, but very grievous sin. I have seen the effects of it but too often and too sadly. It leads to many other sins, and often comes to a sad end. He who would tempt you to break the Sabbath, is one of your worst enemies. Tell him that God is wiser and more your friend than he, and that God says, " Remember the Sabbath-day, to keep it holy." How many mournful cases I might mention here, to show that the companion of Sabbath-breakers shall be destroyed! I should have liked much to say more of this, but I cannot now.

Such are some of the bad companions against whom we are warned. *Why* are we to beware of them ? Because as in the other case, we are in danger of growing like them. You cannot be with them, without being injured by them. It is like touching coal or pitch, the mark will be left behind. As in the case of some terrible, infectious diseases—if you go near, it will be a wonder if you do not catch the infection. You may not like their company at first—nay, you may often shudder; but you will get accustomed to *it* as to other things, and perhaps you will come at last to like it. I believe bad company is one of the greatest of the hindrances that keep children away from Christ. Good impressions are made, there is the wish and the resolution to seek Jesus; but back they go to their old friends, and their goodness, like the morning cloud and early dew, is gone. Bad company has blighted many a hopeful bud; it has disappointed many a father's fond expectation, and broken many a mother's heart; it has brought many a promising Sabbath scholar to misery and ruin —to the prison and the gallows; it has led to almost every evil, in the case not only of grown-up people, but of the young; and what it has done to others, it may do to you. It is the fear of all this, that makes me dwell on it as I do. I wish I could tell you one half of the mischief it has done, that you might be warned. And then think what the end will be. A companion of fools *shall be destroyed.* Good Lot suffered with wicked Sodom. Good Jehoshaphat suffered with wicked Ahab and Ahaziah. The end in your case will be—*destruction.* Think of this, dear children. Though you live in company, you must one day *die alone*; though you sin in company, you must one day be *judged alone*,—only you will not *suffer* alone. But surely that will be little comfort. When a vessel is wrecked, is it any relief to have others shrieking and sinking along with you?—when disease comes, to have others on beds of sickness and death all around you?—when famine comes, to have others dying of hunger beside you? And will it, think you, be any comfort to spend eternity with those with whom you have sinned on earth? Will it not make it all the more terrible? O beloved children! don't be laughed into what is evil—don't be threatened into what is wrong. I find a dying boy, who had before been afraid lest the other boys should laugh at him, saying, "O that I had just another night of the Sabbath-school! I would not care though they should laugh at me now." And if we could but hear voices from the other world, would we not get the same story? Children! have none as your companions on earth, whom you would not like to have as your companions in eternity. Children! begin to-day to break off from the company of the wicked. If you do not know what to say, take David's words: "Depart from me, ye evil doers, for I will keep the commandments of my God." Begin to-day, or with them you may be destroyed.

Make a companion of your *Bible*: you will find it both safe and profitable. In prison, in solitude, on a sick-bed, in the house of sorrowing and of death, it has been a sweet and pleasant companion to many. Cultivate its acquaintance: love it more and more. Still more, make a companion of him of whom it tells—*Jesus*. *That* is one of the best ways of getting rid of others who can only be a curse to you. And what a Friend is he!—a rich friend, a powerful friend, a royal friend, a safe friend, a wise friend, a loving friend, a sympathizing friend, an unchanging friend, an everlasting friend; one to whom you may lay open all your heart—to whom you may go in every difficulty and distress, and always be welcome, and always be blessed; for he is "a friend that loveth at all times—a brother born for adversity,—a friend that sticketh closer than a brother." Say, "This is my beloved, and this is my friend." Whatever other friends you have, make sure of the friendship of Jesus. Take no friends as yours, but those who will be friends to him. And in order to have Christ as your *Friend*, you must have him as your *Saviour*. *That* is the *only way*. He is willing to be the Friend of the youngest, of the poorest, of the most wicked. He says to-day, "Come." He says, "I will in no wise cast out." Walk with this wise friend, and be wise indeed: keep company with him and be blessed; make *him* your companion, and then when you come to die, even when you have to leave all other friends, to die will be gain, and like another dying child, your death-song will be:—

> " Put your arm around me, mother,
>   Draw your chair beside my bed;
> Let me lean upon your bosom
>   This poor weary, aching head.

> Once I thought I could not leave you—
> Once I was afraid to die;
> Now I feel 'tis Jesus calls me,
> To his mansions in the sky."

It is a good rule, to choose those for your companions on earth, whom you may hope to have as your companions in heaven. It is a sweet thought in after-life, that you can go back with satisfaction to the friendships of youth, so that you can thank God for them, instead of remembering them with regret and shame. It is sweet to think of the reunion of such early friends—of those who died in early life, and of those who have since been scattered over all parts of the globe, meeting again there where parting is unknown. Perhaps we may so far accommodate the lines that follow to this closing thought:—

HYMN.

> Who are they whose little feet,
>   Pacing life's dark journey through,
> Now have reached that heavenly seat,
>   They had ever kept in view?
> "I from Greenland's frozen land;"
>   "I from India's sultry plain;"
> "I from Afric's barren sand;"
>   "I from islands of the main."
>
> All our earthly journey past,
>   Every tear and pain gone by,
> Here together met at last,
>   At the portal of the sky;
> Each the welcome "Come" awaits,
>   Conquerors over death and sin.
> Lift your heads, ye golden gates!
>   Let the little travellers in.

Waste Not.

THE HYMN.

LITTLE drops of water,
　　Little grains of sand,
Make the mighty ocean
　　And the pleasant land.

Thus the little minutes,
　　Humble though they be,
Make the mighty ages
　　Of Eternity.

Thus our little errors
　　Lead the soul away
From the path of virtue,
　　Off in sin to stray.

Little deeds of kindness,
　　Little words of love,
Make our earth an Eden,
　　Like the heaven above.

MY DEAR YOUNG FRIENDS,—I have a question to put to you to-day, more than eighteen hundred years old, and yet it is as applicable to you now as when it was uttered long ago;—ay, far more applicable, for then the asking of it was a complete mistake, which I am sure it is not now; then there was no room or reason for it, which I am sure there is now. What the question is we shall see shortly : the asking of it will, I trust, be for good to many.

It has often gone to my heart, and I daresay sometimes to yours, to see in some miserable garret, or cellar, a man or woman, or a family—*very poor*, with scarcely any furniture, or clothing, or food, or fire, even on a winter day. It almost made the tears start to your eyes when you saw it; and when you came away, you could not help saying, "How very sad it is to be so poor! However I may sometimes grumble, I thank God, I am nothing like so poor as that;"—and perhaps that night for the first time you made it your prayer, "Lord, remember, pity, help the poor!" You think their lot hard enough, even though, as some people say, they have never been much better, and have got accustomed to it, and become hardened under it. But when you learn that they were once well off; with a comfortable home, and plenty of money and friends; with every want supplied, living in one of the best parts of the town, and looked up to as better than common, you think, how *very* hard must be their lot! It does not mend the matter a whit, that they have brought all this upon themselves;—that they were extravagant, and kept up great style, and had too many servants, and spent too much money on dress, and had large dancing parties; that by and by they took up with bad companions, and drink began to do its work in the house, and from simple playing at cards, itself bad enough, there came to be regular gambling, till at length, as in such cases generally happens, they lost money, and friends, and character, and home, and one day found themselves outcast, destitute, degraded. The history of their case is just that of the prodigal-son over again: they had wasted their substance with riotous living; and when they had spent all, they began to be in want. Now, they are as truly a *wreck*, as the ship that so gallantly left the harbour and began her voyage, but struck on a rock and was shivered to pieces, or went down entire, her mast still appearing, as I have seen it, above the water, telling all passers-by to beware. I ask to what account you would turn your knowledge of such a case? If you saw others pursuing a similar course, would you not tell them what the end of these had been—would you not try to stop them with all urgency and in all haste—would you not say, "What mean you? why be so foolish?" and with your finger pointing to the "wreck" we have described, "Why will ye die?" It may satisfy others, simply to condemn such—to say it is no more than they deserved, they have only themselves to blame for it, and the like; not thinking that *that* is the bitterest pang of all, and that the voice of conscience which now speaks out, and the remorse that gnaws within the heart, are worse than any outward sufferings could be.

Let him that is without sin among you,—ay, sin of a kind not very different from theirs,—cast the first stone at these. They wasted their substance, as we have seen, and so came to that miserable end. How many among us, even among you young people, have the same sin lying at your door! You may not have had fortunes to spend, you may not have brought yourselves to beggary, and yet you may have thrown away what is unspeakably more precious than mere earthly possessions,—you may be doing it even now; and so, in God's name, I would fain stop you and call you to account, ere you have spent your all, pressing upon you with all earnestness, the question of which I have spoken, which you will find in—

Matt. xxvi. 8.—" To what purpose is THIS WASTE?"

I have already told you that that question was wrongly put in the case before us. The time was drawing near when Jesus should die. There was a woman to whom he had shown mercy and given that precious gift—the gift of pardon. And now having been forgiven much, she loved much, and with a full heart she longed to show how much she loved him. She bought an alabaster box of very precious ointment, grudging no expense, counting it but little after all; she came to the house where Jesus was, broke the box, and poured the ointment on his head, so that the house was filled with the fragrant smell. Thus she meant to tell him how grateful and loving she was,—that she counted nothing too costly to give, nothing too hard to suffer for his sake. And never was money better spent—never was gift better bestowed. Christ was pleased with it, and approved what she did; and so we know that what she did was right, and that those standing by who were so indignant at what they called "this waste" were wrong, and neither understood her nor judged rightly of her deed. And now let me say, by the way, that this mistake is often made,—regarding as "waste," and calling "waste," what is nothing of the kind. For instance, some people seem as if they thought it wrong that children should spend any part of their time in *play*. Now, a fair proportion of children's time spent in play is not time wasted, for it improves their health, and is a help even to their learning. So with *sleep:* it is not waste, it invigorates body and mind alike, and enables us to turn our time really to good account. So when men give money that has been hardly won, to the poor, or to circulate the Bible, or to send missionaries to heathen lands, or otherwise to help on the cause of Christ, some people think it waste, and say they know better than to throw away *their* money in any such way. They ask the question,—as here,—*wrongly*, "To what purpose is this waste?" It is not waste, though it were thousands of pounds. If the motive and the object be such as God approves, it is the most reasonable of all expenditure. It is done to Christ, and given for Christ, who did all and gave all for us. And Christ himself will give us his smile, even although those who profess to be his people should frown. He will be our defender, and we may safely leave the matter in his hands: "Why trouble ye the woman? for she hath wrought a good work upon me." That is the wrong application of the question to which some are very prone; but it has a right application too, and it is to *that* that I mean now to call your attention.

I wish, dear children, to show you the evil, the sin,

the danger of being *wasters*—of wasting any of the good things that God has given you. Some of the things I shall refer to, may not be very important, but others of them are of the greatest consequence, and will affect your well-being in time as well as in eternity. Did you notice, that I spoke of the *sin* of wasting? Now, I daresay none of you can tell me which of the Ten Commandments it breaks. I do not find any one that says in so many words, "Thou shalt not waste; and he that wasteth shall come to poverty, and want, and ruin." You do not find *that*, just as you do not find any command expressly forbidding drunkenness, which yet is none the less—a sin. That is one consideration that led me to take up this subject,—it is made so little account of. One does not feel as if he were doing any great harm. There seems no actual sin committed. Conscience does not reprove here as in the case of other sins; and so the thing goes on and on imperceptibly, till the evil cannot be remedied.

I mean then, not angrily, but in kindness, and with the hope of doing you good, to charge you with the sin of *waste,* in respect of these four things—*Time, Money, Strength,* and *Opportunities;* and to ask regarding them the question of our text, "To what purpose is this waste?"

1. The waste of TIME.—What would you think if you were to see a man—who, by working hard day after day, was able to earn a wage of twelve shillings a-week,— going down each evening after he returned from his work, to a neighbouring harbour, and throwing into the

sea a shilling of his hard-won money, while his rent was running on unpaid, and his clothes were getting worn out, and himself was half starved? What would you think of him thus throwing away a full half of his wages every week,—by his folly preparing for himself a prison or a grave? I am sure you would say the man was mad, and most other people would say the same. But there are other precious things in the world besides shillings and pounds. There is *Time!* You may have heard a saying, "Time is money." For instance, if you were interrupting at his work a mason who is paid by the hour, or one of the young women in a factory who is paid by the piece, they might say to you, "Time is money; every quarter of an hour that you take up, is the loss of so much wage to us." But I go further than that, and say, time is *more* than money, more costly and precious far; money cannot buy it,—you cannot tell its value in gold. Often have the richest men and women been willing to give all they had, for a single hour. They would not have grudged a thousand pounds for five minutes; but though they made the offer, they could not get it. And God has given to none, young or old, more of this costly article than each needs. He has measured out to each just his needful portion, in which to do his work, and to prepare for eternity. What, then, are we to think of him who should do with his time, what we supposed the workman to do with his wages--throw the one-half uselessly away?

Now, dear children, have not you been doing this? Let us just look at one of your ordinary days, and see how you spend it. Suppose you rise at eight in the morning, and go to bed at nine o'clock at night, as many of you do: There is a day of thirteen hours for you. What have you made of it? How much have you used aright, and turned to some good purpose? and how much have you *lost?* If before going to bed, you were each day to take your slate and pencil, and try honestly to note down how these thirteen hours had been spent,— if I am not much mistaken, many here would be found as foolish as the man I have spoken of, throwing away fully one half of their precious time, so that it is as completely lost, as the man's shilling at the bottom of the sea,—beyond recall! And if so many as six or seven hours of a day have been wasted, what a loss that comes to in a month or year! What a tremendous loss in the course of a lifetime! Surely you will not wonder at me sadly asking the question, " To what purpose is this waste?"

The time of Youth, above all precious, is most of all wasted; and the waste can never be made up. There is a boy at school—how does he employ his school time? Whenever his master's back is turned, he is drawing figures on his book or slate, or *talking* when he should be *learning;* or when a neighbour comes in at night, and his mother's attention is diverted, his book is laid aside and he slips out to his play, till it is time for bed. And that can never be made up for in all his after-life. When he grows up to be a lad, he feels the want of it. He might get advancement in his shop, but he has not education enough. He goes to night-schools, but the difficulty and drudgery of learning then, are too much for him; and at length, as an ignorant old man, whose mind has not been stored in youth, when he can no longer work, he does not know what to make of himself, and he becomes a burden alike to others and to himself. Or the careless girl comes to be a mother, and has a soldier-son away in a distant land. Oh, how she wishes she could write to her boy and read his letters herself, instead of having always to get the help of others! But it is too late to learn then. You have all heard of Sir Walter Scott,—of whom his countrymen were so proud that they erected to his honour, one of the finest buildings in Edinburgh,—the "Scott Monument,"—which I daresay many of you have seen in Princes Street Gardens. And yet, famous man as he was, he never ceased to lament the misimprovement of his school-boy days; and in some touching lines he tells how much of his reputation he would gladly part with, if he could hope to secure thereby the advantages which, by his early neglect, he had irrecoverably lost.

There is no time like that of youth, for storing the mind with useful knowledge. I often meet with those whose early education has been neglected, and these almost always bear the strongest and saddest testimony to the truth of what I have said on the subject. There is no time like youth for treasuring up what is good in the memory, as I myself can testify. Chapters of the Bible which I learned when a boy,* are fresh on the mind as when first I learned them; hymns committed to memory when a young Sabbath-scholar, are always coming up again, so that, when alone, I can cheer myself by singing them, and when sitting by the bedside of the sick and dying, I can cheer them by repeating them. But chapters and hymns, which I have spent hours in trying to learn in later years, have flown away, when I thought I had got a thorough hold of them. If any of you think of becoming ministers, or missionaries, or Sabbath-school teachers, and would like when you grow up to be useful to the old, and the sick, and the poor, by telling them what they need most of all to know,—about sin and salvation, and Christ and heaven,—then I beseech you not to waste the only time for getting, yourselves, a thorough hold of Bible-truth.

What shall I say of the waste of Sabbath time, given to you by God to prepare for a fast-coming eternity?

* Such as Isaiah lv., Psalm cxix., John xvii., Romans viii., Hebrews xi., Revelation xxii. As an encouragement to learn in early life that long, but beautiful Psalm (cxix.), I may mention the following: I lately visited an old woman of ninety-one, who had come from the country. "Sometimes at night," she said, "I canna sleep; but I never weary, for I just gang back on the 119th Psalm." To my question, "Can you remember the whole Psalm?" she replied, "On yes; I learnt it when I was a lassie, ten years auld, and I ha'e ne'er forgot it since. Had I been as *active* as I was *clever*, I might have had them a'." This curious thing she also told me: Her sight was very bad, so that, while she could knit her stocking, she could do little in the way of reading. But often, over-night, she dreamed that she was reading passages of Scripture, and when morning came they were so vividly impressed on her mind, that she could quite easily call them up, and thus her wants for the day were supplied. I suppose these must have been passages with which she had become familiar in her youth. She has since gone to the land where "the eyes of them that see shall not be dim" any more for ever.

What shall I say of the excuses of some for neglecting the Bible and prayer? How is it that some, when their mothers would have them daily to read a portion of the Holy Scriptures, say they have no time? Why, where the form of prayer is kept up, is it so hurried over by many young people, that you would think they have hardly had time to repeat ten words, before they are up from their knees again? They say they have *no time*. Then that must be because they have wasted much of the time that God has given them; for he has given them enough for all necessary purposes, and especially for the worshipping and serving of himself. If we did not waste so much of our time, we might have plenty of it for reading God's word and for prayer. Could you not save a little from your *play?* Could you not save a little from your *sleep?* I have heard of soldiers who thought it was wasting time to sleep so long as not to leave an hour for holy exercises, and so if they had to be on duty at three or four o'clock, they rose the sooner for prayer. I have heard of servants and washerwomen, who had to be at work very early, still finding time to worship God. I could show you a whole row of volumes written by a busy minister in America,—now in the hands of many Sabbath-school teachers throughout the country, helping them to understand, and to explain to you, the Scriptures,—every line of them written before breakfast, while most other people were in bed!

How much you might do with your *time*, with the five minutes or quarter of an hour which you often think so lightly of, and throw away as not worth having much ado made about it! I wish when you are wasting these, foolishly and sinfully, you would just look up at the clock, and as you hear it ticking your precious time away, that you would put to yourself the question, "To what purpose is this waste?" Or if there be no clock near you, put your finger on your pulse, which will answer the purpose as well, and ask the same question.

> "My pulse is the clock of my life,
>   It shows me my moments are flying;
> It marks the departure of time,
>   And tells me how fast I am dying."

By-and-by you will think that I have not dwelt on this too much. Some, ere long, when their time is all but spent, and eternity is close upon them, will bitterly bewail that they did not sooner consider and take warning from the question of our text.

2. The waste of MONEY, or *money's worth*. I am not going to speak of the halfpennies and pennies which young people often throw so thoughtlessly away on trifles—toys, and sweetmeats, and other such things. I am not going to counsel you, never to spend a penny, but to put every copper into the Savings' Bank, and hoard up your money there, and become little misers. As to this, there are two kinds of men, neither of whom I would wish you ever to be like—*misers* and *spendthrifts*. "Misers" are so called, as being miserable, wretched men, having no comfort or enjoyment

in laying out their money either for themselves or others, always afraid of losing what they have got; having the same painful craving for money that the drunkard has for drink, or that you have for water when you are very thirsty. "Spendthrifts," again, are those who soon run through all that they have, like the prodigal son, and come to beggary. Both are opposed to God's will and law. I would not have you to be either of these; but I do not mean just now to warn you either against hoarding up your money, or spending it uselessly. I wish to speak against wasting that which *costs money.*

I sometimes notice on the street, or in other like places, a crust of bread, and sometimes more than a crust, trodden under foot of passers-by—a sight I never see without pain. How did that come there? A boy got it to his dinner, or *would* have it after his dinner, and having more than he could rightly manage, instead of putting it into his pocket till he should be hungry, or giving it to some one who would have been thankful enough to get it, he thoughtlessly tossed it away. When that boy goes to school and reads in the Bible-lesson, or hears at family-worship (if there be such a thing in his house), about some of the famines from which Israel suffered—how all sorts of animals were used for food, and the most repulsive things that were eatable were sold at an enormous price; or in the history-lesson, about the taking of Jerusalem, how bread was more precious than gold, and women were reduced to such straits as to eat their own infants;—I wonder if his conscience does not check him; if he never thinks of the bread he so lightly threw away. I wish I could take him to houses which I have seen, and show him that bed-ridden old woman, or these starving little children, crying for bread when there's none to give them—how they would prize and relish a morsel even like that! When he sees these, he will not wonder that I ask, "To what purpose is this waste?" In this, Jesus himself has set us an example, that in this, as in all things else, we should walk in his steps. You remember his feeding the multitude—five thousand men, besides women and children, with five loaves and two fishes. When they had all eaten and were filled, Jesus told them to gather up what was left. Why? Not only that when they saw the twelve baskets full, they might see what a wonder-working Saviour he was,—but, as he himself says, "Gather up the fragments that remain, *that nothing be lost.*" Think of that, dear children, when you would do what is not uncommon.

I sometimes see, in mischief or in thoughtlessness, the stop-cock of the water-pipe left unturned, and whole gallons of water allowed to run to waste. Some children were getting a drink, or amusing themselves, and forgot, or could not be at the trouble, to put things right, and hence the loss. "Nobody suffered by it," you say; "the only loss, if there was any, was to the Water Company." Well, I never like to see such things. How welcome that water would be to many! At that very moment, perhaps, there are travellers passing through the desert; their supply of water is exhausted; the very camels are beginning to fail; one rushes forward to what has been a well among the rocks, but oh, his look of despair—when he finds it dry! Another sees a jar, which those who have gone before, have somehow left; perhaps it may be water; "No," he says, bitterly disappointed,—"it's *only diamonds!*" At that very moment, perhaps, there is a boat at sea—those in it, all that remain of that emigrant ship that is now engulfed in the deep; as the warm sun breaks out, oh, what burning thirst! how priceless would be every drop of a passing shower!—

> " Water! water! everywhere,
> And all the boards did shrink;
> Water! water! everywhere,
> But not a drop to drink."

And how can I but grudge the waste of that which they would give anything to get? Might not such thoughts come into the minds even of children, and teach them a lesson; "To what purpose is this waste?"

I sometimes see children coming to school on a Monday morning, clean and tidy, with every rent in dress or jacket mended. I do not like to see them too much concerned about keeping all right, so that they cannot join with others in play, and would grumble ever so much, because they had rubbed against the dusty jacket of the passing baker's boy or miller. But when I see the opposite extreme, which I do far oftener

—clothes and shoes rubbed and worn, needlessly dirtied and torn,—I do think of that father who has so far to go to his work, and has such a long day of it, and such difficulty in earning the money that provides clothing and food for himself and his family; and of that mother whose washing days are such a serious affair, with her young baby and her delicate health, who finds it no easy matter to eke out the week's wage so as to get ends to meet, and who had to be up so late and so early to get these very clothes made, or mended, or washed, which are so soon calling for the like at her hands again. Children! I am serious in saying all this. I cannot look at what you are doing, without thinking of your fathers and mothers—all they have to do, and all they have to endure—and asking, "To what purpose is this waste?"

Think, then, of what I have said of *money* and *money's worth*, and be warned in this by the end of wasters. There are two young servants in a family: one of them is a *waster*. Crusts of bread, drops of milk, and similar things may often be seen about the kitchen and washing-house. "I often fancy," says her neighbour to her, "that there is never a bit of food wasted in a wilful manner, which may not hereafter come to be wanted by the very person who threw it away. I should not wonder though you yourself may come to be glad of such a dish." But it makes no impression, and out on the dunghill goes the plateful of bones, and meat, and crusts. Some years pass away.

The careful servant is now a respectable and happy wife and mother. Giving a helping hand to her former mistress one day, she is in the old kitchen, when she hears the cry of a child; she opens the back window from which so much good food had been thrown out, and on the ash-heap lies a miserable woman all in rags, her head upon the ashes, her little child, as wretched-looking as herself, gathering up the scraps, and eating a black and mouldy crust, which a dog would almost have refused to eat. The woman can only answer the questions put to her with a groan, for she is dying. And who does she turn out to be? The wasteful girl of former years, furnishing a touching illustration of the proverb, "Wilful waste is woful want."*

3. The waste of STRENGTH. I shall dwell very shortly on this, for I have just two things in view in making this remark. I have already shown that I am no enemy to play within reasonable bounds. But I sometimes notice or hear of *this:* you carry it beyond all reasonable bounds, never appearing till night, when your strength is gone, and you are fairly worn out, and good for nothing but setting off to bed. Now, boys as well as girls should, at home, be like little servants, doing everything they can to help and relieve a loving, hard-wrought mother. But by the time you come home, you have spent all the strength you had, and perhaps *need* help instead of *giving* it; ay, perhaps you are cross and ill-natured, bringing in with you utter

* " Waste not: Want not."

discomfort. Especially is it so on Saturday. You have gone out to the country with other children, and after wandering about all day, you come home at nightfall, wet and weary, selfishly taking all your holiday, and using all your strength for yourselves, instead of being ready and willing to carry your mother's basket to shop and market with her, and carry home her purchases, and lighten her labour, so as to prepare, so far as you can, for a happier and easier day on Sabbath than she has had all the week. When I see the reverse of all this,—when I see you throwing away so heartlessly the strength that would be so serviceable at home,—I cannot but fall back here too upon the question, "To what purpose is this waste?"

And worse even than that: in such a case, you not only leave no strength or heart for work or lessons, but no strength or heart for *prayer;*—you go prayerless to bed, or fall asleep on your knees while mumbling over mere words that you are not even thinking about. Now, my dear child, you have got a precious soul, which it should be your main concern to think about and pray for, and to get pardoned and saved. And day by day you give all your strength to other things—I do not hesitate to say you *waste* it, and leave none to attend to the things of God. And this becomes a habit. When you think about the matter at all, you resolve that next day you will do better; but each day it is the same, and your soul is uncared for as ever. And so perhaps you will go on till your strength fails you altogether, and amid the pain, and disquiet, and weakness of a sudden and fatal illness, you never have opportunity to get ready for eternity, and all unprepared, you are hurried into it. Oh, what is your strength for, but first of all for *this?* what is your strength for, if not to lay hold on Jesus as your Saviour, and to cry to God in prayer, and to wrestle,—ay, even you, children!— for the blessing? You may well give the best of your time and strength to this: nothing is so worthy of it— nothing so much needs it. And when I see you giving your strength to everything except this, however good these other things may be, I must protest against it, and solemnly call you to account with the question, "To what purpose is this waste?" The best of your days, and the *best parts of your best days*, should be devoted to making sure of salvation.

4. The waste of OPPORTUNITIES. You understand what time is, and money, and strength; but some little one asks, "What is meant by an opportunity?" Suppose your friends were in some distant land, and you wished very much to join them, but could find no means of overtaking it. Were I to come to you and say, "There is a vessel to sail from Liverpool next week, for the place you have wished so much to go to, and I have met a friend who has become interested in you, and is willing to take you under his care, and to pay your railway fare and passage-money all through. Such offers are not to be met with every day; now is your opportunity!" You would understand what I meant, and the failing to

take advantage of such a chance would be what I have called—the waste of opportunity.

Now, the opportunities which I have in view are of two kinds,—opportunities of *doing* good, and of *getting* good. (1.) Of *doing good*. How many such, our children have, or might have! Not long ago I was in a country church, and was struck with one voice that sang the psalm very loudly, while from the same quarter, before each line was sung, there came a strange whispering sound. After listening for a little, I discovered what it was. The singer was an old blind man; beside him sat a little boy, who, with Psalm-book in hand, whispered each line into the old man's ear, thus enabling him to join in the praises of the sanctuary, which he could not otherwise have done. It explained beautifully that word, "I was eyes to the blind." That was an opportunity of doing good which that boy had. What good you might often do to the old, and the sick, and the poor! Were it no more than to show them respect, and speak a kind word, and let them feel that you take an interest in them, it would be worth while. You remember what a blessing the little Hebrew maid—to whom I have already referred—was to her master, Naaman the leper, the Syrian captain. We should always be ready to take advantage of such opportunities. We should seek to be like Jesus, who went about continually doing good. When I see such opportunities occurring, and children letting them pass unimproved, intent on reading some interesting story, or through sheer laziness; when I see an aged grandmother trying to lift a load which she has not strength for, and which that boy there could manage with greatest ease; or puzzling herself to get her needle threaded, or to unravel the tangled hank of worsted to complete the stocking which she is intent on finishing, while that girl is sitting listlessly by, whose sharp young eyes and active fingers might put all right in a minute,—I feel that there is room for the rebuke which the question of our text implies.

And what opportunities young people have of a higher kind—for *commending Christ,* and bringing others to him! Out of the mouths of babes and sucklings God has often thus perfected praise. Not that children should be forward and impudent in speaking to those who are grown up; far from it. But if there be love to Jesus in a child's heart, it will gently and sweetly find its way out; so that, like the woman's box of ointment, it will be felt throughout all the house. The other day I saw lying on the counter of a bookseller's shop a little book, called the "Babe of Heaven." The story was simple and touching. Though early taken home, this little girl had been the means of turning at least one heart to Jesus. Travelling in a stage coach, a young gentleman who had been greatly taken with her, and had treated her most kindly, expressed his regret when the journey was at an end. As he was preparing to leave, she said earnestly to him, in her own childish way, "Does you love God?" It was a question he could never forget; it followed him wherever he went; it seemed to ring in his ear,—"Does you love God?" and ere long the child's word was blessed to the man's salvation. Beloved children, what precious opportunities you have of doing good to those about you—at home and at school—among brothers, and sisters, and companions! Do not waste these. Earnestly, humbly, prayerfully *use* them.

But (2.) what opportunities of *getting good*, and what waste there is of these! There is a boy sitting in church, quite inattentive while the gospel of Jesus Christ is being preached,—not even *hearing* what is said. The minister is preaching from some such text as that, "Jesus of Nazareth passeth by,"—telling both about the *way* of salvation, and about this being the *time* of salvation. Others, there, are hearing for their *life*,—taking in the truth, welcoming it, being saved by it. What is he doing? Wasting—what? A most precious opportunity —the opportunity of *being saved*. By-and-by, perhaps, when far away, he will wish for these golden hours back; and when he lies down to die, he will remember them with regret. There is another at the Sabbath school. His teacher is earnestly pressing on his class the need of getting a new heart, and telling of God's willingness to give it; but so little is the scholar concerned, that when the simplest question is put to him, he cannot answer it, for his thoughts are elsewhere; and when it is his turn to read the next verse in some sweet passage, he does not even know where it is. He is wasting a most precious opportunity. There is a boy living in the beginning of such a year as the present. He is making progress at school, active at work, helpful at home; getting the approval of parent, teacher, master; so that if you ask any of all the three how he is getting on, the answer at once will be, "Very well indeed." And is not that enough? No, especially in such years as we have recently had. And how so? Because this is no common time; now there are uncommon opportunities. Old and young are being awakened, and becoming concerned about their souls as perhaps never before. The door of the kingdom of heaven is standing wide open, and multitudes are pressing in. The Holy Spirit is working graciously and wonderfully on the hearts of very many. What a time to live in! What an opportunity, the like of which may never occur again in our day! What if it is *wasted—lost?*

Beloved young friends, I am most of all afraid of your wasting the opportunities that are now. The past year might well be called A YEAR OF GRACE. How many men, and women, and children look back to it as the year of their spiritual birth,—the blessed year of their conversion, so that they count their age from it rather than from the year when first they were born! Within the last few months, I have seen boys and girls like yourselves, giving themselves up to Christ, and getting from him pardon, and peace, and joy of no common kind. How even children have rushed into houses where I have been, and seizing my hand, when I asked them how they were, have said, "O happy, happy, sir!" How I have heard them sing that psalm right heartily, because truthfully,—

> "He took me from a fearful pit,
> And from the miry clay."

In various quarters the young have been getting good to their souls, entering upon the New Year with a new heart, and speaking of the old heart as of the old year, "Old things are passed away, behold, all things are become new." And then God's people in many places have been praying for you. Elsewhere, where the Holy Spirit has been poured out, and where they have already got wonderful answers to prayer, even little children have been offering up such petitions as this, "Lord, send a great revival amongst the young!" What a season of gracious opportunity! How anxious and earnest one and all of us should be! Every day is precious! To-day there is opportunity! Is it to pass unimproved? are you to continue unblessed? Is this day and this sermon to be what other days and other sermons have been—useless, unprofitable? Then I must close sadly with the question, "To what purpose is this waste?"

I would fain have you to be truly happy and truly blessed, both on this side the grave and beyond it; but how shall it be, if you will not listen to the Saviour's call of mercy? However active and successful you may have been in all other respects, if all your attention and care shall have been confined to other things—then, alas, what an end! Your time, and money, and strength, and opportunities shall then be seen to have been *all wasted*. You may rise in the world, you may become great scholars, you may be masters and mistresses—rich and honoured as merchants, as tradesmen, or otherwise; but, after all, yours will have been a *wasted life*, for then you will have laid up nothing for eternity, and you will have lost—*your soul!* And of all the instances of waste that have come before us, none is ever to be compared with this,— a WASTED SOUL; that is, a precious soul trifled away, thrown away for nothing, to no good purpose, getting nothing in exchange for it; leaving the bitter question to be answered in eternity, or rather to be pondered over as unanswerable during eternity's unending ages, "To what purpose was *this waste?*"

But why should it be so? The Lord is asking you now, "Why will ye die?" It is the Lord's question to you now, "To what purpose is this waste?" Do not persist in it. Remember the proverb I quoted, which is true above all else of wasted opportunities and of the soul neglected, "Wilful waste is woful want!" and do not run the fearful risk!

> "Life is the season God hath giv'n
> To fly from hell, and rise to heav'n;
> That day of grace fleets fast away,
> And none its rapid course can stay.
>
> Then what thy thoughts design to do,
> Still let thy hands with might pursue;
> Since no device nor work is found,
> Nor wisdom underneath the ground."

The day is hastening on when the account of this waste—of time, and money, and strength, and opportunities, and *of the soul*—shall have to be rendered by young and old. Are you getting it ready?

THE HYMN.

GOD intrusts to all
   Talents few or many;
None so young and small
   That they have not any.
Though the great and wise
   Have a greater number,
Yet my one I prize,
   And it must not slumber.

Every little mite,
   Every little measure,
Helps to spread the light,
   Helps to swell the treasure.
Little drops of rain
   Bring the springing flowers;
And I may attain
   Much by little powers.

God intrusts to all
   Talents few or many;
None so young and small
   That they have not any.
God will surely ask,
   Ere I enter heaven,
Have I done the task
   Which to me was given.

Truth and Falsehood.

THE HYMN.

WHEN a foolish thought within
    Tries to take us in a snare,
Conscience tells us, "It is sin,"
    And entreats us to beware.
If in something we transgress,
    And are tempted to deny,
Conscience says, "Your faults confess,
    Do not dare to tell a lie."

In the morning, when we rise,
    And would fain omit to pray,
"Child! consider!" Conscience cries;
    "Should not God be sought to-day?"
But if we should disregard,
    While those friendly voices call,
CONSCIENCE SOON WILL GROW SO HARD
    THAT IT WILL NOT SPEAK AT ALL.

MY DEAR YOUNG FRIENDS,—As a minister of Jesus Christ, I have had to come to you under a variety of characters,—as a prophet to speak of the past, and tell of the future; as a doctor to deal with your spiritual diseases, and do what I could, with God's blessing, to heal you; as a watchman, trying to apprehend you when you were doing wrong, and warning you of coming danger. To-day I wish to come to you as a woodman, with axe in hand, anxious to fell a gigantic tree, with deep-struck roots, and great trunk, and wide-spreading branches, and bitter poisonous fruit—ay, striking its roots deep down into your young hearts, and bearing its evil fruit in your lives. I would like at least to give it one of the most deadly blows I can; and if I cannot bring it down—and I fear I can scarcely hope to do that,—I shall at least give the first stroke, and leave the axe at the root of the tree, for some other hand to take it up and do better service. Nay, I would fain put an axe into every little hand, that, having cried to the Strong for strength, as a firm and brave little army, we might make a combined assault, —a united effort, to fell to the ground this deadly tree. I am sure neither God nor man would seek to hinder us; and instead of the appeal, "Woodman! spare that tree!" we should be cheered on by all the good and true, with the cry, "Heaven speed you on your noble enterprise!"

Laying aside figure, I wish to-day to deal with what is one of the *greatest*, and at the same time one of the *commonest* sins,—which is doing a world of damage alike to old and young, and great dishonour to God. The very commonness of it is apt to make us overlook its greatness; and as it meets us everywhere, especially among children, we are in danger of growing familiar with it, and not fearing and hating it as we should. I shall take two texts, the first and shorter for younger children, and the second and longer for the older:—

Colossians iii. 9: "LIE NOT one to another."
Ephesians iv. 25: "Wherefore PUTTING AWAY LYING, SPEAK every man TRUTH with his neighbour."

The tree I have spoken of, you will now see to

be the TREE OF FALSEHOOD—the sin which I have described as so grievous and so common, the SIN OF LYING. But is there anything to justify me in devoting a whole sermon to it? I think there is. When I find it so dwelt upon and denounced in the word of God; when I hear God saying that he so hates it; when I learn that it was A LIE that ruined our world —a lie that introduced sin, and misery, and death;— not a murder, not a theft, not an oath, but *a lie*, "And the serpent said unto the woman, Ye shall not surely die," when he knew they would, and God had said it; when I see it so hurtful to our present and future character; when I am told by one who knows something about children, that "there is no sin into which they so easily fall;" when one of the very proverbs of our country, which contain so much truth in little bulk, says, "*As easy as lying;*" and when I remember that hell's mouth is gaping wide to receive " all liars;" —I am sure you will agree with me when I say, that there is reason enough for *my speaking* and *your thinking* about it.

Let us look at these particulars :—the *nature* of the sin of lying,—the *character* of it,—the *danger* of it,— the *punishment* of it,—our *duty* regarding it.

I. The NATURE of the sin of lying. What is it? I need scarcely explain, even to the youngest child, what is generally meant when we speak about lying. The youngest of us knows the thing too well—the *inten-*

tional leading of others to understand as true what we know to be false. That is a lie; and when I speak of the nature of it, I wish to bring before you some of the ways in which we are guilty of this sin:—

1. It may be by a lying *word*—a sin of the *tongue*—*speaking* a lie.
2. It may be by a lying *look*—a sin of the *eye*—*looking* a lie.
3. It may be by a lying *act*—a sin of the *hand*—*acting* a lie.

1. It may be by a lying WORD—a sin of the *tongue*, *telling* a lie, *speaking* a lie. Shall I try to draw a picture of one who lies in this way—one who does not *speak* the truth? I shall try my hand at a full-length portrait of such a one, first in his week-day, and then in his Sabbath dress. Do you see that boy, skulking about some by-street, or playing with idle boys at some corner, about eleven o'clock in the forenoon? How is he there at that time of day? He was too lazy to rise in the morning, and, though called on again and again, slept in till the clock struck nine. Partly ashamed and partly afraid to go in late, he resolved to say he had not been well, or he had been on an errand for his mother; and having once made up his mind to that, he thinks he may as well, when he is late at any rate, take an hour more of it—it will make his excuse all the more likely to be believed. At school he cannot say his lessons, and says he had forgotten the place, or had lost his book, or at any rate had learned it well the

night before ; when the truth is, he was out so late at play and was so tired when he went home, that he was only fit for bed. In the playground, I see a number of boys gathered round him, listening to him, as he tells them a story that has not a word of truth in it from beginning to end,—it is purely his own invention, for he has a kind of cleverness about him ; or if the things he is telling really happened, he puts in some things to make them *wonder*, and other things to make them *laugh*, leading them to believe all the while that they are true, and wishing to be thought a clever fellow,—as, after a sort, he is. One of his companions has offended him. I hear him vowing vengeance, and saying he will make him suffer for this yet ; and on the first opportunity, he raises some ill report, representing him as having said or done what he would have spurned to say or do, and, perhaps, he is punished for a fault he never committed. When he goes home, he says nothing about the morning, but reports himself as having got a high place in his class, second dux or thereabouts—a place which he might have had, but through his indolence had lost,—making his parents glad, when, had they known the truth, they would have wept. Such is his week-day life; a word about the Sabbath. Having now and then to go alone to church, he professes to have been there, tells who was preaching, even gives the text, when he had gone out to the country to walk, or had spent the afternoon with some like-minded acquaintance, in a way I shall not describe. The same thing takes place at the Sabbath evening class,—going home at the exact hour as if nothing amiss had happened. That boy is a *liar ;* these are *spoken lies.*

Now, let no one say that does not describe him, for I don't at all mean to say that any one boy or girl would be so wicked as to do all these things. I trust I do not address one so far gone as that. But were I to break up my description into so many parts, is there one among us who would not feel that some one or other of them applied to him or her? The truth is, that this is not one, but a group of real portraits—ay, photographs, true pictures, like those taken by the sun. I have in my mind a boy or girl answering almost to every one of them. That is the very reason why I have gone so much into particulars. I wish to get you to regard every one of these as a dark, black, ugly *lie*— not to be laughed at, not to be thought clever, not to be gloried in, far less to be imitated, but to be mourned over before God with deepest sorrow. Whether it was in jest, or to escape punishment, or to be well thought of, or to get some reward—it stands written in God's book as a *sin*.

2. It may be by a lying LOOK—a sin of the *eye*—*looking* a lie. Perhaps you remember one day, shortly before the examination, when the school was in full working order, and the teacher was anxious that all should strive to make the most of the remaining part of the session, you were whispering to your neighbour, and putting off her time as well as your own, when

your teacher looked round, and asked who it was that was disobeying orders. No one said a word, but you looked across significantly to one of the best workers and most hopeful girls in the school; he caught your eye, and understood what it meant, and turning away, said to himself in a tone of disappointment, "Well, Mary, I should not have expected that of you." It was done in a moment, but that ungenerous and unkind look, that falsely accused and wronged the innocent, was a *lie*, and stands written against you as a *sin*.

3. It may be a lying ACT—a sin of the *hand—acting* a lie. This is one of the most common forms of it, and least thought of. Still to keep by school-life: It is the hour for arithmetic. You have got some hard sums to do—too hard for you to master without more time than you have got now. You ask your neighbour to show you his slate, or you look over the shoulder of the boy before you who is always correct, you see you have been mistaken, rub out the wrong figures, fill in the right,—in a moment you are on your feet as having finished your work, read off your sum, get your mark, and, with it, credit for being one of the few who are correct. That is a *theft*, but it is also a *lie;* it is *stealing*, but it is also *lying*. It was not the *tongue*, but the *hand* that did it. And here let me warn you against being parties to the lies of others. Not only copying sums off a slate from a neighbour, is deceptive and untruthful, but *allowing* it to be done, is just about as

bad. It may seem hard and unkind to refuse, and yet you *ought*, for his sake as well as your own. It is not true kindness to him; and on your part it is a lie too, —letting that be passed off for his which is not.

You are a young servant. You have broken accidentally a favourite china bowl. You do not know what to do. It is the first time such a thing has happened with you. You fear your mistress will be angry; perhaps you will have to replace it out of your half-year's wage, small as it is, just on purpose to make you more careful for the future. So instead of making an immediate and full confession, explaining how it took place, and saying you will be more careful in time to come, you take up the pieces, and lay them aside till you have opportunity of getting them out of the way; or you join the broken piece in as neatly as you can, set the bowl in the press, and the discovery is never made that you had any hand in it, till you are in another situation. You have been *acting a lie;* and I can hardly over-estimate the wrong you have done,—most of all to yourself. Or you are reading a book or journal which conscience tells you is wrong: you hear your mistress, or your mother, or your neighbour coming; —in goes the book to your pocket, and you are found sitting quietly with your Bible or your seam in your hand, and so escape detection. You have been *acting a lie*, and, as before, sinning most of all against yourself.

You are walking along the street when you meet

some old acquaintance or school-companion, to whom, had you been alone, you would have frankly spoken. But you have some genteel friend with you, and your school-fellow is beneath you in worldly station, and is poorly, or at least plainly dressed, or is carrying a basket over his arm, or is helping along a widowed mother in feeble health ; and though he is awaiting your recognition with a happy smile, you turn your head the other way,—look as if you never had seen him, and so pass on. Again, I say, you have been *acting a lie*, and a lie of the meanest and most unworthy kind. It was not merely a piece of silly *pride*,—it was a piece of base *falsehood*. It was as much as to say, "You are quite a stranger to me; I have no acquaintance with you."

You profess to be religious, to be a follower of Jesus, to have a real interest in what is good,—none more earnest and solemn-looking than you. You wish to be thought a godly child—to stand well with those who love and fear God—to have the good opinion of your teacher, or minister, or friends. But your godliness is not real. It is confined to certain times and places. You are like those of whom God speaks, as drawing near him with their mouth, and honouring him with their lips, while their heart was removed far from him. Such a profession is a lie ; and *lying* in *religion*,—that is, *pretence* in religion,—or, what we commonly call *hypocrisy*, whether in the young or the old, is one of the worst forms of this sin, peculiarly hateful to God, coming nearest to the case of Ananias and Sapphira, regarding whose acted lie—for it was *acted* before it was *spoken*—Peter said, "Thou hast not lied unto *men*, but unto *God*."

When Jacob put the kid-skins on his hands and neck, and served up dainty meat to his old blind father Isaac, passing himself off for his brother Esau, he *acted a lie;* it was *lying kindness*. When Judas went up to Jesus in the garden, and said, "Hail! Master!" and kissed him, in order thereby to point him out to the soldiers, he *acted a lie;* it was a *lying kiss*. And so in endless ways I might show how lies are acted still. When you try to appear wiser, or richer, or better, or more obedient and kind than you are, you are acting a lie.

Before leaving this head, let me say a word regarding *equivocating*,—that is, saying what has a double meaning—what may be taken up in two ways—the mere *word* true, the *thing* false—a kind of *half-lie*. I can suppose your father, going out of an evening, telling you to take your book, meaning that you are to prepare your lesson. Instead of this you spend the whole hour over a new story-book you have got; and when, on coming in, he asks if you have been at your book, you say, Yes. In one sense it is true, in another it is false; *he* means one thing and *you* another. We may thus make distinctions and justify ourselves, but God condemns all such, as violations of truth. "Old Humphrey," who, under a variety of names, wrote so many good and pleasant things for old and young, in speaking of a painter who overcoloured all his pictures, expressed the defect in these words, "Too much red in the brush;" and in hearing things stated that were not exactly true—that were overstated, he was wont to say, what might often be said to most of us, and what I wish you had a friend at your elbow, when you are overstating things, to whisper into your ear, "Too much red in the brush!" The worst of these half-lies, as I have called them, is, that they generally lead us to worse.

II. The CHARACTER of this sin. It would take long to bring out all the bad features of it. Take the following: 1. It is a COWARDLY thing. No brave boy would lie. Cowards tell lies. One who is vulgarly called a "bully," who keeps all the smaller boys in terror, and is always bragging of his own doings, calling those cowards who refuse to fight with him, or to join in doing what is wrong, upbraiding them for not daring to disobey their mother—*he* is the coward, as you would hear, were you to listen at the door after he has gone home, where he is inventing all manner of lies, for fear his father should whip him. *Fear* lies at the bottom of *falsehood*, and no liar need pretend to be brave. If I were in search of courageous boys, I would seek truthful ones. Our Scottish martyrs, the good Covenanters in olden times, were bright examples of strict adherence, not only to the truth, but to truthfulness; and where shall we find any, more brave? A

lie would have saved their lives—a single lying act—
one lying bow of the head—but they would not. They
would rather die, than be guilty of a single lie, acted
or spoken,—and they *did* die.

2. It is a MEAN thing. It is not manly. Some of the
cases I have mentioned,—showing utter disregard to the
feelings and interests of others, are base, shabby, con-
temptible in the extreme. Never expect much at the
hand of liars. They would sacrifice your interests to
their own any day. You remember the old prophet in
Israel, who, from curiosity, or pride, or some other unworthy motive, wished the man of God from Judah
to stay with him, when God had charged him to return
home as soon as his work was done, without even eating or drinking. When he could not succeed otherwise, he gained his selfish purpose by a lie, though it
cost the other his life; for a lion met him by the way
and slew him, for believing the prophet's lie and disobeying God's command. That liar disregarded the
other's life, in seeking gratification for himself. If you
wished me to set before you a manly boy, I should
not bring a liar, but such a one as George Washing-
ton, who, when questioned by his father as to his
favourite cherry-tree which had been cut down, gave
the well-known noble answer, which cannot be too long
remembered, or too often repeated: "I cannot tell a
lie, papa; you know I cannot tell a lie. I cut down
the cherry-tree with my hatchet." No wonder that we
afterwards read of that truthful boy, who "could not

tell a lie,"—who would rather have been whipped or punished to any extent,—as the brave general and the great man.

> "Dare to be true. Nothing can need a lie.
> A fault, which needs it most, grows two thereby."

We have a fine instance of it in the life of one of the olden kings of France. He was a prisoner in this country, and was released on condition that his two sons should take his place. One of them afterwards grew weary of his confinement, and made his escape, when the father, who could not bear a stain to rest on his royal word, in spite of all persuasions to the contrary, returned to his imprisonment, and died in the Tower of London. That was too manly a thing to be looked for from a liar.

3. It is a God-dishonouring thing. How much is said of God in connection with *truth!* He is called the "God of truth." It is said, he "keepeth truth for ever." Every word of his is so unchangeable that his "truth" is just used for his "word;" they mean the same thing. He is called "God who cannot lie." His people are called "children that will not lie." Lying lips are said to be "an abomination" to him. Truth is part of God's likeness—God's image. What dishonour, then, must be done to the God of truth by lying! What an offence and grief it must be to him! What contempt it shows for him, who sees and knows it all! It seems to throw doubt on God as the omniscient,—the all-knowing One. It is as if the liar mocked God,—as if

he said, "I can deceive God as well as man by my lies." Oh, what an offence must our falsehoods and pretences, whether spoken or acted, be in God's eye! How fit the comparison which Jesus used! how true of liars,— "*whited sepulchres*,"—outwardly fair, but within, full of rottenness and dead men's bones. *You* don't like lying things;—a lying apple, beautiful and inviting without, but rotten within; a lying penny, bright but bad; a lying cat, that invites you to make of it, and seems ever so friendly, and then bites or scratches you; a lying lottery, that promises a prize and gives a blank; a lying branch, that invites your foot to rest upon it, and then gives way and throws you to the ground. And *God* dislikes lying things too,—lying boys and girls, who pretend to be one thing and are another in reality, who say one thing and mean another, who promise one thing and do another,—pretenders,—hypocrites,—deceivers! This is the worst feature in it all—it is so dishonouring to God. This is seen in the way he speaks of it and punishes it.

4. It is a DEVILISH thing. These are strong words, but the Bible warrants me in using them. As much is said of truth in connection with God,—so much is said of lying in connection with Satan. God is the "God of truth," the devil is the "Father of lies,"—is "a liar," ay, and the father of liars. Lying is a thing of hell; it came thence. The first thing Satan did in our world was *to lie*, to deceive our first mother by a falsehood. It is no good relationship. A wise man long ago was once asked

what made men like God. He said, "When they speak truth." We might ask, "What makes men like the devil?" and answer, "When they lie." That marks people out to be like him—to be his. He claims all liars as his children. They are none of God's. When Judas lied, it is said, "Satan entered into him." When Ananias lied, Peter said, "Why hath Satan filled thine heart?" When Peter lied, it was "Satan desiring to have him." Oh, to think that under the fair face and comely dress of some young girl, there should be a black lying heart! I hear one expressing it thus,—on hearing a fashionably dressed young female, as she was passing along the street, saying to another, "And I was contriving what kind of a fib I should tell him." He was startled. He thought— "This is perhaps said of a father, or brother, or teacher, or friend." He heard no more; but he says, "*It made the angel form seem vile.*" Lying is so vile a thing, and the word "lie" is so black, even to the world, even to the wicked, even to careless children, that they try to use it as little as possible, and it is spoken and thought lightly of, under another name—a "fib;" "it was only a fib"—a kind of harmless, innocent falsehood —a *little lie*—a softer name for a bad, black thing.

III. The DANGER of it.

1. It is a GROWING sin. By this I mean it is always increasing. One lie leads to and necessitates another, till no one knows where it will end. It is

like a snowball, the further it is rolled the more it increases in size. Once or twice indulged, it soon becomes a habit. It grows upon one with amazing rapidity. In the case of Ananias, you have first an *acted* lie, and then a *spoken* lie. The one necessitated the other. In the case of Gehazi, the servant of the prophet, you have the first lie to Naaman necessitating the second to Elisha. And how sadly this appears in children! It often staggers one, to hear little children so expert at lying. And a habit of deceitfulness thus formed in early life, gets such a hold on one, that no human power can root it out afterwards. Hence, we are so alarmed when we see it beginning to appear. Dear children! beware of the beginnings of it, for otherwise it will cost you dear.

2. It LEADS TO and is LINKED WITH MANY OTHER SINS. You seldom find lying *alone*. It is something like drinking : it leads to almost every other sin, and all other sins seek its help, and hide themselves under it. I can hardly fancy a liar to be honest—either to fear God or regard man.

3. It DEGRADES THE WHOLE CHARACTER. When a habit of lying has been formed, we may well fear the worst. When truthfulness goes, the whole character goes along with it. There is an end to all confidence. You cannot trust in any one thing. Do you see that mother weeping as if her very heart would break? For whole days I never see her smile. She cannot sleep. It casts a gloom over the whole house. What calamity has

befallen her? Is her darling boy dead? No, but what is next to it has happened—that awful occurrence —*the first lie!* He has told the first wilful falsehood! No wonder that she mourns; the house might well be hung in sackcloth for it. If not checked, it may be her boy's ruin for both worlds. She cannot be too thankful that it *has been discovered*. What a mercy! for now she knows the danger. It is worst of all when not discovered—*when the lie succeeds*. It is the child's safety to be found out in time. There is still hope. "Any vice," I find a father saying of his children,— "*Any vice but falsehood!*"

For a young apprentice, or a young servant, there is nothing I fear so much as untruthfulness. I have seen it lead to so much evil, that I am glad of any opportunity to warn of the danger. Again I repeat it, untruthfulness strikes at the very foundation of one's character. Nothing else can be right, if anything be wrong here. The master or mistress is deceived. Those at home are as much in the dark. Success in deceiving, leads to dishonesty otherwise; and bad company, the theatre, and drinking often follow. It comes out all at once; and a prison, or banishment, and blighted hopes, and broken hearts are the result. Oh, boys and girls! beware of lying—of deceiving. Don't—even for once! It is a grand thing to have it said of you, "We can always trust their word!" It is a character in itself to have it said, "That is a lad that *can be trusted!*" That will carry you all the world over.

IV. The PUNISHMENT of it. This is two-fold.

1. HERE—in the present world. There is the loss of character; the loss of all respect. There is degradation; misery; shame. No one can respect a liar. It carries its own punishment with it. The lie in the school that I spoke of has proved a dear one. Had that scholar not copied from his neighbour's slate that day, the boy might have been spurred on to apply himself to his work, and have mastered it. Now he is in a good situation, and he is not fit for it; he cannot remedy the effects of his neglected education; and especially, when difficult questions in arithmetic come up, he wishes a hundred times over, that he had not acted that lie in copying the account. Generally the sin *comes out*—" for a lying tongue is but for a moment." And then what disgrace is connected with the discovery, so that, ever after, the liar is despised and distrusted! Sometimes there are even visible judgments. There are two pillars set up by the way-side, like Lot's wife, for the warning of all passers by. On the one is the figure of a young man, Gehazi,—a well-instructed, well-brought-up lad, the servant of a mighty prophet. But *he lied;* and, as the punishment, he was sent out of his master's presence, "a leper, white as snow." The writing on it, is our text, " Lie not one to another! Remember Gehazi!" On the other are two figures—of a husband and wife, who persisted in a lie upon which they had agreed beforehand, and one after the other, they dropped down —DEAD. The writing on this pillar is, " Wherefore,

putting away lying, speak every man truth! Remember Ananias and Sapphira!"

Immediate judgments do not always follow sin, but sometimes they do. In the market-place of an English town may be seen the following inscription,—I have copied it for you from a book in which I met with it the other day:—

"The Mayor and Corporation of Devizes avail themselves of the stability of this building to transmit to future times the record of an awful event, which occurred in this market-place, in the year 1753, hoping that such a record may serve as a salutary warning against the danger of impiously invoking the divine vengeance, or of calling on the holy name of God, to conceal the devices of falsehood and fraud. On Thursday, the 25th of January 1753, Ruth Pierce, of Pottern in this county, agreed with three other women to buy a sack of wheat in the market, each agreeing to pay her due proportion towards the same. One of these women, in collecting the several quotas of money, discovered a deficiency, and demanded of Ruth Pierce the sum which was wanting to make good the amount. Ruth Pierce protested that she had paid her share, and said she wished she might drop down dead if she had not. She rashly repeated this awful wish, when, to the consternation of the surrounding multitudes, she instantly fell down and expired, having the money concealed in her hand."

2. HEREAFTER—in the world to come. Remember, dear children! that sooner or later the lie *will be discovered—every lie!* If not here, at any rate hereafter. Were I to make any girl's lie known through this book how she would blush!—how she would say I had destroyed her character!—how she would scarcely ever get over it! And what shall it be *then*, when every lie shall be read out before a world, and when liars shall all receive their portion? God says now, "He that

speaketh lies shall not escape." See the company and the end of the liar. "But the fearful, and unbelieving, and the abominable, and murderers, and whoremongers, and sorcerers, and idolaters, and *all* LIARS, shall have their part in the lake which burneth with fire and brimstone, which is the second death." ALL LIARS! That is not said of any other class of sinners, not, "all murderers," or all "swearers," but only these, as if God would show that it is impossible that *one liar* could escape. Stress is laid upon it. How startling —*all liars!* Young as well as old; poor as well as rich —*all!* Again we read, "For without," that is, without the gates of the celestial city—outside of heaven, "are dogs, and sorcerers, and whoremongers, and murderers, and idolaters, and *whosoever,*"—like the "all;" surely there is something very particular in this: "and *whosoever*"—young or old, it makes no matter, no respect will be paid to what he is otherwise, no excuse,— "whosoever LOVETH or MAKETH a *lie:*" taking in and using, approving, and laughing at the lies of others— loveth, as well as maketh "a lie." *The liar cannot enter heaven.* "There shall in no wise enter into it anything that defileth, neither whatsoever worketh abomination, or *maketh a lie.*" Surely no one is more completely shut out of heaven than the liar. Make up your mind, then, children! You must either give up *lying* or give up *heaven!*

V. Our DUTY regarding it.—"Lie *not: putting*

away lying—*speak the truth.*" Our very first duty is to seek pardon and cleansing in the blood of Jesus, and the renewal of the heart through the power of the Holy Ghost. Of all sinners, the liar needs most to be washed, for he is black, black indeed; and at once you must make up your mind to have done with it— to "*put it away,*" and to speak *the truth*, and only the truth henceforth. But more particularly—

1. STRIVE against it. It is not easy when the habit has been formed; but it is possible,—it can be done,— it has been done. Bridle your tongue, as you would a vicious horse; curb it—hold on at all hazards. And as a help, remember ever that the *eye of God is on you.* Often think of that now, "Thou God seest me!" How often we hear people say, "*God knows* that I am speaking true!" I wish those who often use this word, and who say, "As true as I am here," "As true as you are living," &c., would only think that it is the case that *God knows!*— that *God sees!* "Keep thy tongue from evil, and thy lips from speaking guile." Rather *starve* than *lie*. Rather *die* than *lie!* "Better," says Solomon, "is *a poor man* than a *liar.*"

2. WATCH against it. You must not leave the door open. You must not be off your guard. "I said I will *take heed* to *my ways*, that I offend not with my tongue." "If thou hast thought evil, *lay thy hand upon thy mouth;*" keep it back—don't let it out. Here is a sentence from good Thomas Watson: "The tongue is an unruly member : God hath set a

double hedge before the tongue—the *teeth* and the *lips* to keep it within bounds, that it do not speak vanity. Oh, look to your tongue ! If you would have better tongues, labour to have better hearts. WATCH your tongues. As the tongue hath a *double fence* set about it, so it had need have a *double watch !*"

3. PRAY against it. After you have done your best, and while doing your best, still *cry to God*, "Set a watch, O Lord, before my mouth : keep the door of my lips" (Ps. cxli. 3). Do not attempt it without prayer. The tongue can no man tame ; *none but God !* Pray much, pray earnestly, for grace to overcome

4. Seek to LOVE THE TRUTH. Get the heart filled with the love of Christ, and then you will love the truth, and of necessity hate lying. Every effort will strengthen you, and the more you seek after the truth, the stronger will you become in it. Rather be *simple* than *deceitful ;* rather be the *cheated* than the *cheater*, for it is written, "The Lord *preserveth* the SIMPLE." Oh, labour to get and to keep the jewel of truth, for it is priceless. There is no more beautiful ornament than *thorough, straightforward* truthfulness—straightforward in everything, in dealing with men and with God,—no equivocation in tone, or look, or act. Buy truth at any price, and never sell it.

I give you these lines, taken from an old scrap-book :—

> " If thou wishest to be wise,
> Keep these words before thine eyes :
> ' *What* thou speak'st, and *how* beware ;
> *Of whom, to whom, when* and *where.*' "

THE HYMN.

To speak the truth is always right,
   And therefore always best :
'Tis sinful, in our Maker's sight,
   To tell a lie in jest.

Nor should we seek a fault to hide
   By any false pretence ;
The truth must never be denied,
   Whate'er the consequence.

Falsehood can never prosper long,
   Its triumph soon is past ;
BUT TRUTH, HOWE'ER OPPOSED, IS STRONG,
   AND WILL FOR EVER LAST.

There's One above doth all things know,
   And a strict reckoning keep :
God is not mocked ; and *as we sow
   So shall we surely reap.*

Prayer.

THE HYMN.

THERE is an Eye that never sleeps
    Beneath the wing of night;
There is an Ear that never shuts,
    When sink the beams of light.

There is an Arm that never tires,
    When human strength gives way;
There is a Love that never fails,
    When earthly loves decay.

That Eye is fixed on seraph throngs;
    That Arm upholds the sky;
That Ear is filled with angel songs;
    That Love is throned on high.

But there's a power which man can yield
    When mortal aid is vain,
That Eye, that Arm, that Love to reach,
    That listening Ear to gain.

That power is PRAYER, which soars on high
    Through Jesus to the throne;
And moves the Hand which moves the world,
    To bring salvation down!

MY DEAR YOUNG FRIENDS,—You have heard of people being *dumb;* you have seen such people,—unable to speak, and sing, and laugh like you. When travelling in the country some time ago, there were in the inside of the coach two nice-looking boys, and a man who seemed to be the father of one of them. They looked at each other, and at those about them, but never spoke a word; and by-and-by I found out that they were dumb, and were on their way to one of the hospitals or schools in Edinburgh, where dumb people are taught a language of their own,—where they learn to speak, not with their tongues, as we do, but with their fingers,—a sad, silent language, though many have had cause to bless God that he put it into man's heart to devise it. That father had never heard the voice of his boy. When he was a little child about the age at which children generally begin to lisp their little words, how anxiously his father and mother listened to hear him speak!—how day after day, and month after month, they still waited, and expected, and hoped!—how many little arts they tried, till at length when his age came to be reckoned by years instead of months, the stunning truth was told—*their child was dumb;* and it went like a dagger to their hearts to think they never should hear their darling boy pronounce the word,—Father!—Mother! Many a time have the hearts of parents thus been saddened; but it was God's doing, and he does all things well; so what could be said?

But you can fancy something worse than that: if that boy had been able to speak, and had spoken to everybody but his father—had been dumb only to *him;* if amid all his father's love and kindness to him, providing for his comfort, supplying all his wants, watching most tenderly over him, and only desiring his good, he never thanked his father, or showed any gratitude or love, and refused to ask him for anything he needed, always going to other people and asking them, and if they could not give, resolving rather to want it. I say, would not that be far more trying and grieving to a parent's heart? Or, if he only spoke to him as if he were a stranger, and kept at a distance from him, and would not have any childlike, loving converse with him, would it not be wrong, undutiful, foolish,— wicked?

"How very foolish," you say, "for himself, and how very heartless! What a wicked boy!" My dear child, thou art the boy!—thou art the girl! that is the very thing many of you have been doing; that is just what I charge you with now; that just so far describes your behaviour to your Father in heaven— God. He has done everything for you; he has given you everything you have; he has loved you, and shown his love as none ever did or could do; he has told you his readiness to do still more; and yet you have been to him like a dumb child; you have never spoken to him, never thanked him, never asked his blessing, and while his ear has been open to hear your voice, he has had to wait in vain. Year after year has passed, till it is far beyond the time when you should have been speaking, and it seems likely to be with you as with many grown-up people, who live, and grow old, and die, without ever speaking to their Father at all. Don't you think it must be very grieving to *him?* Don't you think it is very sinful in *you?* What I exactly mean, and what I wish to speak to you about, you will see, if you turn to the last three words of—

ACTS ix. 11: BEHOLD HE PRAYETH.

How many of you prayed to God this morning? how many last night? how many do not pray at all? Perhaps some may even be mistaken who would say they *do* pray; and so I think it well to bring this subject before you somewhat fully. It may help you, if you will put some questions to me about the matter. I shall give you six questions to ask me:—1. *What is prayer?* 2. *What* should I pray for? 3. *Why* should I pray? 4. *Where* should I pray? 5. *When* should I pray? 6. *How* should I pray?

Question I. WHAT IS PRAYER? Many fall into a mistake here. It is not closing the eyes, and clasping the hands together, and standing up as you do in church, and at school, or kneeling as you do at home, and repeating certain words. *That* is not praying. I have heard of a man who "prayed, and did not pray." What would you understand by that? It was an old man who, from his infancy, had never gone to bed at night without repeating the prayer his mother taught him,—

"This night when I lie down to sleep,
I give my soul to Christ to keep;
If I should die before I wake,
I pray thee, Lord, my soul to take."

And yet he had never prayed one real prayer; for *saying prayers* is not *praying*. There may be some of you who have said your prayers from your earliest years; who, though now not very young, have never omitted in the morning, "Our Father who art in heaven," or in the evening, "This night when I lie down to sleep"—(for even many old people have no prayers but these, which they merely repeat like parrots, without understanding even what they mean); you may not have omitted these for a single day, and yet it may be true of you, that you have *never prayed*. If a person were to come to you and repeat certain words which he did not understand; if he did not seem to think of what he was saying; if he kept looking about him all the time, as if he were not speaking to you; if he were to fall asleep while he was speaking; if he went away without ever waiting for an answer, or hearing what you had to say,—what would you think of him? And yet that is what very many do to God; and *that* is what *they* call prayer! What would you think of a person putting a letter into the post-office without an address on it, or putting only unmeaning words, or nothing at all, in the inside of it? Would it be strange if no answer came? would he have reason to say, "I wonder I am getting no reply; other people, I hear, are getting answers to their letters, but I am getting none?" Are not your prayers very much like something of this kind? They are not addressed to God; or they are like a blank sheet of paper neatly folded up, and addressed in a good hand; but there is nothing in them, and so nothing ever comes of them. Like unaddressed letters, they are, as it were, sent to the "Dead-Letter Office," and come back as they went away, or are never heard of more; or like blank letters, there is nothing to reply to, and so no reply is received.

Paul had many a time said prayers before,—oftener, perhaps, than most people now-a-days, for he was very attentive to outward duties; and yet God says in our text to Ananias, "Behold he prayeth!" as if it had now for the first time been true of him—as if he had never prayed before. And so it was. He had often *said his prayers*—he had never *prayed*. What, then, is prayer? You have it in the first word of Matt. vii. 7: ASK. You have it in Ps. l. 15: CALL UPON ME. You have it elsewhere: "They CRIED TO GOD." "Asking" is praying; "calling upon God" is praying; "crying to God" is praying. Look at yon sinking vessel. See yon mother standing on the wreck with her infant in her arms, and yon man clinging to a plank, and others holding on by a boat that has turned upside down, and cut off the last hope of not a few. Amid the loud whistling of the wind and the dashing of the waves, what is that you hear? Listen! above the sound of wind and wave, what shouting and bitter cries, "Help! help! Save me! O save my child!" *That* is prayer. Or see that poor boy. The day is stormy and bitter cold; he has been lying all night under the arch of a bridge, or in some common stair; he has no home, no parents to provide for him, and he comes to your door to ask for help. He is more destitute and more helpless than the robin-red-breasts, that hop about our windows in winter. He is cold and hungry. How he pleads for some of your warm clothing to cover him, and some of your nice food to satisfy the cravings of his hunger!

> "Open your hospitable door,
> And shield me from the biting blast!"

"Help a poor homeless boy. Give me a morsel of bread. Do not send me away." *That* is prayer. Or there is another: a palsy-stricken man, hardly able to walk, ill-clad, wasted and worn-looking, unable to speak so as to be understood. He just stands before you, as much as to say, "Look at me; see how poor and needy I am, how much I need your help; and though I cannot ask it in words, this stammering tongue and trembling hand speak of themselves." *That* is prayer.

Dear children! do not these describe your condition? You are like the sinking, shipwrecked ones, perishing, going down to hell; and you cannot save yourselves. Oh, will you not cry for help,—for deliverance,—for salvation? "Lord, save me, save me; I am perishing!"

> "There is a dreadful hell,
> And everlasting pains;
> Where sinners must with devils dwell,
> In darkness, fire, and chains."

Can you think of going there, without ever asking to be saved, without crying to God to deliver you? Such crying is praying. To pray is just to *beg*, and every praying child is a *beggar*. We are poorer than the poorest, and so we *need* to beg; and if we are like other beggars, there will be no want of praying. Prayer is *speaking to God*—to a real, living person,—as real as we are ourselves. True, you cannot *see* God; but he can *see and hear you* as really as those beside you can now. He is not far away,—he is close at hand! You have heard of the electric telegraph, how quickly messages go and come by it. You can send a message to London, or to any other part of the country, along those mysterious wires, and though hundreds of miles off, your friends will get it and send an answer to you in a few minutes. But God hears, when you speak to him, more quickly than even in this way, for he says, "Before they call, I will answer; and while they are yet speaking, I will hear."

Now, how is it with you, when you pray? Do you feel that you are speaking to God, asking, begging from God, crying to God? What do you think of, when you seem to be praying? Do you desire what you ask? Is your prayer mere words, or is your heart in it? Is it something inflicted on you as a punishment? Is it a task which you must perform every morning and evening? Are you like the praying machines used in some heathen countries; the people writing prayers on pieces of paper, putting them into a kind of roller or barrel, and every time the roller goes round, reckoning it one prayer? Are you like a boy who was proud, because a lady who heard him, said, "How sweetly he prays!" and who, after neglecting his prayers for several days, repeated them over as often as would make up for the omission, lest something should happen to him,—but never really praying, till, when an old man, he felt himself to be a sinner, and cried to God for mercy? Is it a disagreeable duty to ask bread when you are hungry, or help when you are in danger? If you were condemned to die, would you not feel it a privilege to be allowed to ask the Queen for pardon? And will you not regard it as a precious privilege to be allowed to pray to God,—to tell him your wants, to cry to Him for help? If you have never really prayed before, begin to pray now.

> " Prayer is the contrite sinner's voice,
> Returning from his ways :
> While angels in their songs rejoice,
> And say, Behold he prays ! "

Question II. WHAT SHOULD I PRAY FOR? There are two very good guides to follow in praying—the *prayers recorded in the Bible,* and *the promises of God.* Have you ever noticed the hundreds of prayers there are in the Bible? I could not tell you how many. The Book of Psalms is full of them ; and God's people in all ages—whether they have been young or old—have liked to take these prayers, and make them their own. You will find there, prayers for every case. They are fit for children as well as for grown-up people. They are so short that any of you may remember them, and yet so comprehensive as to include everything you can need or desire. First of all, we have the prayer for *a new heart,* and this should be *our* first request, "Create in me a clean heart, O God, and renew a right spirit within me!" For *pardon*,—"Pardon mine iniquity, for it is great!" For *salvation*,—"Lord save us, we perish!" For *mercy*,—"God be merciful to me, a sinner!" My dear young friends, commit these Scripture prayers to memory, and make them your own,—pray them for yourselves.

And then another guide in asking aright is *God's promise.* You are always safe in asking what He has promised. Take his own promise, and plead it with him. Remind him of what he has said, just as you would remind your father and mother if they had promised you anything. He wishes you to do this. He says, "Put me in remembrance." Well, then, his greatest promise is the *Holy Spirit,* and he says, "He will give the Holy Spirit to them that ask him," showing that we are to pray for this blessing. I have already called your special attention to this, as the best thing you can ask or get. It is the Holy Spirit—(who is also God, equal with the Father and the Son)—who leads us to think about our souls and to seek their salvation; who shows us the evil of sin, and the wickedness of our own hearts, and the danger of being forgetful of God, and away from him. It is he who shows us Jesus as the very Saviour we need, who gives us the new heart, who enables us to understand the Bible and the way to be saved, who makes men holy and happy, and who prepares them for heaven. How blessed, then, are they who have the Holy Spirit! All the things in the world are not so precious as this; and for this, blessed be God, you are told to ask. What should I pray for? Pray for the Holy Spirit. What shall I say? "O Lord, for Jesus' sake, give me thy Holy Spirit." Do remember this, for nothing is so important. You might have all the wealth in the world, and yet, without this, you would have no peace, no joy—you would be miserable and poor.

Then there is that wondrous prayer,—" The Lord's Prayer," which we so little think of, and so little understand when we repeat it. Are you grieved, as you hear wicked children or wicked men taking God's name in vain, or speaking amiss of the Bible, or the Sabbath, or the sanctuary, or anything that pertains to God?—"Hallowed be thy name." Would you have the poor heathen to know about Jesus, and the wicked to be made good, and Jesus to be loved and honoured over all the earth?—"Thy kingdom come." Would you be humbly submissive to the will of God, and have this earth to be liker what heaven is?—"Thy will be done in earth, as it is in heaven." Would you have your bodily wants supplied?—"Give us this day our daily bread." Would you have your sins pardoned?—"Forgive us our debts." Would you be kept out of the way of evil, and preserved from bad company and bad things?—" Lead us not into temptation, but deliver us from evil."

Pray for your friends that they may be Christ's,

that they may be saved, that they may be comforted in sorrow, that they may be made holy, and prepared for heaven. If you had a little brother drowning and could not help him, wouldn't you cry to those who could? And if you have brothers or sisters who do not love Christ or believe in Christ, will you not cry to God for them? How it grieves you to see your mother weeping,—how you wish you could comfort her, how you seek to dry the tears that run down her cheeks, even while you weep yourself! Perhaps you think, "If I were only a little older, how I would comfort my mother; I would stand between her and want; I would protect her; I would not suffer an angry word to be said to her; she would lean on my strong arm,—she would share my all!" And can you do nothing now? Yes, very much; you can comfort and help her now; but still more,—you can *pray* for her. "Lord, bless my mother. Lord, comfort my mother. Lord, provide for, and protect, and care for my mother. Lord, be my mother's God as well as mine." When you see godless children around you, who have no fear of God, and no love to God, and no respect for the Bible or the Sabbath, and you think that speaking to them would do no good; still, could you not *pray* for them, that God would convert them, and give them new hearts, and make them what they ought to be?

And so, whatever you need, just go and tell God, as you would your own parents. Open up your heart to him. There is nothing too great to ask, and nothing so little as to be beneath his notice. For health and peace and comfort, for deliverance in danger, for help in distress, for relief when your heart is heavy, for direction when you don't know what to do—pray to God! Your precious soul should be your first concern, and if you have begun to think about your soul, you will be sure to pray about it. During the revival at Dundee in Mr. M'Cheyne's time, when so many were brought to Christ, the prayerfulness of the young people, both alone and together, was one thing very marked. You might have seen young boys kneeling together, sometimes in their own closets or in solitary places, crying for mercy. That was their first and most earnest cry, as it should be yours. "We will easily know if he be earnest," said one of them regarding another, " for then he will not need to be bidden to pray." Do you need to be bidden to pray? Nothing has been more remarkable during the recent outpouring of the Spirit, than the prayerfulness, especially of many young converts ; " *in everything* by prayer and supplication, with thanksgiving, making their requests known unto God."

Perhaps you would like to know how others, just such as you, have prayed.* I find one boy, when he had come to feel himself a sinner deserving hell, crying out, like Peter when he was sinking in the water, " O Jesus, save me, save me." And afterwards, in directing others, I find him saying, "Go and tell Jesus

* See page 258.

that you are poor, lost, hell-deserving sinners; and tell him to give you the new heart." I hear another, five years of age, as he lay on a bed of sore sickness, praying, "Sweet Jesus, save me, deliver me." There is a third. His master is telling him the need and comfort of prayer; but he says, "Sir, I cannot pray, for I cannot read." " You could, John, use the short prayer of the dying thief, 'Lord, remember me.' " And now he is laid on a sick-bed, and as his master sits by his bedside and reads God's word to him, he suddenly stops him and says, " Sir, if you please, I should wish to have you stop reading; I should wish you to hear that I can pray now." And then he says so simply and earnestly, " Lord, remember me! The blood of Jesus Christ cleanseth from all sin. Him that cometh unto me I will in no wise cast out. Lord Jesus "—but he gets no further, and with these words on his lips, he dies. Once more, there is a poor cripple, with little knowledge and few advantages; let us listen to his simple prayer: " O Christ, the Lamb of God, who taketh away the sin of the world, have mercy upon me, have mercy upon me. Wash me throughly from all my sins. Cleanse me from all mine iniquities. Clothe me in the spotless robe of thy righteousness. Sanctify thou my heart and life by thy blessed Spirit, that I may serve thee while here on earth, and be fitted for thy presence in glory. O Christ, hear my prayer. And do thou receive my spirit at the last, when it shall please thee to call it from this body of clay. Amen."

I merely give you these to show what they prayed for. You can find words for yourselves; you can speak to God in your own words. It does not need *long* prayers or *fine-worded* prayers. Only let them be the prayers of the *heart;* asking what you feel you need.

> "Jesus, Saviour, pity me;
> Hear me when I cry to thee.
> I've a very naughty heart,
> Full of sin in every part.
> I can never make it good:
> Wilt thou wash me in thy blood?
> Jesus, Saviour, pity me;
> Hear me when I cry to thee."

Question. III. WHY SHOULD I PRAY? Why does a beggar beg? Because if he does not beg, he will starve. Why does a drowning man cry out? Because if he does not, he will die. Why should a sinner pray? Because if he does not, he will perish. Some one has said, "*You must pray or perish.*" Not that prayer can save us. No, Jesus alone can do that. Prayer only *asks* salvation. What need we have to pray,— as sinful, perishing creatures—we have already seen. I mean, under this head, however, to speak of some *encouragements* to pray.

1. *God commands it.* He says, "Ask"—"Pray to thy Father"—"Call upon me"—"For these things will I be inquired of by the house of Israel to do it for them." He complains of men for not asking. He is angry with the prayerless, and will pour out his fury upon them. It is, therefore, our *duty* in this

to obey God;—and who has such a right to our obedience?

2. *God hears and promises to answer prayer.* "Ask, and ye shall receive"—"Call on me, and I will deliver"—"He will give to those that ask him"—"Thou that hearest prayer"—"He will regard the prayer of the destitute." What more could you wish, than that *if you ask* you will receive? What a privilege! Suppose a man were to say to you,—"Whenever you are in straits, just come to me. When in want of money, or food, or counsel, when perplexed, sorry, downcast, come to me and I'll relieve you:"—would you regard the matter merely as a *duty*, which you *ought* to attend to? Would you not feel, "How happy and thankful I should be, to have such a one to go to! How fortunate! What would I do without this kind, generous friend?" This is just what the godly have to fall back upon; only it is not a man they have to do with, but *God.* Hence, praying people are happy and courageous people. They need not fear want, for if they cry to God, he will relieve them. They have God's bank to draw upon—the Bank of Heaven, which is always full. They need not fear danger, for if they cry to God he will help and deliver them, if it would be good for them. Thus, we are told, that praying men, during the war with the Russians, made the best and the bravest soldiers—they had least fear. Our God is not like the gods of the heathen to whom so many pray. "They have ears, but they hear not." I lately saw some of those gods from

China. The thought cannot but arise, "Why pray to them? They cannot save themselves." When some of the Chinese were enlightened, they took the "god of the Furnace" and threw it into the fire; and instead of saving *them*, it could not save *itself*. It is not so with our God; he hears, and promises to answer; and is able to answer, for he is almighty.

3. *God delights in his people's prayers.* They are said to be a sweet savour or smell to him.

> " These odours are the prayers of saints,
> These sounds the hymns they raise;
> God bends his ear to their requests,
> He loves to hear their praise."

And not least so, is it with the young. When a child first begins to speak, how his parents delight to hear him! What attention they pay to what he says! That lisping tongue of his, which others cannot understand, which others laugh at, has such effect with *them*, that they can scarcely refuse him anything he asks. Such is God's delight in his little ones, when it is said of a child, "Behold, he prayeth!" That infant prayer is very sweet to him, and so it is very powerful with him. If he will hear any prayer, it will be *that*. No wonder that when the great German reformers, Luther and Melancthon, amid their gloom and despondency about the dangers that threatened the Reformation, heard their children in an adjoining room praying for them and their work—no wonder that *then* they took fresh heart, saying, "The GIANTS are praying for us!"

4. *All the good and holy, since the world began, have been given to prayer—have loved prayer.* There never was a good man, or woman, or boy, or girl, who did not pray—who did not love to pray. In the case of how many is it expressly mentioned!—Abraham, and Isaac, and Jacob, and Moses, and Hannah, and Samuel, and Elisha, and David, and Isaiah, and Hezekiah, and Manasseh, and Ezra, and Jeremiah, and Jonah, and Daniel, and Paul, and Peter, and above all—JESUS! How he prayed!—how he loved prayer!—"leaving us an example that we should follow his steps." Prayer is "the Christian's breath"—so precious, so necessary, that he will not give it up, come what will. There is Daniel, persisting in prayer, with the lions' den before him, and willing rather to meet the roaring lions than give up prayer. There is an old slave, called Uncle Ben, noted as a man of prayer. The proprietors have resolved to put an end to praying on their estate, and not finding Ben where they expected him, they take another, put him to death, and with his head upon a pole, march to Ben's dwelling. "Do you know that head, Ben?" "Yes, massa; I knows him." "Well, that's what he has got for his praying; and if you don't stop praying, that's what you'll get. The next time we catch you praying, we'll just do the same with your head." "Massa, do you mean dat?" "To be sure I do; and if you wish to keep your head upon your shoulders, you'll give up praying at once." All are waiting anxiously, when the old negro turns to his fellows

and says, "Bredren, let us pray!"* Did they so love prayer, as to be willing rather to part with life than give it up, and shall not we value the blessed privilege?

5. *Answers to prayer in the past* furnish a strong reason for praying. It has often been said, "Praying breath was never spent in vain." How many wonderful Bible instances are there!—and how many in later times! No really earnest prayer for mercy was ever rejected since the world began. Hopeless cases have yielded to prayer. Prayer has discomfited armies. Prayer has made the sun and moon stand still. Prayer has opened the heavens and brought down rain on a famishing land, or shut up the heavens again. Prayer has driven back death, and foes of every kind;—it has brought in supplies to the destitute; it has opened the prison-door to the captive, and other things of which time would fail me to tell.

There is a little band of Scottish Covenanters, discovered by their persecutors,—with nothing before them but capture or death. There is nothing for it but to pray. And thus Alexander Peden prays: "Send them after them to whom thou wilt gie strength to flee, for our strength is gane. Twine them about the hill, O Lord, and cast the lap of thy cloak on puir auld Saunders and thir puir things, and save us this ae time, and we will keep it in remembrance, and tell to the commendation of thy goodness, pity, and compassion, what thou didst for us at sic a time."

* Dr. Newton.

And, lo! a cloud of mist rises up, and comes between them, and the persecuted escape. There is a house inhabited by a godly old woman, her widowed daughter, and grandson. A brutal soldiery, ravaging the country, threaten them. That old woman prays that God would be a wall round about them; her grandson says she asks an impossibility, and while explaining that she only meant generally that God would protect them, she says God can even build a wall around them if needful. The troops come; every house around is pillaged—*that one* stands untouched, though all that is going on outside is heard by its inmates; and the morning explains it. The snow has drifted so as to form literally a wall between the road and the house, rendering approach impossible! Or see that aged woman, frail, and unable to work, and destitute. What shall she do? She prays, and ere her prayer is ended, there is a knock at her door, and a stranger she has never seen before, brings her full supplies, sent by Him who hears and answers prayer. Or see that little girl. She has got a nice new parasol, and the very first day she has it out, she gets the handle of it broken. She fears to go home, for her mother is a passionate woman, and never lets such a thing pass unpunished. The poor girl prays to God for help, and comes back hoping to see the parasol mended; but there it is, just as it was, and again and again, as she comes back, it is still the same. At length she goes home, and just as she is about to enter the room, she prays once more, "O

Lord, do help me;" and to her surprise, instead of scolding and punishing her, her mother is kind and sympathizing as she never was before. She soon saw she had been wrong, not in praying to God for help, but in expecting the parasol to be miraculously mended. The answer came, though not as she expected; and since then what a comfort, when any trouble comes,—at once to tell the Lord! We need not go back to Old Testament times for answers to prayer. They are to be counted by thousands in every age, so that I might fill a whole volume with those that have occurred in our own day—many of them almost as remarkable as any of those recorded in the Bible. Indeed, such a volume has been published, entitled "The Power of Prayer," in connection with the recent religious movement in America, giving the details of numerous instances of the most interesting and remarkable kind, and these, not extending over a number of *years*, but all confined to a very few *months*. The cases I have mentioned are therefore to be taken merely as specimens, and are given as showing what God has been pleased to do in answer to prayer, and as an encouragement to you *in everything* to make your requests known to God. It is no vain thing, whatever some may think. It is the greatest comfort on earth. "If ye, then, being evil, know how to give good gifts unto your children, how much more shall your Father who is in heaven give good things to them that ask him?"

Do *you*, then, pray? Have you ever prayed—for

the pardon of sin—for the new heart—for the Holy Spirit—for God to be your Father, and Christ your Saviour? If not, begin now—to-day. Offer up your first prayer now—where you are sitting. Don't be put past it. Cry to God for help,—for mercy. And though we cannot see you, may the word be spoken of one, and another, and another of you, as of Paul, "Behold he prayeth! behold she prayeth!" Let God have no dumb children among you!

THE HYMN.

WHAT various hindrances we meet
    In coming to the mercy-seat!
Yet who, that knows the worth of prayer,
But wishes to be often there?

Prayer makes the darkened cloud withdraw;
Prayer climbs the ladder Jacob saw,
Gives exercise to faith and love,
Brings every blessing from above.

Restraining prayer, we cease to fight;
Prayer makes the Christian's armour bright;
And Satan trembles when he sees
The weakest saint upon his knees.

Have you no words? ah! think again;
Words flow apace when we complain,
And fill our fellow-creature's ear
With the sad tale of all our care.

Were half the breath thus vainly spent,
To heaven in supplication sent,
Our cheerful song would oftener be,
"Hear what the Lord has done for me!"

Prayer.

(CONTINUED.)

THE HYMN.

GO when the morning shineth —
   Go when the noon is bright—
Go when the eve declineth—
   Go in the hush of night;
Go with pure mind and feeling,
   Fling earthly thoughts away,
And in thy chamber kneeling,
   Do thou in secret pray.

Remember all who love thee—
   All who are loved by thee;
Pray, too, for those who hate thee,
   If any such there be.
Then for thyself, in meekness,
   A blessing humbly claim,
And link with each petition
   Thy great Redeemer's name.

Or, if 'tis e'er denied thee
   In solitude to pray,
Should holy thoughts come o'er thee,
   When friends are round thy way;
Ev'n then, the silent breathing
   Thy spirit lifts above,
Will reach His throne of glory,
   Who is Mercy, Truth, and Love.

Oh, not a joy or blessing
   With this can we compare—
The grace our Father gives us
   To pour our souls in prayer!

> Whene'er thou pin'st in sadness,
> On Him who saveth call;
> And ever in thy gladness
> Thank Him who gave thee all.

MY DEAR YOUNG FRIENDS,—You know there are some countries which abound with wild beasts—lions, and tigers, and wolves, and the like; and the people stand in great fear of them, for to be overtaken by them, alone and unprotected, would be almost certain death. They often carry off lambs and sheep, and do not hesitate to spring upon cattle and horses, or even upon men and children, when they are hard pressed with hunger, and have the opportunity—devouring them, and leaving nothing but the bones behind. Now, if there were one notable lion that kept the whole country-side in terror, that was always doing some mischief, so that when his roar was heard, and his flashing eyes were seen, even at a distance, it made man and beast tremble, the flocks hastening to their folds, and children running to their fathers and mothers lest they should be devoured—would it not be strange, if some day this terrible lion were seen playing with lambs, and kids, and calves, instead of devouring them as he used to do,—eating straw like the ox, and suffering himself to be led about by a little child? Would not people be astonished, and exclaim, "What a wonderful change is here!"

Now, if instead of a *lion* you suppose a *man* answering to this description, as cruel, as blood-thirsty, as much feared,—would it not be just as strange, if such a change were to come over him? Such a man there was in Africa, so dreaded both by white men as well as by those of the same colour with himself, that he might have been called "The African Lion;" and we actually find the missionaries writing of him thus: "It is hoped the soldiers will succeed in ridding the country of such a monster." And yet you might have seen this very Africaner (for that was his name) sitting peacefully in the missionary's tent with those for whose blood he had thirsted, singing the praises of God. And such another there was, long before his day, in another country, who bitterly hated Christ and his people, getting them cast into prison and put to death, so that we read of him, " He was exceedingly *mad* against the Church "—another ravening lion, so that if he had come on such meetings as you sometimes attend, nothing would have satisfied him but getting even you children imprisoned or killed. And yet we hear of him too, as sitting at length at the feet of Jesus as a little child, one of his most humble, loving, devoted followers. Perhaps you say, " What a wonderful change !" It is indeed, and yet no more than the Bible speaks of as being necessary in your case and mine—a change of heart—a change of nature—becoming a "*new creature :*" " Old things are passed away; behold, all things are become new." Dear children, has such a change ever taken place on *you?* Perhaps you would like to know, how the change, in those of whom I have spoken, began to show itself—what was one of the very first indications of it—one of the very first ways in which it appeared. You will see by turning again to the last three words of—

Acts ix. 11: "BEHOLD HE PRAYETH."

One of the first things that told of the change on Saul of Tarsus and on Africaner, was, that they prayed to God; not merely repeated words; not merely said prayers—for even wicked people can do that—but *prayed*. And what was true of them at the beginning of their new life, was true of them all through, till they died—they were *men of prayer*—they delighted in prayer—they could not live without prayer. And if prayer was so important to them, so helpful to them, so loved by them, as in the case of all God's people still, surely it is well for us to learn as much about it as possible, that those who pray already may pray more, and love prayer more, and that those who do not pray may begin to pray now.

In my former address I gave you six questions to put to me, three of which I answered: 1. What is prayer? Not the repeating of certain words, but speaking to God, asking, begging from God, crying to God. 2. What should I pray for? I mentioned two guides to be followed in praying—the prayers recorded in the Bible, and the promises of God; referring especially to the new heart, pardon, salvation, the Holy Spirit. 3. Why should I pray? (1.) God commands it; (2.) God hears and promises to answer prayer; (3.) God delights in his people's prayers; (4.) All the good and holy since the world began have been given to prayer, and loved it; (5.) The answers to prayer in the past. The other three questions, you will remember, were: 4. *Where* should I pray? 5. *When* should I pray? and, 6. *How* should I pray? These we shall take up now.

Question IV. WHERE SHOULD I PRAY? I give you two answers to this question. Turn to Matthew vi. 6, "Thou, when thou prayest, *enter into thy closet;*" and 1 Timothy ii. 8, "I will therefore that men pray *everywhere;*"—not in one place only, but *in every place*. There were some long ago, who were fond of making a show of their praying, doing it in public places that they might be seen of men, and that men might say of them, How good these people are! It is a dangerous thing to do that; it is dishonouring to God,—it is mocking God. And so Jesus says, "Don't do that; but when you pray, enter into your closet and shut your door, and then, alone and unseen by any, pour out your hearts to God." It is well to have our "closet," a place to which we can look back in after years as a place of prayer,— such as the Mount of Olives was to Jesus. We like, when we are grown up, to think of *our home*—in town or country, in which we spent our early youth. We like to think of the fireside around which we sat or played, ere yet the family circle was broken up. And besides being a *pleasure*, the remembrance of these and the like, comes in many cases to be a *help*. And so it is when we have had a closet, or place for prayer. The remembrance of it may follow us through life. When under some heavy trial, when on the brink of some great temptation, the recollection of my closet, where I knelt in my early days, ere yet the world had got such a hold of me, may start up, and be the saving of me. Have you, dear children, such a place? Jesus chose the Mount of Olives because it was quiet and retired, away from the noise and bustle of the city, where he might be unseen and undisturbed. So should we choose our place for prayer—our closet, when we can.

But some one says, "I am sure you know our houses better than that,—in the very heart of the town, where it is scarcely possible to be free from noise and interruption; and besides that, you know that many of our houses have not their three, or four, or six rooms, so that we can get a closet to ourselves when we like. Many of us have only one room for a whole family, and what are we to do; how are we to get a closet—how are we to pray at all?" My young friend, I know it well; and yet I say even *you* may have a closet, and *should*. It need not be literally a *closet*—a little room with four walls, and a door and window. You have but to shut your eyes, and you may be in your closet at once. Whenever you have got *alone*, and have closed your heart on all but God, feeling alone with God, you have "entered into your closet, and shut your door." Just as the soldier kneeling by his bedside in the large barrack-room, or the sailor beside his hammock, with scores of mockers all around, may, even there, enter into his closet; so in your one room, with all the family around you, you can shut yourself up in your own heart, you can be alone while yet not alone, you can make a closet to yourselves. I know some don't like closets of that kind, and are ashamed to enter into them, ashamed to be seen praying by others—some older than you, and some like yourselves. Some of you bigger boys may have gone to the country for a while to spend your holidays, or to work at your trade; you were living with friends, or you had to take lodgings, and in the same room with you, were some who laughed at sacred things, and never prayed, and you were afraid —ashamed to kneel before them and pray—to go into your closet; and sometimes prayer has thus been laid aside,—the first step in a backgoing course. I have heard of a boy in such a case. He had a prayerless companion, and the first night he did not know what to do. Satan whispered, "You can pray in your heart, without seeming to pray outwardly,—God will hear it as well; or you can pray after you have gone to bed, and then no one will see you, and it will be all the same— it is not necessary to pray on your knees." But that boy had been taught by a kind mother, now in her grave, to kneel by his bedside, and he could not think of giving it up now; and besides, he felt that that would be to be ashamed of his religion and of his God. That night he got out of the difficulty, by waiting till his neighbour was in bed and asleep, and then he knelt and prayed as he had been used to do. Next night he got first to his room, and, being alone, he fell on his knees. While so engaged, he heard his comrade's foot upon the stair. He hesitated what to do. The wicked one suggested, "Rise; he'll see you, and laugh at you, and you'll get no peace,—you'll never hear the end of it." His better feelings said, "No—pray on." It was the turning point in his life. The door opened,—he continued praying;—it was a real victory, and while he lived he thanked God for it. The battle was fought on his knees, as in such a case it often is. It was the hardest battle he ever fought, but it was a glorious triumph. I would to God it were so with every boy and girl, and every grown-up person whom I address, whether living at home, or in service, or in lodgings, or among strangers. When thus tempted, remember that brave boy, and never be ashamed;—enter into thy closet there.

The following little narrative, of what occurred quite recently, has just been sent to me by a friend, and is so beautiful, that I cannot but insert it. It may encourage to perseverance in a right course, amid much opposition :—

"On board a man-of-war there was a midshipman, who, in spite of the ridicule of his companions, was in the habit of kneeling in prayer at his berth. This was such an unusual practice, that the other middies resolved to put it down; so they watched him, and the moment he knelt, he encountered a volley of caps and shoes. This was repeated again and again, but still the midshipman persevered in his devotions. At last some one of the superior officers informed the commander of the ship, who summoned the whole midshipmen, and calling the persecuted one to the front, asked him to state his grievance. The lad said frankly he had no complaint to make. His commander said he knew he had good cause of complaint, and told him to speak out. But the praying midshipman persisted in stating he had nothing to complain of. The commander then dismissed them, at the same time signifying that he knew how matters stood, and trusted there would be no more of it.

"That evening the middy knelt as usual in prayer, but without experiencing the smallest annoyance. While so engaged, he heard footsteps quietly approaching, and was expecting some disagreeable interruption; but, to his surprise, a middy—the youngest on board—knelt down by his side. Shortly afterwards came another, and another, till fourteen of his companions, under the influence of his noble example, were kneeling beside him.

"This was told at a public breakfast, and Mr. ——, who was there, said that the gentleman who was sitting next to him was much affected by it. The cause of this was explained when the gentleman whispered to him, 'That lad is my son, and I have only now for the first time heard of it!'"

It matters not how you may be situated, or where you may be; you can have a closet *anywhere*. Let us see where some have had their closet. Jesus went out into a solitary place, and there prayed; he had his closet often in the wilderness or on the mountain. Eliezer (Abraham's godly servant) made a closet for himself beside the well, kneeling beside his camels; and Isaac in the fields; and Jacob amid the solitude of Bethel, or at Peniel beside the running stream; and David in the cave; and Jonah in the whale's belly; and Jeremiah, and Paul, and Silas in the prison; and Peter on the house-top. Soldiers have had their closet on the field of battle, and sailors on the sea, and miners deep down in the bowels of the earth, and shepherds on the hills. And so you may have your closet in your own house, or in the church, or in the school, or on the street, or in the fields, or in the workshop, or anywhere. Dr. Milne, the famous missionary in China, when a youth, was, after leaving home, situated in an ungodly family, as unfavourably as any of you; and so he used to retire to a sheep-cot, where the sheep were kept in winter, and there, surrounded by the sheep, he knelt on a piece of turf which he kept and carried with him for the purpose, spending many an hour there, even in the cold of winter, in sweet communion with his God. That was his closet. Or there is a little chimney-sweeper, harshly aroused in the early morning, and hurried off to his work before he is thoroughly awake,—where does he find a place for prayer? Not in his master's house; but when he has reached the chimney-top, where he has to remain for a few minutes, while his master is doing his part of the work below, he finds a closet *there*. After that, who will say he has no place to pray? Who will say he can get no closet?

There is no place in all the world in which you may not pray. It matters not in what part of the country or of the world you be,—in India, or China, or Australia, or America: "I will that men pray *everywhere.*" God is equally near, and he hears equally well, at all these places. I spoke, in my former address, of prayer being like the electric telegraph, only a more rapid means of communication even than it. You can send a message at any instant from earth to heaven. It is better than the telegraph in many respects. There are places where you are *out of the reach of the telegragh*, in some remote parts of the country, or away at sea; so that, however anxious, you cannot avail yourself of it. But wherever you are, on land or at sea, you have always the telegraph of prayer ready to your hand: "I will that men pray everywhere." Sometimes *the telegraph will not work;* in certain states of the atmosphere it is useless; or a mischievous hand may destroy it—and that may be the most important time of all, when life and property are at stake. It need never be so with prayer. You have *to pay for the use of the telegraph,* so that the very poor must do without it. Prayer is free—free to all;—the very poorest may pray. And once more, you can send messages by the telegraph, but *it can bring back to you nothing but words.* It may be days or weeks before you get what you want, however pressing the case may be. If you are ill, it does not bring you medicine or a physician; if you are sorrowful, it does not send you comfort; if you are dying, it does not bring a mother or mother-like friend to smooth your pillow, and watch by your bedside. Prayer does all this; it brings back the blessing needed and desired, when it would be good to have it. What a comfort! What a blessing! Thanks be to God for his unspeakable mercy!

Question V. WHEN SHOULD I PRAY? Here, too, I have two answers to the question. Turn to Ephesians vi. 18: "Praying *always;*" and Philippians iv. 6: "In *everything* by prayer and supplication, let your requests be made known unto God." I might answer this question in various ways:

1. I might say, "always"—*at all times of life*—from youth on to old age. You should pray in *youth*, in earliest childhood. It is never too soon to pray. None are too young to pray, for none are too young to die—to be saved or lost—to go to heaven or hell. Prayer is not confined to grown-up people. God hears the very youngest. We saw in our last address how God likes to hear the prayers of children, and how he delights to answer them. For the encouragement of the *very little ones*, I set the picture before you again. See that father with his little boy of two years old upon his knee. Why is he looking so lovingly, and smiling so gladly? Because he likes to hear the first lispings of his little one,—he likes to be asked for things with that stammering tongue. And so God our heavenly Father feels towards his little children. Their little prayers he will not disregard. Little children! do you pray? Many like you have prayed, and got their prayers answered. Little children need the new heart, and therefore they should pray. Little children need to be forgiven, and therefore they should pray. Little children need to be saved, and therefore they should pray.

2. I might say "always"—*at all times of the day*. It is never too early in the day,—never too late at night. I find David saying, "Lord, thou shalt *early* hear my voice;" and again, "At evening, morning, and at noon;" and again, "Seven times a-day it is my care." I find Daniel praying three times a-day. I find Jesus

rising up a great while before day to pray. I find little Samuel praying during the night. I find that the Chinese Christian children, when they awake out of sleep at night, don't lie down again without praying. I find John Welsh of Ayr, that good minister and godly man, keeping his plaid lying by his bedside, to wrap about him when he rises during the night to pray. Prayer is not fixed as to *time* any more than as to *place*. If you were to ask some petition of man, you would perhaps find the door shut, and be told you were too late. If you were going to the Dispensary at four o'clock to get medicine for a sick brother, you would not get in, and above the door you would see, "Open from 12 till 3 o'clock;"—you should have gone an hour sooner. *This* door stands always open; you can never come amiss. And so you should come often, because always sure of a welcome. You will do so if you take Jesus for an example. "He *ofttimes* resorted thither"—to pray; and if He prayed often, how much more should we! None ever regretted having prayed too much, too often, too long; many, because they prayed so little, or never prayed at all. How often, my young friends, do you pray? Do you pray in the morning; do you ask God then for protection, and guidance, and pardon; or are you in so great a hurry to get away to school or to work, that you have no time? Do you pray at night; or are you too tired and sleepy—though only tired and sleepy when you have *to pray?* Do you ever think of praying during the day, or are your thoughts too much occupied with other things? "Always," says Christ; "Without ceasing," says Paul. They knew how sweet prayer was. Not that we should be always on our knees, speaking words of prayer; but yet we should be always in the *spirit* of prayer, and often sending up our cry to God.

3. I might say "always"—*in all circumstances.* You should pray *at meal times.* Do you ask a blessing on your meals? " Lord, I thank thee for my food; bless it to me. May it strengthen my body, and make me more fit for thy service." Can you take the food God gives without ever thanking him for it, or praying for a blessing with it? See that Highlander, on a summer day, down at the burn-side, where he has gone to get a drink; why does he lay aside his blue bonnet and look up to heaven before he drinks? To ask his Father's blessing. There is a boy, the son of godly parents, visiting at the house of ungodly friends. He has had a long walk, and is both tired and hungry, and yet, though the dinner is on the table and his plate before him, he does not eat, and when urged refuses. " Why, little boy, will you not eat your dinner?" and at length he bursts into tears and says, " *You haven't blessed it.*" He could not think of taking a meal, without a blessing being asked. Or see that sick boy with his medicine in his hand; what is he doing? Asking a blessing; for says he, "If God do not bless it to me, it can do me no good." It is an opportunity for praying, and we know not when our last prayer may be, what may be our last oppor-

tunity, so it is well to avail ourselves of it. The train is whirling along between Edinburgh and Manchester. It stops at Carlisle, and, after the long journey, two little passengers are taken into the refreshment-room to get their dinner. There is little time to put off, and there are many strangers and much noise and bustle. See that little boy, a mere child; there is not time to take off even his gloves and hat, but he clasps his hands, and says aloud, " O Lord, bless my food, and pardon my sin, for Jesus' sake. Amen." It was his last prayer; the accident occurred to which I have already alluded, and ere long that praying boy was where prayer is needed no more.* Children! take him for your example. Go ye and do likewise.

When at your lessons, pray, "Lord, help me." You will learn your lessons all the better if you ask and get God's blessing. You have heard of the boy who was always dux of his class, and of his reply when asked how it was. It was *because he prayed*. That night his school-fellow, who asked the question, prayed that he might get up in his class; and next day, when he was booby as before, and expressed his surprise at it, since he had prayed like his neighbour, he was asked, " But did you learn your lessons?" "Oh no; I just prayed." " Then that explains it. I learn my lessons as well as I possibly can, and I pray to God to help me while I am learning them." There is a saying, " Prayer and pains will do anything." That holds good of lessons

* "The Way Home."

and of everything else. *When at work*, pray. So did Moses: "Let the beauty of the Lord our God be upon us, and establish the work of our hands upon us; yea, the work of our hands establish thou it." *When tempted to do what is wrong*—to go where you should not; when in the midst of wicked companions who would lead you astray, and press you to sin, to throw off parental authority, to leave your home, to disregard and cast aside the restraints of the Sabbath and the sanctuary, and the Bible, and honour, and honesty, and decency, and truthfulness,—O children! pray, "Lord, deliver me. Enable me to resist this temptation, and to do what is right." The power of prayer is wonderful at such a time,—how it nerves a man or woman, and even a child! *When you do wrong*, when sin is on the conscience, and you can get no rest, and you feel that God is angry with you, O pray! Come as the publican came, and pray as the publican prayed: "God, be merciful to me a sinner." Ask forgiveness, and a broken heart, and grace not to do the like again. *When anxious about your soul*, grieving over your sin, and fearing lest you should be lost for ever, and longing for the Saviour to be your Saviour — pray. That was just what Saul did in such a case; of him as awakened and anxious, we read, "Behold he prayeth!" *When in sorrow*, it may be for the loss of a parent, or brother, or friend; *when in perplexity*, not knowing what to do; when at your wit's end, unable to get yourself out of some difficulty, or to overtake some duty, or likely to sink under some trial, feeling yourself utterly helpless—pray! I once heard it mentioned that the fishermen along the coast, when they were becalmed and could make no way, "lay upon their oars, and *whistled for the wind.*" It suggested a fine thought: when you are in straits, and can get no help of man such as you need, like these fishermen whistling for the wind—to your knees! Cry to the Lord! And if it be about others that you are concerned, when you have done all you can, and can do no more, cry to the wind—to the Holy Spirit—"Come from the four winds, O breath, and breathe on these slain, that they may live!"

When danger threatens, or any sore trial comes, just as the child's first cry is "Mother!" and his first thought is to run to *her*, so the child of God will run to his knees, to his closet, to his God, and cry to *him*. *When you are laid on a sick-bed*, unable, it may be, to bend your knee, or even to lift up your head, or raise your hands to heaven, yet there and then you can pray—pray so as to be heard—pray so as to prevail. As you lie on your little couch, and your mother watches over you, or paces the room with the tear in her eye, and a beating heart, eager to relieve you, but unable, when you cannot even tell her what you are suffering, when you can open neither the closed lips nor the closed eye, still, dear children, you can pray. And *when death comes*, when the sick-bed becomes a death-bed, and you must leave all you love, and your dearest friends can do no more for you, and can go no further with you, and you are about to enter the eternal world *alone*,—still, still, beloved children! you can pray, " Lord Jesus, receive my spirit."

> " And when I'm to die, receive me I'll cry,
> For Jesus has loved me, I cannot tell why;
> But this I do find, we two are so joined,
> He'll not be in glory and leave me behind."

In *everything* then,—*always*, we should pray.

Question VI. HOW SHOULD I PRAY? *With the heart* —not in mere words; *earnestly*. Like Jacob when he said, "I will not let thee go except thou bless me." Like Esau when he cried, "Bless me, even me also, O my father!" Like Jesus, who prayed with strong crying and tears. Like the blind man who followed Jesus, saying, "Have mercy on me, O Lord, thou Son of David;" and, who, when they bade him hold his peace, only "cried the more a great deal." Like a drowning man crying for his life. Pray *believingly*. Expect an answer. "In the morning," says David, "will I present my prayer to thee, and *will look up*." "Whatsoever things ye ask, *believing*, ye shall receive:"—trusting God's promise, giving him credit for what he says. Pray *perseveringly*. "Men ought always to pray, and *not to faint*." Don't grow weary; don't be discouraged. If you were very anxious for anything, you would not be satisfied with asking it once; you would ask it again and again. Do you see that beggar following me? I refuse to give him anything, but he does not give up; the faster I go, the faster he goes, and the more earnestly he pleads with me, till I can't refuse him. Pray *humbly and submissively*—

leaving it to Him to give or to withhold, as he sees best. Tempting cherries have just come into the market, and the child asks his father for them; but he knows it would be dangerous for his boy to have them,—that if he got them, the bitter medicine would have to follow, or illness, and perhaps death; and so he says, "No, my son, I cannot give them to you,"—and he is the best judge. So leave your requests with God. That explains why some of your prayers have not been answered, or at least answered in your own way. You wished to be rich,—to be great,—to have some particular thing. You are like a child whom I love, to whom I say, "I'll give you whatever is good for you." Well, he sees a beautiful serpent in its glass enclosure, sparkling and attractive as can be. How he would like to have it, to handle it, to take it home with him, to lay it in his bosom! Would it be a proof of my love if I gratified his wish? Would it not be just the reverse?

Pray *unitedly*. It is a fine thing to see two brothers or two sisters, or two school-mates or friends, joining together to *pray*. When religion is in a lively state, this is no uncommon thing. The Lord loves to see it; hence his promise, "If *two* of you shall agree as touching anything that ye shall ask, it shall be done unto you. When *two or three* are gathered together in my name, there am I in the midst of them." You meet for other things, why not for this; to *play*—why not to *pray?* There are six Sabbath-school boys just such as you. Their teacher has been pressing on them the need of getting a new heart, and God's willingness to give it. They would like to have it. They agree to pray together for it. They take their place under the shade of a spreading tree; but they have never prayed before others, and no one likes to take the lead. What is to be done? They fall on their knees. They open their Bibles at Ezekiel xxxvi. 26; they put their finger on that verse, each of them, and lift up their eyes to heaven; and in silence, without speaking a word, they pray! Yes, children! *that* is prayer, believing prayer, united prayer; and God hears it and answers it. Will you not try the same thing? Will you not, whether old or young, alone or together, turn to this verse, or some other such, this very night, put your finger on it, as much as to say, " Lord, thou hast said it; do as thou hast said?" Let us all try this way of praying; who can tell what might come of it? Once more: *Ask all in the name of Jesus.* I do not mean merely that you are to close all your prayers by saying, "For Jesus' sake." I mean more than that. If you were going to the Queen, would you not need to have some one with you—some one who had influence with the Queen, and knew the ways of the palace, to present your petition and speak a good word for you—all the more if she had said, "I can only receive petitions that come through such a one"—a minister appointed for the purpose? So is it with the great God, the King of heaven; he has appointed Jesus our Advocate with the Father —our great High Priest, who offers in his golden censer his people's prayers. Him the Father heareth always. "Whatsoever ye shall ask the Father IN MY NAME, that will I do."

And now I have answered all the questions I proposed. The next question is, What are we to make of them? Will praying save me? No; don't make that mistake: Jesus alone can. As I said before, praying is only *asking for salvation.* Believe, and be saved. Repent, and be saved. Give yourselves to Christ, and be saved. But if we do not ask to be saved—if we do not pray for salvation—how can we expect to get it? I know there are some among you who once did not pray; I know there are too many among us to-day, old and young, who *never pray;* and isn't it a terrible thing? Drowning, and never to cry for help! going down to hell, and going in silence, without one cry, "Lord, save me!" It will be a terrible thought in eternity, *not to have prayed!* I might have had pardon, and peace, and salvation for the asking,—but I would not pray! I might have had heaven and glory,—but I would not pray! As I said before, it is "PRAY, or PERISH"—which will you choose? Will you not go straightway and pray for the new heart, for converting grace, to have Christ as your Saviour now, and heaven at length as your home? Surely if ever prayer was needful, it is needful in our time. There is evil enough in the country, quiet and peaceful though it be—how much more in large cities! What abounding temptations! those theatres —nurseries for hell, which, alas! too many of our young people frequent; those public-houses, where bodies and souls alike are ruined, to which, alas! so many of our children are sent to purchase the poison, the more dangerous because it has another name—so early trained to familiarity with that which is the grand instrument of Satan in our day for men's destruction; those "Sunday shops," holding out so many attractions, so many inducements to dishonesty and Sabbath-breaking, and that but the beginning of evil; those Sabbath-evening streets of ours, which you have but to look at, to see what danger there is from bad company and otherwise. I say nothing of the very homes of many. Enough to show that for parents and children, for young men and maidens, for Sabbath scholars and church attenders, there is the most urgent call to prayer.

You cannot begin too soon; you *may* begin too late. The day is coming when many who never prayed before will pray for the first time—the first time in real earnest. Oh, what a prayer-meeting there will be then of those who never attended a prayer-meeting before! What a prayer in which they must all unite!—"Then shall they cry to the mountains, Fall on us, and to the hills, Cover us." And their last and only prayer will not be answered; the mountains and hills will be *deaf*, and *God* will be deaf. He will not hear prayer *then*.

> "Their lips by anguish shall be taught,
> But taught too late to pray."

Children will be there! little children! and they will pray that terrible prayer. "Then shall they call on me, but I will not answer." *When* should I pray? *Now.* Dear children! begin at once; there is no time to lose. Now is the time for praying. Begin to pray while you are in health,—in youth: you may be glad enough to pray when sickness comes,—when death comes; but you will be more likely to be heard *now*. Be praying children, and we may expect you, if spared, to be praying men and women on earth, and praising saints in heaven.

THE HYMN.

PRAYER is the soul's sincere desire,
    Uttered or unexpress'd;
The motion of a hidden fire
    That trembles in the breast.

Prayer is the burden of a sigh,
    The falling of a tear;
The upward glancing of an eye,
    When none but God is near.

Prayer is the simplest form of speech
    That infant lips can try;
Prayer, the sublimest strains that reach
    The Majesty on high.

Prayer is the contrite sinner's voice,
    Returning from his ways;
While angels in their songs rejoice,
    And cry, "Behold he prays!"

Prayer is the Christian's vital breath,
    The Christian's native air;
His watch-word at the gates of death;
    He enters heaven with prayer.

O Thou, by whom we come to God,
    The Life, the Truth, the Way!
The path of prayer Thyself hast trod;
    Lord, teach us how to pray!

The following prayer for young children has been drawn up by a Christian mother, whose pen has touchingly pled the cause of the little ones. It has been largely circulated in the form in which it is given here:—

FOR BOYS AND GIRLS.

Dear Young Friend—Will you offer this Prayer daily, and ask your companions to do the same?

O HEAVENLY FATHER! give me thy Holy Spirit *now*, to make me thy loving and obedient child. Teach me to feel that I am a great sinner, and to look to Jesus as my Almighty Saviour. Enable me to honour my parents and teachers, and to walk willingly in the right way. Make me like what Jesus was when he was a child. Help me to serve thee while I am young, and go on serving thee all my days. Give thy grace likewise to my companions, and send a great revival amongst the young, for Jesus Christ's sake. Amen.

Jesus Passing By.

THE HYMN.

COME, ye sinners, poor and wretched,
    This is your accepted hour;
Jesus ready stands to save you,
    Full of pity, love, and power:
      He is able,
    He is willing; doubt no more.

Come, ye weary, heavy laden,
    Lost and ruined by the fall;
If you tarry till you're better,
    You will never come at all:
      Not the righteous—
    Sinners, Jesus came to call.

Lo! th' incarnate God ascended,
    Pleads the merit of his blood;
Venture on him, venture wholly,
    Let no other trust intrude:
      None but Jesus
    Can do helpless sinners good.

MY DEAR YOUNG FRIENDS,—If I had been addressing you from the pulpit instead of speaking to you through this book, I should have said I was going to preach a GOSPEL sermon to you—a GOOD-NEWS' sermon. I would like you to be truly happy—to have a joyful heart and a cheerful countenance; and just as when you carry good tidings to any one, you make their heart glad, and it shows itself in their very look, so nothing would give me

greater joy, than to bring such a message to you, as would fill your hearts and your homes with rejoicing, as you said, "We have heard good news to-day." If the Queen or some great person were passing along our streets, bestowing precious gifts on all the children in the neighbourhood who came for them; looking to each door as she passed, to see whether any were coming out of that house—nay, were it only smiles and friendly recognitions that she was giving to those who lined the street on either side—if you were sitting asleep at home, or doing a piece of work in some back room, where you saw and heard nothing of what was going on, would you not be thankful to the friend who came running in all breathless, to tell you that the carriage was just at your door now, and bidding you be quick, that you might not miss the sight, and that you might get your share of the good things that were going? I am sure you would say, *that* was good news indeed. If a doctor were passing through the town, who had great skill in healing a certain sore disease, which your own doctors with all their skill could not cure, and if you were one of the sufferers—if some kind neighbour who had been in the town were hurrying in to you, so joyful and in such haste as never to knock at the door, or ask, "May I come in?" saying, "Have you heard the news? Dr. So-and-so, who has wrought such wonderful cures, and of whom we have read so much in the newspapers, is in the town, at such a hotel, in such a street. Crowds of people are going and getting cured; and he is such a kind, considerate, homely man, that any one may go to him. Now's the time for you?"—would you not be right glad and thankful, and say it was good news? Now, that is the burden of my present message. And that I bring such tidings to you, I am sure you will admit when you have read my text—

"And they told him that JESUS OF NAZARETH PASSETH BY."—
Luke xviii. 37.

First of all, I must give you the story. Jesus had been in another part of the country called Galilee; and when he would return to Jerusalem, he did not take the direct road through Samaria, but crossed the Jordan and came down the country on the other side of the river, till he was opposite Jericho, when he recrossed, and proceeded on his journey to Jerusalem. By this time, his mighty works had been heard of, all over the country; and as the people from all quarters crowded along the roads leading to Jerusalem, on their way thither to keep the Passover, they seem to have gathered round Jesus, and, almost as in a triumphal procession, to have followed him as he went along. Just outside the city of Jericho, which lay in their way, there sat a poor blind man by the road-side. It was a public highway, along which many travellers passed, especially at that time of the year. Many a year had he sat there begging, so that those who went up to the Passover knew him well, and spoke of him as Blind Bartimeus—giving him many a piece of money, or otherwise showing kindness to him as they passed. He was quite accustomed to little groups of country people passing by, the godly among them still, as in former days, singing those beautiful Psalms, from the 120th to the 134th—

> "I joy'd when to the house of God,
> Go up, they said to me," &c.

But this time it was something more than ordinary. He could gather from what he heard that there was a great crowd. There was the hum of half-suppressed voices, and every now and then were heard the joyous shoutings of new comers, as they learned who this was; and with the eagerness of one who could not see for himself, he asked those who were hurrying past him, "What's the meaning of all this?" "And they told him that *Jesus of Nazareth passeth by.*"

What a change has all at once come over the man! How his face is lighted up with joy! What has happened? Has some one told him that a fortune has been left to him, so that he'll need to sit and beg there no longer? Has the news been brought to him that his kind mother—who used to watch so tenderly over her blind boy when no one else cared for him, and for whom he has never ceased to mourn as his best and only earthly friend—has been restored to him again? Is it something of that kind? No. It is this: He had often listened to the tale of passers-by, as they talked about the Great Prophet that had appeared, and the wonderful things which he did. Perhaps some one, more sympathizing than the rest, had sat down beside him, and told him of what had been done in Galilee, at Capernaum, and Bethsaida; how one, and another, and another, blind like him, had got their sight, even though blind from their birth. How he treasured up that name! How he thought on it by day, and dreamed of it by night! How, day by day, he wondered if it would ever be his happy lot to come in the way of the Stranger—never doubting but that if He were near, he would do for him what he had done for others; and while he had despaired before of ever seeing, and had become contentedly blind, now he began to hope, and his blindness seemed to him more terrible than ever. And whenever it was told him, "Jesus passeth by," how at once he recognised the name— "*Jesus of Nazareth!* That's the man of whom I have heard so much!—that's the man I have been so waiting for, praying for!—that's the man who gives the blind their sight!—that's the man for me!" And the next you hear is his shrill voice, loud above all the noise and tumult—"Jesus, thou son of David, have mercy on me!" And Jesus heard him and healed him; and from that hour he was no more "Bartimeus the blind," or "Bartimeus the beggar," but Bartimeus the follower of Jesus, loving him and living for him— glorifying God, as well he might.

Now, dear children! I have the same news for you to-day, that the people gave to Bartimeus that day; and it is as good for you now, as it was for him then.

The good news is, that Jesus of Nazareth, the divine Saviour, passeth by; that he is at your door—the door of each one of you—within call, within reach; that you may get from him, all you can need or rightly desire, *immediately* and *freely;* that you will not be sent away, but welcomed; that he will not say to one of you, that you are too young, or too wicked, or too ignorant, or too poor. He sends me with this message to you to-day; and if ever you said it, you may say it now, "How beautiful upon the mountains are the feet of him that bringeth good tidings!"

I need scarcely stop to show you your *need of a Saviour.* Some of you know that full well already. Some of you have been *feeling* it. Some of you understand that word in a way you never did before—*lost.* Perhaps if you were speaking out, you would say, "I'm a poor lost sinner. I wonder I could be so careless, and so fearless, and so prayerless before! I wonder I could live in sin and in neglect of God so long! I wonder I could be content to be without God and without Christ so long! I have been sinning all my life-time against the great God. I have been crucifying the Lord Jesus. I have been grieving the Holy Spirit. I have been doing the devil's bidding. I have been living under the wrath of God. I have been walking on the brink of hell; and if I had died, I should have been lost for ever. I have been all this, and I didn't know it, and had no concern about it; but I know it now, and can get no rest because of it. The blind, and dumb, and deaf, and leprous, and palsied, and those possessed with devils, who came to Jesus, were just in body what I am in soul. I see in them just a picture of myself, as God sees me, who looks upon the heart. And as nobody could cure or help them, so nobody can cure or help me. My mother cannot, my teacher cannot, my minister cannot;—these have all tried it and have failed. O wretched one that I am! who shall deliver me?"

If you have any thoughts of this kind, you will feel you have an interest in what I have now to say, about an almighty and loving Saviour, and a saving time. These are my two heads: I. *An Almighty Saviour* —JESUS OF NAZARETH; and, II. *A saving time*—HE PASSETH BY.

I. AN ALMIGHTY AND LOVING SAVIOUR.—Sometimes you meet with people who are *able* to help you, but *will* not. Sometimes you meet with people who are *willing* to help you, but *cannot*. I have, therefore, two things to say about the Saviour of whom our text speaks: He is *able* to save you, and he is *willing*.

1. He is ABLE to save you. How do I know it? Because he says it, because he has done the like before,—because he is GOD. Why did Bartimeus so rejoice, when he heard that Jesus was within reach? Because he had made other blind people to see, and, therefore, he knew he was able to do as much for *him*. And so it is still;—so it is for *you*. He has saved sinners like you before, he is saving sinners like

you elsewhere, and so you know he is *able* to save *you*. And what a comfort is that! I go into a house and find a little child very ill, tossing about on his bed, unable even to tell what he is suffering; and as I stand by his bed-side, it goes to my heart to see him. How I wish I could give him some healing medicine, and restore him to those who love him so well! But I cannot, and the doctor cannot, though none could be more willing; and he dies. I am willing, but I am not able to save him. I go along the road, and overhear some one weeping bitterly; and when I speak to him, I find he is an orphan boy. It is the day after the funeral of his mother, and he is inconsolable for his loss. I try to comfort him. I speak kindly to him. I weep with him. I tell him about the Father and the Friend in heaven, whom he may have as his; but though I *would* be his comforter, I *cannot;* and I have to leave him as I found him,—weeping alone. I meet with one who has begun to think about her sin, and to care for her soul. There is a heavy burden lying on her young heart; and when I ask her what ails her, I get no answer but this—"Oh, it's heavy, heavy! It's my sin, my sin!" And what can I do? I cannot take her burden away; I cannot make her holy, without which no one can be happy; I cannot deliver her from her sin, and turn her sorrow into joy. I am as helpless as with the dying child—more helpless than with the orphan boy. How gladly I would give her relief; but I cannot. In such a case, even a child feels that "vain is the help of man."

Ah, but children! we must not stop here. One there is, who *is able*—Jesus of Nazareth, the divine Saviour, the Great Physician, the Sinner's Friend;—the same who gave the blind their sight and raised the dead; the same who received publicans and sinners, and changed their hearts; the same who has brought to heaven every saved soul that is there, and who has converted every child of God now on earth, old or young, and made him what he is. It is the same Jesus, of whom I have to tell you to-day. He is the same Jesus that ever he was. He is mighty to save. He is able to save to the uttermost all that come unto God by him. There is no one too far gone for him to save. There is not a heart too hard for him to break. There is not a will too stubborn for him to bend. There is not a sin too great for him to pardon. There is not a heart too filthy for him to cleanse; for the blood of Jesus cleanseth from *all* sin. There is *nothing* too hard for the Lord. That is the Saviour for you. He has saved those every way like yourselves,—some who seemed past all hope—some who thought they could never be saved—some whose parents and teachers said they must give them up as desperate cases. He saved *them*, and so he is able to save *you*. But,

2. He is WILLING as well as *able*. Perhaps you don't doubt his ability, but you think he will not care for or receive the like of you. "If I were a man or woman, he might think it worth his while; but I'm only a child. If I were not so bad, he might take some no-

tice of me; but though I'm young, I have been such a sinner, that I don't wonder he should just leave me to myself, and refuse to have anything to do with me." Nay, my young friend, you mistake altogether the character of him of whom I am speaking; he is no less *willing* than *able*. How do I know it? Just as in the other case, because he says it, because he has done the like before—because he is GOD. Bartimeus never doubted that if he could only bring his case before Jesus, he would give him what he needed. And you may be just as sure as he. Who was it that received little children, and laid his hands on them and blessed them, when others rebuked them and sent them away? It was Jesus of Nazareth. Who was it that received the most wicked of men, the chief of sinners, the persecuting Saul, the woman that was a sinner,—the dying thief? It was Jesus of Nazareth. Who was it that made many of our godly friends what they are—saved them, blessed them, prepared heaven for them, and is now preparing them for heaven? Jesus of Nazareth. Who was it that brought pardon and peace to any soul now living, making that soul, once just like yours, wise unto salvation, and happy and holy as never before? Jesus of Nazareth. When the blind beggar cried to him, while others scolded him, we are told, "Jesus *stood still*, and called him," showing how willing he was. So he does to you; he says, "Behold, *I stand!*"

Dear children! will you not believe that Jesus is willing to save you? I saw, some time ago, a letter from India, from one of our brave Highlanders, one of those gallant men who went to relieve our countrymen, who, during the mutiny, were shut up in Lucknow. He tells how desperately they fought their way through the town, to get to where the British were,—how their ranks were thinned, man after man shot down,—how their colours were riddled,—how at every turn new enemies met them, so that even after having conquered again and again, and rescued many from blood-thirsty foes, it seemed as if they would fall at last by the hand of traitors. If you had been one of those whom they went and risked their lives to save, would you have doubted their willingness? As they pressed forward to where you were,—as at length they stood victorious before the gates,—would you have said, "I know they are *able*, for they are lion-hearted men every one of them, or they never could have done what they have done already, but I fear they won't care for the like of us?" Would not that have been strange? Have they done this very thing over and over again—have they come so far— have they shed their blood for this very purpose, and can I have a single doubt? And will you doubt this Jesus of Nazareth? Would he have done all he has done, and said all he has said, if he had not been willing? Would he have lived and died—would he have sent his gospel and his messengers to you, as he does to-day, if he had not been willing? Again, I say, that is the Saviour for you. Will you not have him as your Saviour? Is it not then good news I have to bring you, that there is an almighty and loving Saviour, Jesus of Nazareth?

> "He is able—he is willing;
> Doubt no more."

II. A SAVING TIME.—I ground this remark on the words, "Jesus *passeth by.*" That was the time for Bartimeus. He felt it so; he believed it to be a special opportunity, perhaps an only one, and so resolved not to lose it. Here, also, I call your attention to two things—*Times when Jesus may be said to "pass by;"* and *the need of improving these.*

1. Times when Jesus may be said to "pass by"— times that may be called *saving times.* I said that what I had to tell you about Jesus, was good news;— His ability and willingness to save you. I have better news still—that this able and willing Saviour is passing by you; that he is near, within hearing, within reach, close at hand. In one sense this is always true. Every time the gospel is preached, he may be said to pass by; every time you read his word, every time the offer of mercy is made to you, it may be said he is passing by. He is always to be found by any seeking soul. He is always within reach, wherever you are. But there are certain times when he is nearer to you than at others, when he is *very near*, when he comes close to you, and knocks at your door more loudly than usual.

(1.) Such a time is the SABBATH. You may sometimes be sorry when Saturday is past, and Sabbath comes on; because there is no play, and you have not your ordinary story-books,—just always that old Bible; and you must listen to dull and tiresome sermons that have no interest for you, and which you sometimes think were never intended to have any interest for you; so that instead of singing—

> " Happy, happy, Sunday,
> Best day of all the seven!"

you would say, if you spoke the truth,—

> " Weary, weary, Sunday,
> Worst day of all the seven!"

Ah! but here is something that should make you prize it—it is THE LORD'S DAY: and every Sabbath, in a special sense, Jesus is passing by. It is thus well called the "PEARL OF DAYS." When you are in the house of God, hearing his word, praying and praising—when you are in the Sabbath school, getting instruction about eternal things—when you are sitting quietly at home in your own corner, reading your library book, or your Bible, or listening to your father or brother as he reads aloud for the benefit of the rest, Jesus is passing by, so that you can speak to him and go to him. He is there for the very purpose. He says, "Where two or three are gathered together in my name, *there am I*." Many have found Jesus on his own day. After the hard work or the difficult lessons of the week, the blessed Sabbath comes for the very purpose, just to give opportunity of seeking the Saviour. O remember, each Sabbath says, as it comes, "Jesus is passing by to-day!" Not that you are any day to put off till Sabbath; but **prize and improve it** when it comes.

(2.) Such a time is AFFLICTION. There is a girl laid upon a sick-bed. She used to be up early in the morning, to kindle the fire, and clean the house, and help her mother in every way she could; or to learn her lessons and prepare for school,—always punctually there. But now, books are laid aside, lessons are never thought of, work is out of the question. There is pain and weakness, and the thought sometimes comes up, "Perhaps this is my last illness; perhaps I shall never rise from this sick-bed, and only leave it to be carried to my grave." She cannot help going back over the past, and forward to the future, asking, "Am I ready for the change? What is to become of my precious soul?" At such a time, Jesus is passing by that bed-side. Or a little brother or companion is very ill, and anxiously you inquire for him. Day by day you see him growing paler, and thinner, and weaker, till he dies; and you feel as you never felt before; and, as you stand beside his little grave, you wonder where his soul will be—saved or lost, in heaven or in hell. As you stand beside that new-made grave, and think, and weep, Jesus is passing by. Such times as these, dear children, have been saving times. One little girl of nine years of age, who afterwards became an eminently godly and useful lady, tells us that it was at such a time that the Lord touched her heart, and drew her to himself.

(3.) Such a time is YOUTH; then Jesus is passing

by indeed. What a mistake it is, to think that it is not for children to be concerned about their souls and about Christ—that they should just think about their lessons and their play, and leave more serious things till another time! The truth is, there is no time like childhood for seeking and for finding salvation. The Holy Spirit often works in the hearts of children. Impressions are most easily made on the hearts of children. Special invitations and special promises are given to children, so that to every young person whom I address I might say, as I could not say it to the old, "My dear child, Jesus of Nazareth is now passing by." Ask that old grey-headed man, so happy as he goes tottering down to the grave,—when it was that Jesus first passed by *him*, when it was that he made choice of Christ, and he says, "In the days of my youth." Ask that aged grandmother who speaks in such a winning way about Jesus to the little ones about her bed, how long it is since Jesus passed by her,—since first she knew and loved him; how her dim eye kindles up as she answers, "Forty, or fifty, or sixty years ago, when I was a little girl, at school like you. Well do I remember that Sabbath night, when my godly mother, now in glory, pled with me and prayed for me; and I got a sight of my own heart, and a sight of Jesus, and took him to be my Saviour." Many, many could tell you that, who are the Lord's people on earth, and many more who are now in heaven. Some seek and find Jesus when they are old; but most when they are young. Surely, then, youth is a saving time, a converting time, a time when Jesus is passing by—when he is very near. Don't think it is too soon for you to be inquiring after Jesus; it is the very time—the best time of all.

(4.) Such a time it is, when there is a SPECIAL OUTPOURING OF THE HOLY SPIRIT. Then, most of all, Jesus is passing by. And how are we to know such a time? When those around us, and many elsewhere, are asking what they shall do to be saved, and are finding peace and joy in believing on Jesus. When we feel ill at ease, because we know we have never been converted, and cannot go on in our old careless and thoughtless ways, and are anxious to know the way of salvation, to have sin taken away, and the heart renewed, and our soul in the safe keeping of Jesus. When sin becomes burdensome, and seems a very evil thing, and we long to be delivered from its power. Then, I say, the Spirit is striving, and then, of a truth, Jesus is passing by. Such a time, dear children! is this. I suppose there has not been a time like it, since you and I were born. From all quarters we are hearing of what the Lord is doing, and doing among the young; not only in churches and among grown-up people, but in schools, and among boys and girls. First, tidings reached us from America of the wonderful things God was doing there, opening the hearts of old and young, who, heedless of what men might think or say, were to be seen, first mourning for sin and crying for mercy, and then rejoicing in Jesus as an all-sufficient Saviour. Then we have been seeing and hearing of the like, in different parts of our own country,—in Ireland, and Scotland, and England, and Wales. Sometimes whole schools have been awakened, so that in one play-ground you might have seen forty children distressed about their souls, and praying for pardon, their fellow-scholars praying with them, and trying to direct them to Christ; ay, even infant schools, in one of which, as I learn from a private letter, "there is a universal cry for Jesus, nothing but Jesus!" Surely there is something particular in all this, something encouraging, something solemnizing,—something that should lead old and young alike to seek the Lord. Surely there is reason to believe that Jesus is passing by.

If you ask how I know that Jesus is passing by now, I say, others tell me who have seen him,—not with the bodily eye, but with the eye of faith,—in their homely Scottish dialect, saying, "Eh, but he's bonnie!" just as David said, "Thou art fairer than the children of men;" and Solomon, "He is altogether lovely." Those tell me who have been with him. We see what he has been doing; we see the work of his hand. If you had seen a man, long ago, whose eyes had been opened, you would have said, "Jesus must have been here." If you had seen one who had been possessed with devils, sitting clothed and in his right mind, you would have said, "Jesus has been here." And so, if you see some great sinner changed, some careless child becoming thoughtful, and earnest, and Christ-loving, you cannot but say, "Jesus has been here." And all this is going on *now*; therefore I say, Jesus is passing by; it must be true. O surely, it is Jesus of Nazareth!

A few months ago, I visited a school where many were anxious, and some were full of joy as having found the Saviour. When asked to speak to them, as I took the Bible out of the hands of the dux of the class, my eye fell upon these words (Ps. lxxv. 1), "Unto thee, O God, do we give thanks; unto thee do we give thanks: *for that thy name is near, thy wondrous works declare.*" I could not but look round on the children; and feeling how true these words were, I made them my own. Do you ask what he says as he passes by? I shall let him speak for himself. "Suffer the little children to come unto me, and forbid them not." "Come unto me, all ye that labour and are heavy laden, and I will give you rest." "Him that cometh unto me I will in no wise cast out." Oh, what a precious time this is: may we not find it out only when it is past!

2. *The need of improving such times.* Why? Because they are so precious and so short. Why was Bartimeus so anxious, why did he cry so often and so loud? Because Jesus was passing *by*—was going on his way, and he feared lest he should lose the opportunity, and lose it for ever. And so it is now. Jesus is "passing by," he is not standing still, he is going, and will soon be away—away perhaps never to come back. That is the only time we read of Christ being in Jericho; it was his *one visit;* and if Bartimeus had

taken the advice, not to be in such haste, to have a little patience, to wait till Jesus should be more free to attend to him, or till he should return, as he might, at some future time, he had missed the blessing, and been a blind man to his dying day.

When that wonderful Comet was sending its light streaming across our sky, so that people were on the watch night after night, all eager to see it when it was largest and brightest, what was it that made them so anxious ? Do you think they would have been so, if the comet had been to go on shining for a whole year ; or if it had been to make its appearance again next year, or even a year or two after, when they might have seen it again ? No, it was because they were told that it would not appear again in our day, that when next it came back, we would all be in our graves,—that this would be the only opportunity. And so, some fathers awoke their children, and got them out of bed, and had them up to see this wonderful sight, for they would never see the like again. And so, dear children ! it is when Jesus of Nazareth passeth by. It *may be* the like again in our day, but it *may not*. It is a special opportunity now. Parents may well try to get their children to see Jesus, like the mothers who brought their children to him long ago. Young and old may well be like Zaccheus, when he climbed up the sycamore tree, to get a passing glimpse of the Stranger.

And how are you to improve these times ? Just by doing as this blind man did. He cried to Jesus ; laid aside his garment, rose and went to him; believed on him, rejoiced in him,—followed him. Go you and do likewise. *Cry to Jesus* as he did, "Lord Jesus, have mercy on me!" Don't be discouraged if others are angry with you, if even professing Christians rebuke you, if people should try to laugh you out of your concern, and say, "There is no need for all this ado." Don't stop or be silent; nay, cry all the more, for fear you should miss the blessing. Eternity depends on it,—you must not give up. Some cry once, and stop there. Not so Bartimeus; he cried again, and again, and again; louder, and louder, and louder. And *he was heard*. And *you* will not cry in vain. When the children were brought to Christ, even the disciples rebuked them, but Jesus said, "Suffer them to come to me, and forbid them not." So is it still.

Like him, *lay aside all that would hinder you.* He was so eager and so much in haste, that, lest it should hinder him, or trip him and cause him to fall, he laid aside his garment and ran to where Jesus was. So let nothing keep you back, let nothing come between you and Christ,—no lawful thing, no sinful thing. Don't let your dress, or your play, or your friends, or anything else stand in your way. *This* is of more consequence than anything else. Lay aside your garment. Rise and go to him. He calls you. Go,—go at once, and don't keep him waiting. Take him as your Saviour. Oh, how happy you would be,—how gladly you would follow him,—how greatly you would love him!

Jesus of Nazareth passeth by. Perhaps he *has passed!* He has been speaking to some, and they did not know him. He has been dealing with some, and they did not recognise him. And now he is *past!* Well, but he is still within hearing; will you not run after him yet? Perhaps he is looking back, taking a last look, to see if no one will apply to him. Perhaps he is listening to hear if there is no one even now crying after him, "Jesus, thou Son of David, have mercy on me." Dear children, if you don't cry to him *now*, you may be too late. Don't say *to-morrow*, for he says, "Boast not thyself of to-morrow; thou knowest not what a day may bring forth." He may before then be quite out of the way. Many will wish that Jesus of Nazareth had never passed by. If we do not take him as our Saviour, it will be worse for us than if he had never come near us.

> "Oh sick at soul! oh blind at heart!
> Why lift ye not *your* cry?
> Since He who hath all power to save,
> *To-day is passing by!*"

My dear children, this may be with many of you the deciding time for eternity. That is the reason why Christ is so earnest with *you*, and why you should be so earnest with *him*. He says, "Seek ye the Lord *while he may be found*, call ye upon him *while he is near;*" which is the same thing as saying, Go to him when he is passing by. Don't think, "He'll never mind *me;* he'll take no notice of *me*." Nay, but see how he noticed a poor blind beggar; and will he, after that, pass over *you?* Will he not care for *you?* The present is a time to seek him for yourselves, and to get others to seek with you. Tell your parents that Jesus of Nazareth passeth by. Tell your brothers and sisters; write to your friends the good news, that Jesus of Nazareth passeth by. Plead with them, and plead with Jesus for them. Bring them to him in the only way you can—*in prayer;* and who can tell what the end may be? Let us seek great things. None can ever ask too much.

About twelve or fifteen years ago, you might have seen drifting out from an English sea-port, a fishing-boat with neither pilot nor oarsman, its sole occupants six little children, between five and nine years of age.* It was amusement at first, but soon the tide carried them out, and there they were on the wide sea, with a dark sky above them, and not a soul near to hear their cries! When morning came, a sailor saw them;—there they lay like little birds in a nest, clasped in each other's arms, fast asleep down in the bottom of the boat. You may fancy how glad he was to save them. But what a scene on shore!—men searching every nook and corner, mothers wailing, boats pushing off. What fear, and grief, and anxiety, during that long, dreary night! When the morning dawns, a vessel is seen approaching, with the missing boat behind. Every eye is turned towards it, every heart beats quick:

* "The Rescue."

no child is to be seen, and every mother fears the worst, till at length the truth is told—is seen, and the cry is heard through all the gathered crowd, "THEY'RE ALL SAFE! THEY'RE ALL SAFE!" Oh, to have seen these mothers then, as they clasped their little ones to their bosom, and wept over them tears of joy; and to have heard weather-beaten seamen sobbing like children for very gladness, and the whole town rejoicing, as from street to street, and from house to house, the tidings flew, "They're all safe!" Beloved young friends, we often feel and fear for you, as they did for their missing little ones;—sometimes we can only hope, and weep, and pray. But oh, what a burst of joy would break forth from parents, and teachers, and ministers, and all the godly, if we could say of our children, "*They're all safe!*"—safe in the arms of Jesus! In the midst of a godless world, they're all safe; in the midst of temptation, and trial, and sorrow, they're all safe; in the midst of sickness and death, they're all safe; standing by the lifeless body, looking on the little coffin, giving the last kiss to the pale, cold brow, weeping beside the little grave,—amid our very tears, we could still thank God as we whispered the words, "They're all safe! they're all safe!" And why should it not be? Why should we not seek it when Jesus is passing by? Why should we be content with anything less, when, like the oil in the widow's cruse, the blessing might continue, till we had to say, "There is not a vessel more?" Oh, I think if regarding all our children we could say it, we might take up the words of old Simeon, as having got our heart's wish, "Now, Lord, lettest thou thy servant depart in peace, for mine eyes have seen thy salvation!" Then in taking farewell, we might say, "Farewell: we'll meet again!"

THE HYMN.

JESUS Christ is passing by,
   Sinner, lift to him thine eye;
As the precious moments flee,
Cry, " Be merciful to me."

Jesus Christ is passing by,
Will he always be so nigh?
Now is the accepted day,
Seek for healing while you may.

Fearest thou he will not hear?
Art thou bidden to forbear?
Let no obstacle defeat;
Yet more earnestly entreat.

Lo! he stands and calls to thee,
"What wilt thou then have of me?"
Rise, and tell him all thy need;
Rise, he calleth thee indeed.

" Lord, I would thy mercy see!
Lord, reveal thy love to me!
Let it penetrate my soul,—
All my heart and life control."

Oh, how sweet! the touch of power
Comes—it is salvation's hour;
Jesus gives from guilt release,—
"Faith has saved thee, go in peace."

Glory to the Saviour's name!
He is ever still the same;
To his matchless honour raise
Never-ending songs of praise.

The History of a Lost Soul.

THE HYMN.

RETURN, O holy Dove, return!
　Sweet messenger of rest;
I hate the sins that made thee mourn,
　And drove thee from my breast.

The dearest idol I have known,
　Whate'er that idol be,
Help me to tear it from thy throne,
　And worship only thee.

So shall my walk be close with God,
　Calm and serene my frame;
So purer light shall mark the road
　That leads me to the Lamb.

MY DEAR YOUNG FRIENDS,—I daresay there are few here who do not know and love that sweet passage in the book of the prophet Isaiah (xlix. 15): "Can a woman forget her sucking child, that she should not have compassion on the son of her womb? yea, they may forget, yet will I not forget thee." The Lord would have his humble people to know, how unquenchable is his love to them. Oh, how unwearied his care for them! and so he likens his love, for strength and tenderness, to that of a mother, intimating that even that comes far short of his. "They *may* forget,"—such a thing can scarcely happen, still it is possible; "yet will I not forget thee."

I don't know anything in all the world to be set alongside of a mother's love; and I don't know anything in all the world so strange and sad, as the treatment that mother sometimes meets with, at the hand of her child. What a glad and joyful mother was she when that babe was born! how she watched over him by night and by day! how she bore with his fretfulness, and yearned over him in his sickness, and never grudged her labour, and fatigue, and sleepless nights! and when, once more, she saw the smile on his face as he slept in his cradle, and the glow of health on his dimpled cheek, or listened to his prattle as he sat on her knee, how she thought there never was a fairer child, or a happier mother than she! But soon the evil that is in the heart of a child began to appear—the thorns grew out around the rose; and as that mother saw the outbursts of passion, and overheard the unholy word, and detected the untruthful story, and looked on that once sweet face, now crimsoned with guilt and shame,—who shall tell the grief that filled her heart? And yet he was ready to confess his fault, and was sorry for it, and instead of setting her at defiance, promised amendment; and so though grieved, she was yet hopeful. Another stage, and the youth has a will of his own, follows his own inclinations,—though in direct opposition to hers,—does not scruple to run in the face of her express commands; and when she would win him back, showing him his error and pleading with him to be other than he is, he will not yield, and in spite of his better feelings and his sense of duty, still holds out. And yet, even now, the case is not felt to be hopeless : his resistance may yet be overcome and his heart subdued. But at length the boy becomes a man ; he is his own master, throws off all restraint, runs headlong in a course of sin, till his old mother is driven from her home. Once and again she returns, if perchance she may reclaim her son; for she loves him still. But his dishonour to her God and his cruelty to herself become unendurable. There is nothing for it but to leave him. You might see her on a cold winter night, pacing the street, often looking up to that lighted window where she knows her son is. Her heart beats quick every time she sees his shadow. She longs to see him another man ; and, loath to give him up, she groans out the prayer, "O God, save my lad !" But there is no opening for her return ; and lest her old heart should break, she sorrowfully takes her departure. As I see her leaving, casting many a lingering look behind, I think, though not so sadly, of Hagar and her boy in the wilderness, when the water was spent in the bottle, and it seemed as if Ishmael must die : "And she went and sat her down over against him, a good way off, for she said, Let me not see the death of the child. And she sat over against him, and lifted up her voice and wept." And never does the hardened man come to himself till it is too late,—till his mother's head is in the grave, and place of repentance for him there is none ; her gentleness, and love, and patience making his sin all the greater, and at last increasing the bitterness and unbearableness of his remorse. "Ah," you say, "that does not describe me. I never was, and never will be such a one, to friend or mother. God forbid that I should ever be so far left to myself as that!"

Well, my dear children, I trust with all my heart you never will be; and yet, perhaps there is something not unlike it even now—something that may at least one day come to be like it. In a former address, I sought to introduce you to a Friend whose help you needed, and who was willing to have befriended you all your life long; One who has long been near you, though you did not know it; without whom you can never be happy in life or in death; who has had wonderful forbearance with you, and has many a time had provocation enough to make him leave you,—a kind, gentle, loving Friend. Think how you have been treating him—how you are treating him now. You will understand what I mean if you look at my three texts:—

>Eph. iv. 30: "GRIEVE not the Holy Spirit of God."
>Acts vii. 51: "Ye do always RESIST the Holy Ghost."
>1 Thess. iv. 19: "QUENCH not the Spirit."

You may remember that the text on which I spoke to you before was, "If ye, being evil, know how to give good things to your children, how much more shall your heavenly Father give the Holy Spirit to them that ask him?" That address was mainly taken up with a description of this,—God's precious gift to men. As inducements to you to ask the Holy Spirit, I gave you these seven particulars regarding him : 1. He convinces us of sin—the Reprover. 2. He renews the heart—the Regenerator, the Quickener. 3. He teaches us to pray,—how to pray, and what to pray for—the Advocate, the Intercessor. 4. He enables us to understand the word of God—the Teacher, the Interpreter, the Enlightener. 5. He strengthens us to resist what is evil, and to do what is right—the Helper and Upholder. 6. He comforts us—the Comforter. 7. He makes us holy, like God, and fit for heaven—the Sanctifier.

Now, all the three texts that have been read, refer to our treatment of this great and good Friend. The first is addressed to believers, to those who belong to the fold of Christ, and so is especially for you who are the Lord's dear children ; the other two are for those who are still strangers to Jesus. I think, however, we may weave the whole three into one web, and set before you the history of a lost soul. Suppose then that this address were a book by itself, the title of the book would be—

THE HISTORY OF A LOST SOUL:

Set Forth in Three Successive Stages.

The book would be divided into three chapters :—

CHAPTER I.—A COURSE OF CARELESSNESS AND SIN *BEGUN;* THE HOLY SPIRIT *GRIEVED.*

CHAPTER II.—A COURSE OF CARELESSNESS AND SIN *PERSISTED IN:* THE HOLY SPIRIT *RESISTED.*
CHAPTER III.—A COURSE OF CARELESSNESS AND SIN *COMPLETED:* THE HOLY SPIRIT *QUENCHED.*

I have never taken up a more solemn subject. May the Spirit plead his own cause with you to-day!

CHAPTER I.—A COURSE OF CARELESSNESS AND SIN *BEGUN:* THE HOLY SPIRIT *GRIEVED.*

It is with sin as with everything else, people do not become perfect in it at once. It is progressive. It has a beginning, and a middle, and an end. Men do not become confirmed thieves, or drunkards, or swearers in a day. Men do not get hardened in sin all at once: they become so by degrees. And the Holy Spirit does not leave men all at once: he bears with them, strives with them, gives them many opportunities, and only when all has been in vain, gives them up and goes away. Perhaps you ask, "How do we grieve the Spirit?" I shall try to answer the question.

1. We grieve the Spirit when we *harbour his enemies;* by that I mean when we indulge in sinful thoughts, and words, and actions. There are certain people who hate your father very much, and do all they can to vex and annoy him,—who, if they could, would by some means or other, get him out of the way altogether. Well, one day, coming home unexpectedly, he finds you with these in the house, entertaining them, giving them his own best room, making friends of them,—joining them in mocking and speaking ill of him. What would

he think? how would he feel? would he not be grieved? would it not pierce him to the heart? Could you do *that?* Or you have been left alone, friendless and uncared for. Some neighbour, on whom you had no claim, came in to cheer and comfort you when you were mourning your loss; promising to act the part of a father to you, to help you on in the world; telling you to come to him in every difficulty, and he would show you what to do; giving you proof that he was both able and willing. If you knew that there was something that he disliked very much, that he would not come near, that he could not bear the sight of,— how do you think he would feel, if you were to take that hated thing, to carry it about with you, and put it in his way, so that he could have no dealing with you without coming in contact with it,—would it not wound him and grieve him most bitterly? Could you do *that?* There is a little plant called the Sensitive Plant, beautiful in form, and of a pretty green colour; whenever you touch it, the leaf falls down, as if it were a living thing, shrinking back from, unable to endure your touch,—hence its name. It cannot bear to be meddled with.

Now, children, when you tamper with sin, you do all I have been describing. Your thinking sin, or speaking sin, or acting sin, is like entertaining your father's hateful foes, or rewarding your friend's kindness by doing what most annoys him, pressing upon him what his very nature revolts from. You are grieving the Holy

Spirit,—beginning a course that may end in his leaving you.

You lost your temper, and, in the heat of the moment, said some sharp, bitter thing, to a friend or companion. You saw it had "told,"—your friend's countenance fell, his mouth was shut, and you came off conqueror. When your better feelings returned, it pained you as you thought you had grieved *him*. Ah! it did more than that,—it grieved the Holy Spirit. You spoke some unhallowed word, and just as you spoke it, your mother came in sight, and you almost fancied you saw it go like a dagger to her heart. That word, unintended for her—it was a mercy she heard it, for it told her of her boy's danger—how you wished it recalled! how you wept as you thought you had grieved *your mother!* Ah! it did more than that; though she had never heard it, it grieved the Holy Spirit, who sees and hears all. You were tempted to commit some sin, and fell before the temptation; and now that it is discovered, you can scarcely hold up your head,—it seems as if everybody were pointing his finger at you, and crying, "Shame!"— or without it being known to others, your own conscience condemns you, and you think how foolish you were to make yourself so unhappy for a moment's pleasure; it grieves *you* to have done it. Ay, but more than that, it has grieved the Holy Spirit. Of such things as these was Paul speaking when he wrote our text. Never, then, think lightly of them.

2. We grieve the Spirit when we *neglect prayer and*

the reading of God's word. A son is leaving his home for the first time. His godly mother makes him promise, that he will never retire to rest at night, without reading a portion of God's word, which she has learned to prize above all things else. He is now lodging at some distance from town or village. It is late at night, and his candle is burnt out, and he has not read his chapter. There is not another candle in the house ; there is no gas-light or lamp—none to be had without going miles for it. The night is dark ; everything seems to say, "Wait for your chapter till morning—light enough then !" But that youth knows how it would grieve his mother's heart to think he had begun to neglect his Bible ;—rather than that, he would do anything. The long road, and the dark night, and the late hour are disregarded ; he gets his candle, and reads his Bible as perhaps never before. Ah! I wonder how many among us are as much afraid to omit their morning or evening prayer, or their morning or evening chapter, lest they should grieve the Holy Spirit. Perhaps you ask, "But how should that grieve the Spirit ?"

There is a prisoner confined for some serious offence. Others would leave him to his fate, and say he richly deserved the worst he could get. But there is a kind-hearted advocate who goes down to his cell, offers to help him in drawing up a statement of his case,—leaves with him a schedule to be filled up, and a paper of instructions telling him both how to proceed now, and, in the event of his being pardoned, how to conduct himself afterwards. And as he comes down day after day, he finds things just as he left them—the schedule unfilled up, the memorial not sent off, the paper of instructions unlooked at, and the whole matter treated with neglect; the man sometimes saying he had forgot, and sometimes he had not had time, and sometimes he had been so tired and sleepy! What would you think of him? Might not his generous-hearted friend well be grieved? Children! you are that poor prisoner, and you need one to help you in your application for pardon —to tell you from whom you are to get it, how you are to ask for it, and how you are to live after you are pardoned; and that one is the Holy Spirit,—and prayer and the Bible are the only way in which you and God can converse with each other; and while the Spirit would help you both to speak to him and to understand what he says to you, he finds you careless about both. And, in so doing, how can you but grieve him? Oh, think of this, prayerless, Bible-neglecting children! If nothing else has any weight with you, surely this might move you.

3. We grieve the Holy Spirit, when we are *careless about our souls*, and *about Christ*. When I was in Switzerland I saw many of the people—little children as well as men and women—suffering from a terrible disease, called goitre; great lumps growing from their neck, sometimes almost as large as their head. It is very sad, as you pass through the villages and along the roads, to see this, and nothing seems to be done to cure it. Suppose I were

to make earnest inquiry everywhere, going to all quarters of the globe in search of a remedy—of some one who could effect a cure; were I to hurry back, my heart bounding with joy at having made the discovery, expecting them all to be as glad and thankful as myself, when I offered to show them the way to be cured—to guide them to one who could make them healthy and well;—would it not be strange, if I found them all unconcerned about it, preferring to live a miserable life, and to die a miserable death, rather than take advantage of my help? *Would* it not,—*must* it not grieve me? and would I not come back from my thankless, fruitless task, miserably disappointed?

Beloved young people! the Holy Spirit was promised, and has been given, to make you acquainted with your disease—the disease of which your soul is ill, and, unless cured of which, you must die eternally—and to make known to you the great Physician, the grand gospel remedy. He came to show us ourselves, and to show us Jesus. It is his work and his delight to commend Christ, and to guide men to him. He rejoices to hold up Christ to the view of poor sinners, as Moses did to lift up the serpent to the dying Israelites. He rejoices to bring glory to Christ in the salvation of souls. And when we have no care about all this, or think we can do better ourselves, and find out some way of our own,—then we do not honour Christ, and we forsake our own mercies, and the good and loving Spirit is grieved. Dear children! let us at the outset, before the evil go any further, hear the voice that says to us, "Grieve not the Holy Spirit."

> "Come, Holy Spirit, from above,
> With all thy quick'ning powers,
> Kindle a flame of sacred love
> In these cold hearts of ours."

CHAPTER II.—A COURSE OF CARELESSNESS AND SIN *PERSISTED IN:* THE HOLY SPIRIT *RESISTED.*

The first chapter might have been also the last, and have ended the whole matter; and the Spirit, thus grieved, might have gone away. But he did not, and now we advance a stage further. To "resist" means to *fight against,*—to *oppose;* and that is just its meaning here. You ask, "How do we resist the Holy Spirit?" I might mention many ways; I shall only speak of three :—

1. We resist the Holy Spirit *when he shows us the evil of our sin, and yet we will not part with it.* There is a child playing with a sharp knife, which he has been forbidden to touch. He has some notion he is doing wrong, and his father, when he sees him, is grieved at his disobedience. But when the evil of his conduct has been set before him, and the danger of it is explained, and he is reasoned with, and still refuses to give it up, then it is open resistance—worse by far than before. There is a man with a cup of poison in his hand; it is sparkling and beautiful, and, as he tastes and finds it so sweet, though he knows it is poisonous, he still sips on. But when a friend comes

up, and, seeing what he is doing, shows him his danger, tells him what the end of it in other cases has been; and when, unable to reason him out of it, he grasps the cup and would wrench it from his hand; and when he will not be prevented, but drinks deeper and deeper,—his case, too, is worse than before, and his conduct more inexcusable. So when we sin, as we have already seen, we "grieve" the Spirit; but when we come to see more clearly what we have been doing, and find the Scriptures condemning it, or people coming to us and dealing with us about it, our own conscience now rising up and protesting against it as never before, —all this is the Spirit showing us our sin, with a view to driving us out of it; and when still we *will* cling to the sin we love, knowing that it is displeasing to God, and that it will be our ruin,—then we "resist" or fight against the Holy Spirit. Are any of you now doing this as regards any sin? Then, think what it is to be fighting against God!

2. We resist the Spirit *when he works conviction of sin in us, and we try to throw it off.* When I say this, some will understand what I mean, and some will not. I will try to explain. A young apprentice has done something wrong, and is found fault with by his master. He speaks back, as boy should never do to master, and is turned off. His pride is touched, and, rather than go home disgraced, or confess and ask forgiveness for his fault, he sets out for some strange place, as people say, to "push his fortune." A stranger meets

him, learns his history, shows him how wrong his conduct is, and entreats him to return; to fall back on the word I used, he *convinces* the boy of his sin. He feels he has done wrong—sees how differently he should have acted—knows he ought at once to go back—is every way most unhappy; but, instead of returning, seeks something to drive it out of his mind, takes up with wicked boys, gets deeper into sin, and drives all good thoughts away. Some of you once took things very easily. Had any one asked you if you were a sinner, you would have said—yes; but your sin gave you little concern. One day, as you were hearing a sermon, or reading your Bible, God sent the word home to your heart, and you saw yourself to be a sinner as never before, and you wept as you thought of what you had been; and, when night came, you could not sleep for thinking about your sin,—you felt as if a burden were lying on your heart,—you almost feared lest before morning you should be lost. How was all this—what brought about such a change—whose doing was it? It was the Holy Spirit, from whom all this came, and this is what I mean by his working in you conviction of sin. And when, after all this,—feeling as if there were no sinner like you—as if you deserved, and could not escape from hell—as if you had crucified Christ, and could not hope for mercy from him, young though you were—next day, or some days after, you tried to get quit of these feelings, and hurried back to your careless companions, and sought to be as little alone as possible, and went direct from your play to bed, or got some interesting story-book to fill up the vacant hour, and did all you could, not to think about these things at all, drowning these convictions which the Spirit had wrought in you;—then you *resisted* the Spirit, and fought against him. Ah, dear children! I fear some of you understand all this, better than I can tell you; and to-day, you do not like to hear about it. That is the very reason why I remind you of it, for when you have lost your convictions, there is cause indeed for alarm.

3. We resist the Holy Spirit *when he strives with us to bring us to Christ, and we delay or refuse to come.* I have never heard of a drowning man, when another had swam out to save him, telling him he wanted none of him, refusing his help, or saying he would take it by-and-by, asking him meanwhile just to leave him to himself. And yet this is what some of you have been doing. You felt some concern about your soul; you had some desire to be Christ's; you began to inquire about the way; you asked how you were to find Christ; you spoke and prayed about it at home and among your companions. And whence did this unusual concern come? who brought it about? It was the Holy Spirit. It was he—striving with you. His great work is to bring sinners to Christ—his great word to sinners is, "Come!" for "the Spirit and the bride say, Come." It was he who was urging you to come, and to come at once without delay; for "the Holy Ghost saith, *To-*

day!" And it seemed as if then you would be saved; you were almost persuaded; but no—you stopped, and when he would have drawn you on, you refused to come—you *would not* be saved; and in so doing, you fought against—you resisted the Holy Spirit. Perhaps some of you have so resisted, as to give up prayer, and the reading of the word, and the house of God, keeping out of the way of those who would be likely to speak to you about your souls, and you wish just to be let alone,—which means, that you wish *to be lost!* Perhaps, even some of you young people, have got as far advanced on the downward path as this.

CHAPTER III.—A COURSE OF CARELESSNESS AND SIN *COMPLETED:* THE HOLY SPIRIT *QUENCHED.*

What a startling word that is! How it rings in my ear! I cannot forget it, for it sounds to me like an echo from the regions of despair. I cannot trust myself to say much under this head. It is too solemn and sacred a subject to be much meddled with, by such a hand as mine. For many a day I thought of it as a text from which to preach, but each time I shrunk back from it, almost afraid to touch it. And when at length I came fairly to look at it, and to follow out the thoughts suggested by it, I had to lay aside my pen and—to weep. I'll tell you why. It called up a scene that is often to be witnessed. On that bed is one on whom the hand of death seems to be laid. Gradually he has been sinking, and now the end is evidently drawing near. Weeping friends stand all around, watching every symptom, each more eager than another to wipe the cold sweat from the brow, or to moisten the parched lips, trying to relieve the cough, or to change the position of the pillow, anticipating every wish,—all looking on with drawn breath and trembling heart. The hope still lingers in one breast that a change for the better may be even yet, and that hope so sustains, that in her eye you cannot see a tear. But as the sound of the breathing gets lower and softer, and then is not heard at all—in an instant, one has his finger on the pulse, another lays his hand on the heart, but both have ceased to beat; and when the mirror, held close to the lips of that loved one, bears not the trace of a breath on its clear surface, telling surely that the spirit has fled, I hear the words, "He is gone!" and after a momentary pause, these eager on-lookers instinctively turn away;—further effort would now be vain; a sheet is thrown over the lifeless body, and they give way to uncontrollable sorrow.

This is just what suggested itself to me as a sad but truthful picture of some of you. Here is a boy whose case was hopeful once. He knew the better way, and seemed for a time on the threshold of the kingdom of heaven. You might have seen him in the Boys' Prayer-meeting, devout-looking as any, and heard him pouring out earnest petitions before God, bestirring himself to get others to join in seeking the Lord. But he went back; he tampered with sin; he sought the companionship of the worldly and the godless. One heart still yearned over him, and hoped against hope. How she listened at his door, if peradventure she might hear the voice of prayer, as in earlier and happier days! How she stole into his little room, when he had left it, to see whether there was any indication of that long-neglected Bible having been taken up again! How, when a time of awakening came, efforts were made to get him to meetings where others had met with Christ, and one friend after another sought to do him good! But all in vain. He is hardened; he fights against the truth; he will not leave an open door for any holy influence to reach him; and he dies as he lived, unsoftened,—unsaved. As I stand beside his grave, our text comes sadly to mind; and if asked for a truthful passage of Scripture to inscribe on his tombstone for the benefit of others, I should give this,—" Quench not the Spirit!" Oh, sure there is cause to weep!

The figure here used is expressive: "*Quench* not!" Two little children have been left for a while by themselves, to play by a bright and cheerful fireside. In their mother's absence, bent on amusement, they resolve to drown out the fire. A pail of water is conveyed to the hearth, and the work begins. Time after time their little hands lave the water on, but though, at first, the flame goes down, it soon burns up again. Once and again it rallies, but in course of time it begins to give signs of yielding. The flame is gone, the glow of the still live-coal is getting dim; when I come in there is yet a spark—it may yet be saved. I cry, "Hold, boys! hold!" but they make haste to finish what they have begun,—another handful puts out the one remaining spark, yet another follows, so that even the smoke that still survived the spark disappears, and I hear the shout uttered with childish glee, "It's out! it's out!" Out? Yes; and now do what you will, it matters not. Fan it, supply the best of fuel, blow with all your might, do all for it that can be done, and you will find all in vain, for it is "quenched;"—all is black, and damp, and cold, and dead. The last handful did the deed; but for that, it might have been revived; that destroyed the very possibility of recovery.

Dear children! this is just the effect of repeated dealings with the Spirit, such as we before described,— the natural consequence of grieving and resisting him, when he had begun his blessed work. When there have been repeated times of awakening, when impressions have been made, when there has been great anxiety, and when repeated efforts have been made to throw all this off and get quit of it,—if such a course be persisted in, if such efforts be successful, so that anxiety, and conviction of sin, and care for the soul are all gone,—then, if I may not say the Spirit is quenched, I may at least say that things are on the way to it, and that every such effort is like another handful of water thrown upon the fire, which, in due time, must extinguish it altogether. It cannot go on always; it is impossible. "The longsuffering of God *waited* in the days of Noah;" but there was a limit, and at length you hear him saying, "My Spirit shall not *always* strive with man." Even so is it now. And when the Spirit has ceased to strive, when the Spirit is quenched, you have the completion of the history of a lost soul, at least as regards its experience on earth.

After such times as those in which it has been our happy lot to live, when Jesus of Nazareth has been passing by, when the Spirit has been working so largely and so graciously, there is great danger. Dear children! be on your guard. It may seem a small matter, to do many things which you are doing constantly; and yet every means of grace neglected, every careless reading or hearing of the word, every unmeaning and heartless prayer, every opportunity lost, every warning of conscience disregarded, is throwing another drop into the cup that is ready to overflow, and so is bringing you ever nearer to the point at which the Spirit ceases to strive, at which the Spirit is quenched.

And then what is the soul's case? Like the dead man, or the extinguished fire, or a tree of which I have now to speak. When addressing the lambs of my flock on this subject, I called their attention to a tree that stood in front of the church in which we were assembled. For years it had stood there, stretching out its bare unyielding arms, the same unchanging thing all the four seasons over. When spring came round, and other trees were sending forth their buds and opening out their leaves, rejoicing the eye with their freshness after the desolation of winter, no bud or leaf appeared on it; the birds did not build their nests nor sing their merry song among its branches, the dews did not refresh it, nor the sunshine gladden it, nor the rain nourish it. No, for it was *dead*. Some wished it away, as serving no good purpose; but I pled that it might be spared, as a remembrancer of former days, and still more as furnishing a picture to our children of what it is to be spiritually dead. A proposal was made to clothe it with ivy, and twine other creeping plants around it, that it might be fairer to look upon; but that would not have made it *live*, so I preferred that it should appear to be—just what it really was. Some months after, a rough blast or some rude hand brought it down, and now nothing but the unseemly stump remains; and long ere this, I fancy, the tree has been committed to the flames. That tree preached many a sermon to me as, in passing, I looked at it. I wish you would let it preach a sermon to you. It would take as its text the last of the three,—" Quench not the Spirit." Its sermon might be after this fashion: " Children! look at me—useless, leafless, fruitless, sapless, dead; and see in me the likeness of every dead, unconverted soul, that has grieved, and resisted, and quenched the Holy Spirit. Nothing tells upon me now—neither cloud nor sunshine, day nor night, heat nor cold. Nothing does me any good now—summer and winter are all alike. I am just waiting the hour when I shall be hewn down and cast into the fire."

Beloved young friends, what are you going to do? Are you to go on grieving and resisting the Spirit, as many of you are doing? Have you made up your minds for it? Will you rather run the fearful risk, than give up some present sin, some present misnamed pleasure? Then realize what it involves, and speak the language of truth. Let us hear it come from your lips; speak it with unfaltering voice if you can: "Farewell ye bright expectations of childhood and youth! Farewell ye cherished hopes of my better days! Farewell ye sweet feelings and impressions of my early years! Farewell my companions in seeking the Saviour! Farewell all ye good and holy on earth! Farewell ye saints and angels in heaven! Farewell joy! Farewell peace! Farewell Christ! Farewell heaven! Farewell glory! I have made a covenant with death, and with hell I am at agreement. I have gone after strangers, and after them will I go." Will you not rather listen to the Father's voice, "Return, ye backsliding children, and I will heal your backslidings?" There is a possibility of return now; it may not be long; make haste. Turn the hymn at the beginning of this address into a prayer to Him whom you have so sinned against:—

"Return, O holy Dove, return!
 Sweet messenger of rest;
I hate the sins that made thee mourn,
 And drove thee from my breast."

Make David's prayer yours: "Cast me not away from thy presence; take not thy Holy Spirit from me."

While there is yet place of repentance, out with the cry, "Hast thou but one blessing, my Father? Bless me, even me also, O my Father."

THE HYMN.

WHEN the harvest is past and the summer is gone,
    And sermons and prayers shall be o'er,
When the beams cease to break of the blest Sabbath morn,
    And Jesus invites thee no more;

When the rich gales of mercy no longer shall blow,
    The gospel no message declare,
Sinner, how canst thou bear the deep wailing of woe—
    How suffer the night of despair?

When the holy have gone to the region of peace,
    To dwell in the mansions above,
When their harmony wakes, in the fulness of bliss,
    Their song to the Saviour they love:

Say, O sinner that livest at rest and secure,
    Who fearest no trouble to come,
Can thy spirit the swellings of sorrow endure?
    Or bear the impenitent's doom?

The Account.

THE HYMN.

GREAT God, what do I see and hear?
   The end of things created!
The Judge of mankind doth appear
   On clouds of glory seated.
The trumpet sounds; the graves restore
The dead which they contained before;—
   Prepare, my soul, to meet him.

The dead in Christ shall first arise,
   At the last trumpet's sounding,
Caught up to meet him in the skies,
   With joy their Lord surrounding.
No gloomy fears their souls dismay;
His presence sheds eternal day
   On those prepared to meet him.

Great God, what do I see and hear?
   The end of things created!
The Judge of mankind doth appear
   On clouds of glory seated.
Beneath his cross I view the day
When heaven and earth shall pass away,
   And thus prepare to meet him.

MY DEAR YOUNG FRIENDS,—We have now come to the closing address, and it has not been easy to decide upon what should be the parting word. The thought crossed my mind, that I should try to fancy I had all my readers gathered together, on the last day of the old year, or the first of the new; and the question came up, "What should I say to them then?" It seemed not unsuitable to take the text, "Redeeming the time," reminding you how fast your time was hurrying by—like a swollen stream in winter, how soon it would all be gone, even with the youngest among us, and what need there was to make the most of it, to let none be wasted, and especially to use it as God intends we should, in first of all seeking Christ, and pardon, and salvation through him, improving ourselves and doing good to others,—serving God and preparing for eternity. But as I thought of various things connected with a Christmas or New Year time, another subject came up. What is such a time remarkable for? How would you know it to be such? Perhaps one says, "By seeing people, who never shake hands all the year round, shaking hands then, and saying, with a smile on their face, 'A merry Christmas to you!' or, 'A happy New Year!'" Another says, "By seeing people, who are sober and well-behaved all the rest of the year, drinking then as if they had special leave, and as if they were bound to do so, and making themselves—I'll not say what—but making their families and friends very anxious and very sorrowful." Another says, "By seeing the bakers' windows filled with all manner of fine things; or by not having to go to school for a week or more; or by seeing our fathers and brothers going idle—doing no work for days together; or by getting a nice little book, such as the 'Voyage of Life,' at the Sabbath school; and in many other ways." Shall I tell you of one other?

There is a word that, whether it be strange to you or not, is by no means strange to your fathers and mothers at such a time of the year,—at least those of them who do not always pay ready money for what they buy. I mean the word—ACCOUNT. Go in to call upon a merchant, and he says he is busy making out his accounts. Go in to other people, and if you want money from them, it is likely they will say, "You could not have come at a worse time: we are getting in accounts of all kinds,—bakers' accounts, and butchers' accounts, and grocers' accounts. And agents of various kinds have to give account to their employers, of how things stand between them—whether they have been gaining or losing during the year. And servants, whose masters have been from home till the Christmas holidays, are called to give account of what they have been doing, what they have been making of their time, and how they have been caring for their masters' interests, and watching over their property, and spending their money. Almost everybody has then something or other to do with accounts, and in one way or other is thinking about them; and so I thought I could not do better than take up the subject with *you*, and say something about *your* accounts. "Our accounts!" some one says; "we are in nobody's books, we are nobody's servants, we have nobody's money in our hands,—we have nothing to look after, for which we must give account. For once, you are quite beside the mark." Well, let us see; turn to—

THE ACCOUNT.

Romans xiv. 12: "Every one of us shall give ACCOUNT of himself to God."

That surely is not out of place for such a time as I have referred to, or for the close of a book like this— that tells of an account which we are all running, which we should often look narrowly into, of which the solemn reckoning time is nearer than ever it was before—our LIFE-ACCOUNT WITH GOD. We shall begin at the middle of the text, then go to the end of it, and then come back to the beginning. I think this may be the best way to take it up. Here, then, is the order: "Shall give account of himself—to God— every one of us." I shall ask three questions, and try to answer them:—

Question I. What is the Account? *Answer.* "Shall give account of himself."

Question II. To whom is it to be given? *Answer.* "To God."

Question III. Who are to give it? *Answer.* "Every one of us."

Question I. WHAT IS THE ACCOUNT?

Answer. "OF OURSELVES." I need scarcely explain what this means. There is a boy who left his home in the morning to go to school. At dinner-time he does not appear, and in the afternoon at five o'clock, there is still no word of him. And when his mother goes to make inquiry, she finds he has not been at school all day. She becomes anxious about him, afraid lest he should have met with some accident, or have been led away by other wicked boys, or, it may be, even have run off to sea to be a sailor; and the neighbours are all astir, and they are fancying the worst, till at length, when it is just about time for going to bed, the runaway appears—wet, and cold, and dirty, and tired, and hungry. The first thing his mother says to him is, "Johnnie, where have you been? what has come over you? what have you been doing? *Give an account of yourself.*" You all know what she means when she says that. And there is another boy, who has gone to be apprentice to a grocer. His master is as kind to him as any master can be, for he is an orphan; and behaves to him like a father, and so he is grieved more than I can tell, to learn that his young apprentice is going far wrong. He is taking his master's money, and putting away his goods, and wasting his time whenever his back is turned, and taking up with bad company, and learning to drink, and to smoke, and going to the theatre, where Satan likes young people to go, because there they learn so much that is evil, and get so quickly ready for doing his work on earth, and going to be with him in hell. Well, there is nothing for it but he must turn him away in disgrace, and so he takes him into his little room, and sits down right opposite to him, and looking him full in the face, he says, "What is this you have been doing? *what account have you to give of yourself?*" You know what he means when he says that.

Well, just so is the day coming when God shall require account from his truant, wayward, disobedient children—his unfaithful, ungrateful servants. Few people think of that, whether children or men and women. They go on in their sin, and enjoy themselves the best way they can, and disobey God, and forget God, and serve the devil, as if they had nothing else to do, as if nothing else were expected of them,—as if there were no account to be rendered. Solomon seeing them in his day, just as now, living as if they were mere butterflies, as if they had no precious souls to be saved or lost, and no heaven or hell to look forward to, and no God to answer to, puts in the solemn warning, "But know thou, that for all these things God will bring thee into judgment." Yes, dear children, hear what God's word says, "It is appointed unto men once to die, but after this *the judgment!*" Have you ever thought of this "judgment," in which we shall have to give account of ourselves? It is an account of *ourselves* we have to give—not of other people, not of our neighbours, not of this or the other boy or girl, but each of himself and herself; and that is the most difficult account of all, the hardest, that which people like worst. It is an easy thing to give an account of others,—we are all ready enough to do that, whether young or old; we can tell what this one and the other one has done. But to give account *of one's self!* and to have no way of getting away from it!—that is the difficulty. I have two things to say about this account:—

1. It will be a FULL account; going back to infancy, and coming down to the day you die, with all that has been between—nothing awanting, nothing left out, nothing forgotten. Everything done in all your lifetime will be brought up, dragged out of its hiding-place; all the sins you ever committed, openly or secretly, in company or alone—*all;* every untrue, or unkind, or unholy word; every sinful, discontented, angry look; every wicked thought; every evil desire; every wrong action. Men only take notice of what we *do* amiss or *say* amiss, and only punish that; but in this account notice will be taken of what we *think* amiss or *feel* amiss, which man never knew, perhaps never suspected. Your *temper:* outbursts of passion or feelings of anger, sullenness, and obstinacy. Your *habits:* idleness, or dishonesty, taking little things that did not belong to you, which no one ever saw or knew of; or untruthfulness, telling "little" falsehoods, or *acting* them, pretending one thing when you knew it was another; or disobedience to parents and teachers; or Sabbath-breaking; or speaking bad words; or keeping bad company, associating with those who would lead you into sin—all will have to be told. The question will be asked, " How have you spent your *time*—at school and at home, at work and at play, on Sabbath and on week-day?" and you will have to account for every day and every hour. Take the last year with its eight thousand seven hundred and sixty hours, what have you made of them all—how were they occupied? And

then your *opportunities*, your *privileges*, your training at home, your Bible, your teaching in the church and Sabbath school, the good books you have had—to what purpose have you turned them? Many have never been taught as you have been ; many have never heard of Jesus or of salvation, of hell or of the way to heaven ; many little children have no Bibles, and could not read them if they had; many attend schools where they are taught only to steal, and to lie, and to say and do all bad things —what are *you* better than *they?* Yes ; you will have to give an account of the way in which you have used your Bible, and of every hour you have spent in the house of God, and of all the advantages you have had above others—and what sort of account will you have to give? And lest you should think it is only my word, I'll tell you what Christ himself, the great Judge, says regarding what gives us little concern—*words:* "But I say unto you, that every idle word that men shall speak, they shall give account thereof in the day of judgment." Oh, what an account! I could not count up the number of your sins :—

> " Than are the hairs upon mine head,
> They more in number be."

Have you ever tried to count them? We are told of a boy who was always doing wrong, to whom his father gave a hammer and a keg of nails, making him fasten a nail into a door, every time he did a wrong thing. You may suppose it was not long till the keg was empty, and the door was all studded over with nails. And it is just as if *for every sin, there were thus a nail*—so many that you could not count them up.

> "It passed away, it passed away,
> Thou canst not hear the sound to-day;
> 'Twas water lost upon the ground,
> Or wind that vanisheth in sound;
> Oh! who shall gather it, or tell
> How idly from the lip it fell?
>
> 'Tis written with an iron pen,
> And thou shalt hear it yet again!
> A solemn thing it thus shall seem
> To trifle with a holy theme.
> Oh! let our lightest accent be
> Uttered as for eternity."

2. It will be a TRUE account. There will be nothing false. If other people were to give account of us, they might be far enough from the truth; they might speak well of us, and tell this and the other good thing about us; and they might be quite sincere,—they know no better, they cannot see our motives, they cannot read our hearts, and so they are often mistaken in their opinion of us. But it is not the account, either good or bad, which other people give of us, of which the text speaks, but *our account of ourselves*. Others may be deceived or mistaken, but we know better; and there will be no hypocrites and no hypocrisy then. There will be honesty, truthfulness, straightforwardness—we will be compelled to speak the truth. And again I say, what an account!

Perhaps you say, you could not remember all

these things I have mentioned, however anxious you might be to do it—that it would be an impossibility. Yes, you will remember them; they will all be brought to your mind. You have often spoken unkindly and acted rudely to your mother, and your harsh words and actions passed away from your mind with the day that saw them; perhaps they have been repeated often since, and you thought little of the sorrow you caused to that mother's loving heart,—you never took any notice of the sigh that once and again escaped from her, or of the tear that trickled down her cheek, and you little thought of the anguish that filled her soul, which you might have read, if you would, upon her face. But your mother dies, and when you stand beside the lifeless body, and take her cold hand in yours, or when you stand beside her grave, and come back to a motherless home,—oh, how you then remember all you had forgotten! the past all comes back; your looks, and words, and tones, everything as fresh and vivid as yesterday; and what seemed to have passed clean away from your mind, seems now as if it had been burnt into your heart, and would leave a mark never to be wiped out. I say, you see in that, how things long-forgotten may come again to mind, and so it will be then.

And there is a thing within us called *Conscience*, that tells us when we do wrong, and warns us against it, and makes us uncomfortable and unhappy after it. But it does more: it not only *speaks*, it also *remembers;*

it not only warns, it also keeps account when the warning is disregarded. Conscience has a *pen* as well as a *tongue*, and it writes down after it has spoken. Yes, dear children, that pen outruns the quickest writer among you; and its writing is not like that of some of you, difficult to read, so that when you meet with it afterwards you can hardly make it out. It is plain and in large hand, so that any one can read it,—ay, even those who have never been at school, and never knew the alphabet, and could never sign their own name—they'll all be able to read *that writing* THEN. Oh, take care what work you give conscience to do, take care what you make it write!* It is your *clerk, and keeps correct accounts*; and you cannot wash out its writing. Sometimes the writing of conscience has to be read, ay, *read aloud*, even in this world. There, for instance, is a murderer. No eye saw him commit the crime: it was in the dark, he was alone. Nobody suspects him, he is far from the place, and seems likely to carry the secret to his grave. But no. Conscience told him it was wrong at the time; he argued with conscience, he brought forward many reasons,—he wanted to get money, or he had been ill-used and would be revenged; and he did it; and conscience wrote it down, and has held up the writing before him ever since, so that he can-

---

* We are told of a good bishop of the Church of England, when on trial before his blood-thirsty enemies for faithfully preaching the gospel of Christ, that "when he heard the pen going behind the hangings, he was careful in his answers." Remember "*the pen going behind the hangings*," and take care!

not forget it, cannot get it out of his mind, cannot get it out of his sight even in his sleep,—he dreams about it, he can get no rest, and at last he has to become his own accuser, and tells it all, and "gives account of himself" even to men, and in this world. "Be sure," says Scripture, "your sin will find you out."

You would wonder how fresh one's memory sometimes becomes, when danger is near—when a thunderstorm comes on, and all is dark and judgment-looking —when death lays hold on those beside us—when it comes near to ourselves. People who have been shipwrecked, and had no prospect but that of finding a grave amid the roaring waters, tell us, that at that moment, when death appeared near and certain, their whole life seemed to pass in an instant before them,— all their past sins came up and stood like an army in their presence. It was just as if they had got a strange kind of telescope, that looked back to their very infancy, and showed them at one view all that they had been and all that they had done. And then, they tell us, they could understand how men should be able to give the account, of which our text speaks.

Question II. To whom is the account to be given?

Answer. To God. I said it would have to be a full and true account; and if you ask further, Why? I say, Because it is *to God*, who sees everything—who hears everything—who remembers everything—who keeps account of everything. There will not be any need of witnesses to prove our sin; as I have said already, we shall give account *of ourselves*. And then it is *to God*, who saw it all—who was present—whose eye was on it—who has it written down in *his* book; for he keeps a book as well as conscience: and when the books shall be opened by him as he sits on the great white throne, and you give your account of yourselves, the two books will be found to correspond. Hence we read, "And I saw a great white throne, and him that sat on it, from whose face the earth and the heaven fled away; and there was found no place for them. And I saw the dead, small and great, stand before God: and THE BOOKS WERE OPENED; and another book was opened, which is the book of life: and the dead were judged out of those things which were written in the books, *according to their works.*" Sometimes people give in false accounts of themselves and of what was intrusted to them, and they are not detected. But no servant would do this, if he believed that his master knew it all himself. One Sabbath afternoon, I heard a little boy speaking some terrible words through the keyhole of a door where an infant Sabbath-class was met; and when I went to see who it was, and laid hold of the boy in the very act, he took guilt to himself—he did not deny it—he did not attempt to hide it, for he saw that I knew it. And so it is with God. He knows it all. He can see through stone walls, and iron doors, and the darkness of night. And he can hear *whispers*,

—ay, even *thoughts*. His eyes are as a flame of fire, and they are in every place. We are told by some, that, when in prison, they were watched by the keeper's eye night and day; do what they would, go where they would, they could never get out of its reach. There was a little opening, and the only living, moving thing about them, was the eye at that opening. It was never off them for a moment—when they ate, when they slept, when they awoke. Oh, that terrible eye! So, "thou God seest me,"—always, everywhere. There are many people in the world, but God sees them all, and knows them all, just as well as if there had been only *one;* and so each will have to give account of himself to God, as particularly as if there had been only one man in all the world. There can be no deceiving, for remember the prophet and his servant: "Gehazi, whence camest thou? Thy servant went no whither. *Went not mine eye with thee?*" So was it with Adam: "Adam, where art thou? Hast thou eaten of the tree whereof I commanded thee that thou shouldest not eat? And the Lord God said unto the woman, What is this that thou hast done?" They had to give account—to God.

I said God has *his* book of remembrance, and conscience has *its* book—ay, and Satan has *his* book too. He remembers too; he keeps account too. There was a trial the other day in which there were two guilty parties; one of them turned the accuser, or "Queen's evidence," as it is called, and the other, on that evidence, was condemned. So Satan, though he now tempts to sin, will keep it in mind, and then accuse the sinner. Hence he is called "the accuser of the brethren." Oh, what a thought it is, that so many and such strict accounts are kept of our sin, by those who know best about it!

There is a custom becoming very common now in this country. When a man or a boy does a wrong thing, and runs away—flees from justice, the officers of justice get his photograph—his likeness as taken by the sun, and, therefore, taken correctly, for the sun is an honest painter and good—just like those portraits you see in the shop windows wherever you go. Well, they send these to all parts of the country; the police are furnished with them, and, when the criminal is taken, he may deny the thing—he may have changed his name, and say he is some other person—but the likeness is brought out, and the faces correspond; doubt about the man there can be none. And just so, my young friends, is it with you. It is as if a picture were taken, of every act you do,—the very acts you commit in secret, and under the cover of night. It is as if all these pictures were hung up on the wall,—exactly what occurred each day and each night. *There* are the proofs of your guilt; they cannot be denied. There is thus a pictorial history, if I may so call it, of every one of us, true to the life. And so it has been said, "*Every day we live, our likeness is being taken for eternity.*" Oh, when tempted to sin, remember this, that it will appear, just as it occurred, on the great day of account!

> " Then shall the soul around it call
> Impressions which it gathered here;
> And, pictured on the eternal wall,
> THE PAST SHALL RE-APPEAR."

There is yet another thought connected with this second question. What a word that is,—" Shall give account of himself TO GOD!" A member of my class, now no longer within reach, so that I need not hesitate to tell it, once went home on a Sabbath evening late, and told her mistress she had been at my class, and that that was what had kept her so long, when I had not had a class that evening at all. Her mistress said she did not believe it, and that she would ask me. The girl pled with her not to do it, and has kept out of my way ever since;—she could not bear to give an account of herself to *me*. I knew a boy, who, having gone into a river to which he had been forbidden to go, was carried beyond his depth; and, when taken out half-drowned, the first words he spoke after he came to himself were, "Don't tell my mother!" He was afraid to give account of himself *to his mother.* Ah, but this is TO GOD! What shall we say of *that?* If one so shrinks back before a mother or a minister, frail and sinning as themselves, what must it be to appear before the great, wise, holy God, and give account to *him?* Ay, and it will be *before all the world* as well! When we have anything wrong to confess, we like everybody to be out of the way; we look carefully round to see that the door is shut, and then we whisper it into the ear, as if afraid of being overheard What would you think of having to give account of yourself before a large congregation? Would it not make you tremble? And the whole world will be present, when this account of yourself shall be given to God. "For there is nothing covered that shall not be revealed, neither hid that shall not be known." "Until the Lord come, who both will bring to light the hidden things of darkness, and will make manifest the counsels of the hearts." And if it be asked, "Why should God require account of us at all, if he knows everything already?"—the answer is, "Out of thine own mouth will I condemn thee, thou wicked servant." He will thus have the sinner's guilt established on his own showing, and will set forth his justice before all.

Question III. WHO ARE TO GIVE THIS ACCOUNT?
Answer. EVERY ONE OF US. There is no exception. Whatever our age, whatever our rank or condition, in all our relations in life, as parent or child, servant or master, minister or people—"every one of us." "But surely," you say, "very young people will be left out —passed over; young people like us." I know you would not like to be passed over as regards *some* accounts. I know many of you have your account at the Savings' Bank, some of the youngest of you; you are not too young for *that*. And so the very youngest

has his account with God, and the day is coming when the accounts will all be summed up, and given in by "every one of us."

"Every one of us!" Oh, what a gathering there will be! You have seen great crowds sometimes: when our beloved Queen pays a visit to our town; or when a fire breaks out; or when,—as at the close of the Russian war,— peace is proclaimed, and fireworks, on a large scale, are exhibited; or at a Review of the Rifle Volunteers,—what crowds of men, and women, and children there are! But none of all these crowds can be compared with the gathering that shall be then;—all who have ever been in the world, all who lived before the flood, and all who were drowned in the flood, and all who have been since; all who are in the world now, and all who shall ever be in it. The dead committed to the grave, and the dead buried in the sea, and the dead devoured by beasts and birds of prey, and the dead consumed in the fire, and the dead unburied, whose bones withered in the sunshine,—all will be present, and all will give in their account. And there will be children of all ages, and from all lands,— from India, and China, and Africa,—from Scotland, and England, and Ireland,—from our own town or village— ay, from our own church and Sabbath-school; every one who reads this sermon, from the youngest boy or girl up to the eldest,—"*every one of us,*" shall give an account of himself to God! "We must *all* appear before the judgment-seat of Christ." Dear children! are you getting ready? Are you making preparation? Do you ever think of your account? do you ever look at it? When you are sinning, when you are tempted to sin, when you are idling away your time, when you are wasting your opportunities—does *your account* ever come into your mind? When you hear of so many little children dying close beside you, body and soul parting from each other, and no more heard of in the world; when you look at their little graves and find them as little as yours would be,—does it ever come into your mind? When you hear or read of others like yourselves rejoicing, even amid suffering and death, as having found a Saviour to take their sins away and make them friends with God, so that they can die, not only without fear, but joyful, in prospect of the white robe, and the golden harp, and the crown of glory,—does it ever come into your mind? Have you ever handed over your account to Jesus?

When a man is at court, charged with committing some crime, he gets an advocate to plead his cause,—either to show that he is not guilty, or to make some excuse for him, or to appeal to the judges for mercy. And so we need an advocate at the court of heaven, not to prove our innocence, not to make excuses for us, but to plead for mercy, *because of what he Himself has done.* And those who have fled to Jesus as their refuge, and laid hold on him as their Saviour, can say, "We have an advocate with the Father, Jesus Christ the righteous." But many among us have no such advocate,—they will not have him. They have none to plead for *them*, none to ask mercy for them, none to say a word on their behalf; and then, when the time for giving in the account comes, it will be too late—then there will be no mercy, no pardon, no escape, and none to ask it; for the Advocate shall then have become the Judge! Let me tell you a dream which a godly man had. The scene was the final judgment: before him was the judgment-seat; around him were his young, gay, thoughtless companions. He was summoned to stand before the Judge: question after question was put to him; *he* answered not, but there was One who answered for him, and he was at length joyfully dismissed. Then came others of his acquaintance: the same questions were put to them; they too answered not, but there was no one to answer for them. There was *silence*—intense, solemn stillness, but they looked in vain for one to speak a word on their behalf, and they were driven in wrath from the presence of the Judge. Oh, dear children! will you be of the number of those, who shall thus be condemned and sent away into everlasting punishment? Will you not rather take Jesus as your advocate now, and be reconciled to God through him?

It is a dreadful thing to think of *living* with such a load of sin to account for: it is a more dreadful thing to think of *dying* with it. How can you be happy in such a case—how can you live happily, committing sin every day—sin still unforgiven? How can you expect to die happily, while this text stands written in the Bible, "Every one of us," &c. Can you lay down this book as you took it up—careless? Can you go to rest this night again, unpardoned—what if you should never awake? Will you not go straightway and offer up the prayer, "Lord, have mercy upon me, and take away my sins, for Jesus' sake?" You know there are some substances that take out marks made by ink: nothing in all the world but one can take out the marks of sin. Who can tell me what it is? THE BLOOD OF CHRIST. Who can give me the text that says it? "The blood of Jesus Christ, God's son, cleanseth us from all sin." The dying time is coming, will you not get ready for it? will you not be like that young Hindoo, just about to die, saying, "Sing, brother, sing?" "What shall I sing?" "Sing of salvation through the blood of Jesus. Sing, thanks be to Him who giveth us the victory through the blood of Jesus;" and then he sinks back and dies.

And now our parting word must be a word of love. I would like to leave you with this, as the word that should leave its echo behind, when we have parted company—THE LOVE OF JESUS! Oh, what love was his! I have read of a mother who was travelling on a cold wintry night, with an infant in her arms, being overtaken by a snow-storm. When morning came that mother was found *alone*,—cold, and stiff, and dead. Search was made for her child, and at length he was discovered under a ledge of rock hard by, alive and well. The story was soon told. Unable to proceed further, the drifting snow bewildering her, and her limbs benumbed and losing their power, she would yet, even though she should perish, save the life of her little one. She stripped herself of her warm clothing and wrapped it round her boy; and, having left him in what seemed a place of safety, she lay down herself and died. Such was the love of a mother! "Greater love hath no man than this, that a man lay down his life for his friends ; but God commendeth his love toward us, in that while we were yet *sinners*, Christ died for us." Christ gave himself for you to save you from coming wrath ; will you not be saved by him ? will you not take hold of his hand ? Will you not give up your hearts to him who is so worthy of them, and who alone is worthy ? And then with Paul you may sing :—

"I know that safe with him remains,
Protected by his power,
What I've committed to his trust,
Till the decisive hour.

Then will he own his servant's name
Before his Father's face,
And in the New Jerusalem
Appoint my soul a place."

Let me set alongside of the "*every one*" of our text, another "*every one*." "Then Peter said unto them, Repent and be baptized, EVERY ONE OF YOU, in the name of Jesus Christ, for the remission of sins, and ye shall receive the gift of the Holy Ghost. For the promise is unto you and to your children, and to all that are afar off, even as many as the Lord our God shall call."

"Teach me to live that I may dread
The grave as little as my bed ;
Teach me to die that so I may
Rise glorious on the judgment day !"

THE HYMN.

JESUS! thy blood and righteousness
 My beauty are, my glorious dress:
'Midst flaming worlds, in these arrayed,
With joy shall I lift up my head.

Bold shall I stand in that great day;
For who aught to my charge shall lay?
Fully absolved through these I am,
From sin, and fear, and guilt, and shame.

When from the dust of death I rise
To claim my mansion in the skies,
Ev'n then shall this be all my plea,—
"Jesus hath lived and died for me!"

This spotless robe the same appears,
When ruined nature sinks in years;
No age can change its glorious hue,—
The robe of Christ is ever new.

Oh, let the dead now hear thy voice;
Now bid thy banished ones rejoice;
Their beauty this, their glorious dress,
Jesus! thy blood and righteousness!

HYMNS AND MELODIES

FOR THE YOUNG.

(*Copyright.*)

HYMNS AND MELODIES

FOR THE YOUNG.

1.—I want to be like Jesus.

2.
I want to be like Jesus,—
  So frequently in prayer;
Alone upon the mountain-top,
  He met his Father there.

3.
I want to be like Jesus,—
  I never, never find
That he, though persecuted, was
  To any one unkind.

4.
I want to be like Jesus,—
  Engaged in doing good;
So that of me it may be said,
  "She hath done what she could."

5.
Alas! I'm not like Jesus,
  As any one may see:
O gentle Saviour, send thy grace
  And make me like to thee!

FAR, FAR AWAY—continued.

2.
There never trembles a sigh of regret,
 Far, far away; far, far away;
Stars of the morning in glory ne'er set,
 Far, far away; far away.
There I from sorrow for ever would rest,
Leaning with joy on Emmanuel's breast;
Tears never fall in the homes of the blest,
 Far, far away; far away.

3.
Friends there united in glory ne'er part,
 Far, far away; far, far away:
One is their temple, their home, and their heart,
 Far, far away; far away.
The river of crystal, the city of gold,
The portals of pearls such glory unfold,
Thought cannot image, and tongue hath not told,
 Far, far away; far away.

4.
List what yon harpers on golden harps play!
 Come, come away; come, come away:
Falling and frail is your cottage of clay,
 Come, come away; come away.
Come to these mansions, there's room yet for you;
Dwell with the Friend ever faithful and true;
Sing ye the song, ever old, ever new;
 Come, come away; come away.

♩ = 66.

3.—Mothers of Salem.

:s | d¹ :t .l | s :s .s | l .s :l .t | d¹ :s .s
When mo-thers of Sa-lem their chil-dren brought to Je-sus, The

:m | m :s .f | m :m .m | f .m :f .r | m :m .m

| l .s :f .m | l .s :f .m | r.s :s .,s | s : .s
stern dis - ci - ples drove them back, And bade them de-part. But

| f .m :r .d | f .m :r .d | t₁.m :r.,d | t₁ : .t₁

| m .s :s .s | l .s :s .s | m .s :s .s | l .s :s
Je - sus saw them ere they fled, And sweet-ly smil-ing, kind-ly said—

| d .m :m .m | f .m :m .m | d .m :m .m | f .m :m

| d¹ :r¹ .d¹ | m¹ :d¹ .d¹ | r¹ .d¹ :t .s | d¹ ||
"Suf - fer the chil - dren to come un - to me."

| m :f .m | s :m .m | f .m :r .f | m ||

MOTHERS OF SALEM—continued.

2.
"For I will receive them, and fold them to my bosom;
I'll be a Shepherd to these lambs: oh, drive them not away;
For if their hearts to me they give,
They shall with me in glory live,—
Suffer the children to come unto me."

3.
How kind was our Saviour to bid these children welcome!
But there are many thousands who have never heard his name;
The Bible they have never read,
They know not that the Saviour said,
"Suffer the children to come unto me."

4.
And oh! how we pity those poor deluded creatures
Who worship gods of wood and stone, which they themselves have made:
Dear Saviour, hear us when we pray
That they may hear thee to them say,
"Suffer the children to come unto me."

5.
And soon may the heathen of every tribe and nation
Fulfil thy blessed word, and cast their idols all away.
Oh, shine upon them from above,
And show thyself a God of love.
Teach them, dear Saviour, to come unto [thee.

4.—Little Things.

2.
Thus the little minutes,
Humble though they be,
Make the mighty ages
Of Eternity.

3.
Thus our little errors
Lead the soul away
From the path of virtue,
Off in sin to stray.

4.
Little deeds of kindness,
Little words of love,
Make our earth an Eden.
Like the heaven above.

2.
Not the labour of my hands
Can fulfil thy law's demands:
Could my zeal no respite know,
Could my tears for ever flow,
All for sin could not atone;—
Thou must save, and thou alone.

3.
Nothing in my hand I bring,
Simply to thy Cross I cling;
Naked, come to thee for dress;
Helpless, look to thee for grace;
Vile—I to the fountain fly;—
Wash me, Saviour, or I die!

4.
While I draw this fleeting breath,
When my eyes are closed in death,
When I soar to worlds unknown,
See thee on thy judgment throne,—
Rock of Ages, cleft for me,
Let me hide myself in thee.

6.—Luther's Hymn.

2.
The dead in Christ shall first arise,
  At the last trumpet's sounding,
Caught up to meet him in the skies,
  With joy their Lord surrounding.
No gloomy fears their souls dismay;
His presence sheds eternal day
  On those prepared to meet him.

3.
Great God, what do I see and hear?
  The end of things created!
The Judge of mankind doth appear,
  On clouds of glory seated.
Beneath his cross I view the day
When heaven and earth shall pass away,
  And thus prepare to meet him.

2.
He is fitting up my mansion,
  Which eternally shall stand;
My stay shall not be transient
  In that holy, happy land.
    On the other side of Jordan, &c.

3.
Pain or sickness ne'er can enter;
  Grief nor woe my lot shall share;
But in that celestial centre
  I a crown of life shall wear.
    On the other side of Jordan, &c.

4.
Death itself shall then be vanquish'd,
  And its sting shall be withdrawn,—
Shout with gladness, O ye ransomed!
  Hail with joy the happy morn.
    On the other side of Jordan, &c.

5.
Sing, O sing, ye heirs of glory,
  Shout your triumphs as you go!
Zion's gates will open to you,
  You shall find an entrance through.
    On the other side of Jordan, &c.

8.—Prayer to the Holy Spirit.

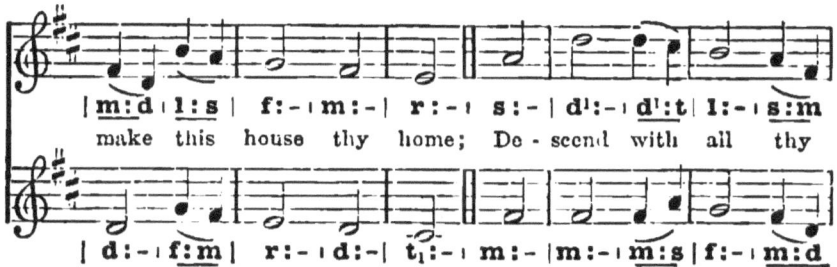

Spirit divine! attend our pray'r, And make this house thy home; Descend with all thy gracious pow'r,— O come, Great Spirit, come!

2.
Come as the LIGHT—to us reveal
 Our emptiness and woe;
And lead us in those paths of life
 Where all the righteous go.

3.
Come as the FIRE—and purge our hearts
 Like sacrificial flame;
Let our whole souls an off'ring be
 To our Redeemer's name.

4.
Come as the DEW—and sweetly bless
 This consecrated hour;
May barren minds be taught to own
 Thy fertilizing power.

5.
Come as the DOVE—and spread thy wings,
 The wings of peaceful love;
And let the Church on earth become
 Blest as the Church above.

♩ = 84.

9.—Not lost, but gone before.

```
:s  | s :m :f | s :- :d¹ | r¹:d¹ :t  | d¹:- :s
Say,  why should friend-ship  grieve   for those Who

:m  | m :d :r | m :- :m | f :m  :r  | m :- :m
```

```
| l :d¹ :l | s :- :m | s :f :m | r :-
  safe  ar-rive  ou  Ca - naan's shore?

| f :l :f | m :- :d | m :r :d | t₁:-
```

```
:s  | r¹:- :t | d¹:- :s | m¹:r¹:d¹ | d¹:t :t
Re-leased from  all   their  hurt-ful  foes, They

:m  | f :- :s | m :- :m | s :f :m | m :r :r
```

```
| d¹:t :l | s :- :m | l :s :f | m :- :m | r :- :r | d :- ‖
  are  not lost, They are not lost, but gone be-fore.

| m :s :f | m :- :d | f :m :r | d :- :d | t₁:- :t₁| d :- ‖
```

NOT LOST, BUT GONE BEFORE—continued.

2.
How many painful days on earth
 Their fainting spirits number'd o'er!
Now they enjoy a heav'nly birth,
 They are not lost—but gone before.

3.
Dear is the spot where Christians sleep,
 And sweet the strains which angels pour;
O why should we in anguish weep?
 They are not lost—but gone before.

4.
Secure from ev'ry mortal care,
By sin and sorrow vex'd no more,
Eternal happiness they share,
 Who are not lost—but gone before.

5.
To Zion's peaceful courts above,
 In faith triumphant may we soar,
Embracing in the arms of love
 The friends not lost—but gone before.

6.
On Jordan's banks whene'er we come,
 And hear the swelling waters roar,
Jesus, convey us safely home
 To friends not lost—but gone before.

10.—"My all in all."

I am a poor sinner and nothing at all;
Jesus Christ is my all in all. Jesus Christ,
Jesus Christ, Jesus Christ is my all in all.

♩=84.   11.—Return, O Holy Dove.   H.

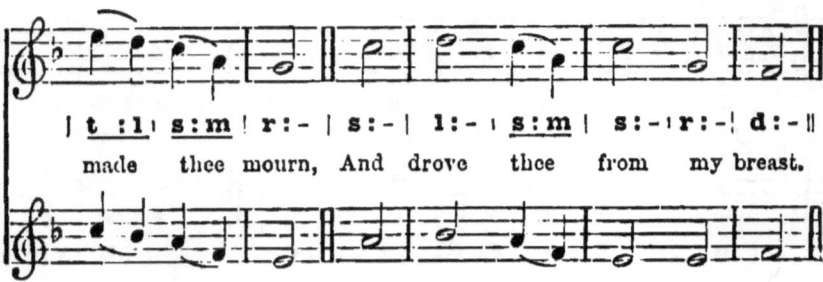

2.
The dearest idol I have known,
Whate'er that idol be,
Help me to tear it from thy throne,
And worship only thee.

3.
So shall my walk be close with God,
Calm and serene my frame;
So purer light shall mark the road
That leads me to the Lamb.

12.—Return, O Wanderer.

2.
Return, O wand'rer, to thy home,
  'Tis Jesus calls for thee!
The Spirit and the Bride say, Come!
  O now for refuge flee.
          Return! return!

3.
Return, O wand'rer, to thy home,
  'Tis madness to delay;
There are no pardons in the tomb,
  And brief is mercy's day.
          Return! return!

2.
Bold shall I stand in that great day;
For who aught to my charge shall lay?
Fully absolved through these I am,
From sin and fear, and guilt and shame.

3.
When from the dust of death I rise,
To claim my mansion in the skies,
Ev'n then shall this be all my plea,—
"Jesus hath lived and died for me!"

4.
This spotless robe the same appears,
When ruin'd nature sinks in years;
No age can change its glorious hue,—
The robe of Christ is ever new.

5.
Oh, let the dead now hear thy voice;
Now bid thy banish'd ones rejoice;
Their beauty this, their glorious dress,
Jesus! thy blood and righteousness!

14.—The All-Seeing God.

To be sung to the Music on opposite page.

1.
Among the deepest shades of night,
　Can there be one who sees my way?
Yes; God is like a shining light,
　That turns the darkness into day.

2.
When ev'ry eye around me sleeps,
　May I not sin without control?
No; for a constant watch he keeps
　On ev'ry thought of ev'ry soul.

3.
If I could find some cave unknown,
　Where human foot had never trod,
Yet there I could not be alone,—
　On ev'ry side there would be God.

4.
He smiles in heav'n, he frowns in hell;
　He fills the air, the earth, the sea;
I must within his presence dwell,—
　I cannot from his anger flee.

5.
Yes! I may flee—he shows me where;
　Tells me to Jesus Christ to fly:
And when he sees me weeping there,
　There's mercy beaming in his eye.

15.—Lost, but Found.

I was a wand'ring sheep, I did not love the fold; I did not love the Shep-herd's voice, I

2.
The Shepherd sought his sheep,
  The Father sought his child;
They follow'd me o'er vale and hill,
  O'er deserts waste and wild.
They found me nigh to death,
  Famish'd, and faint, and lone;
They bound me with the bands of love,—
  They saved the wand'ring one!

3.
They spoke in tender love,
  They raised my drooping head;
They gently closed my bleeding wounds,
  My fainting soul they fed.
They wash'd my filth away,
  They made me clean and fair;
They brought me to my home in peace—
  The long sought wanderer!

4.
Jesus my Shepherd is,—
  'Twas he that loved my soul;
'Twas he that wash'd me in his blood,
  'Twas he that made me whole.
'Twas he that sought the lost,
  That found the wand'ring sheep,
'Twas he that brought me to the fold,—
  'Tis he that still doth keep.

5.
I was a wand'ring sheep,
  I would not be controll'd;
But now I love my Shepherd's voice,—
  I love, I love the fold!
I was a wayward child,
  I once preferr'd to roam;
But now I love my Father's voice,—
  I love, I love his home!

♩=84. 16.—Delight in the Scriptures.

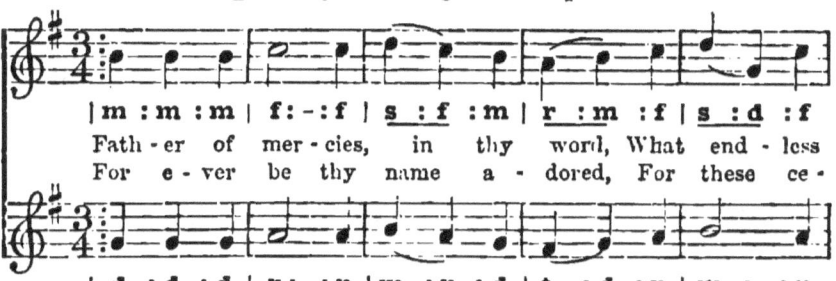

3.
O may these heavenly pages be
My ever dear delight;
And still new beauties may I see,
And still increasing light!

4.
Divine Instructor, gracious Lord,
Be thou for ever near;
Teach me to love thy sacred word,
And view my Saviour there.

17.—Jesus is mine.*

J. H. Dürrner.

* This piece, with pianoforte accompaniment, can be had of Messrs. Wood and Co., Edinburgh, by whose permission it is here inserted.

JESUS IS MINE—continued.

2.
Tempt not my soul away,
    Jesus is mine!
Here would I ever stay,
    Jesus is mine!
Perishing things of clay,
Born but for one brief day,
Pass from my heart away,
    Jesus is mine!

3.
Fare ye well, dreams of night,
    Jesus is mine!
Mine is a dawning bright,
    Jesus is mine!
All that my soul has tried
Left but a dismal void,
Jesus has satisfied,
    Jesus is mine

4.
Farewell, mortality,
    Jesus is mine!
Welcome, eternity,
    Jesus is mine!
Welcome, ye scenes of rest,
Welcome, ye mansions blest,
Welcome a Saviour's breast,
    Jesus is mine!

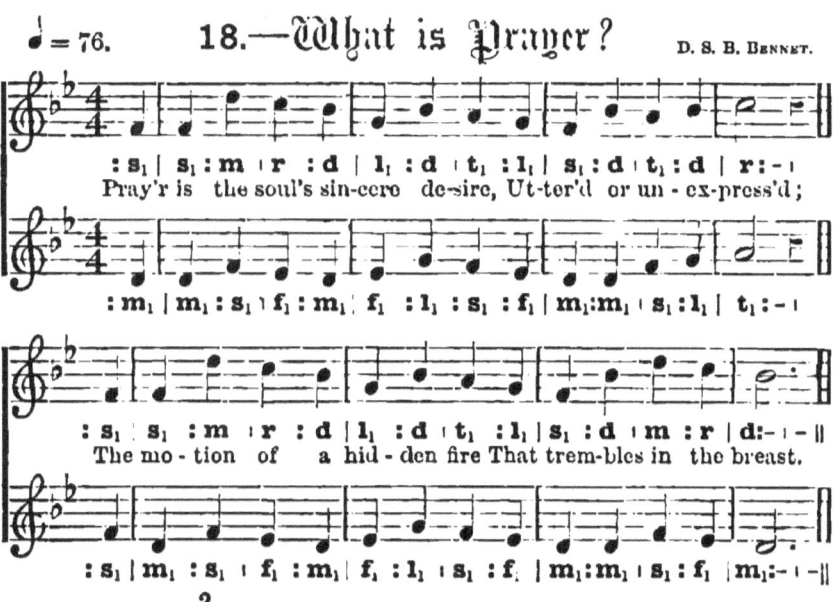

18.—What is Prayer?

D. S. B. Bennet.

Pray'r is the soul's sincere desire, Utter'd or unexpress'd;
The motion of a hidden fire That trembles in the breast.

2.
Pray'r is the burden of a sigh,
  The falling of a tear;
The upward glancing of an eye,
  When none but God is near.

3.
Pray'r is the simplest form of speech
  That infant lips can try;
Pray'r, the sublimest strains that reach
  The Majesty on high.

4.
Pray'r is the contrite sinner's voice,
  Returning from his ways;
While angels in their songs rejoice,
  And cry, "Behold, he prays!"

5.
Pray'r is the Christian's vital breath,
  The Christian's native air;
His watch-word at the gates of death,—
  He enters heaven with prayer.

6.
O Thou, by whom we come to God,
  The Life, the Truth, the Way!
The path of prayer Thyself hast trod;
  Lord, teach us how to pray!

♩= 72.   19.—Sun of my Soul.

```
: l₁   | s₁ ., s₁ : s₁ : d  | t₁ ., l₁ : l₁ : l₁
  Sun    of    my  soul, thou Sav-iour dear,  It
: f₁   | m₁ ., m₁ : m₁ : m₁ | s₁ ., f₁ : f₁ : f₁

| f ., r : d : t₁ | r ., d : d : l₁ | s₁ ., s₁ : s₁ : d
  is   not night if  thou  be near; O  may  no earth-born
| l₁ ., f₁ : m₁ : s₁ | f₁ ., m₁ : m₁ : f₁ | m₁ ., m₁ : m₁ : m₁

| t₁ ., l₁ : l₁ : l₁ | f ., r : d : t₁
  cloud  a - rise  To  hide  thee from thy
| s₁ ., f₁ : f₁ : f₁ | l₁ ., f₁ : m₁ : s₁

| r ., d : d : s₁ | d ., m : s : m
  ser-vant's eyes!  A-bide with me from
| f₁ ., m₁ : m₁ : s₁ | d ., d : m : d
```

SUN OF MY SOUL—continued.

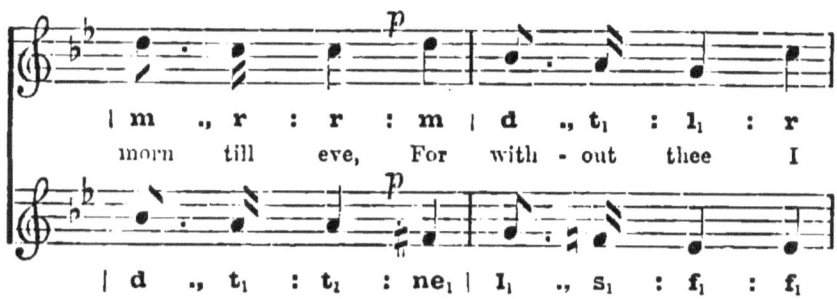

2.
When the soft dews of kindly sleep
My wearied eyelids gently steep,
Be my last thought—how sweet to rest
For ever on my Saviour's breast.
Thou Framer of the light and dark,
Steer through the tempest thine own ark;
Amid the howling wintry sea,
We are in port if we have thee.

3.
Watch by the sick: enrich the poor
With blessings from thy boundless store:
Be every mourner's sleep to-night
Like infant's slumbers, pure and light.
Come near and bless us when we wake,
Ere through the world our way we take;
Till, in the ocean of thy love,
We lose ourselves in heaven above.

♩ = 63. **20.—My times are in thy hand.**

Fa-ther, I know that all my life Is por-tion'd out by thee, And the chang-es that will sure-ly come, I do not fear to see; But I ask thee for a pre-sent mind In-

MY TIMES ARE IN THY HAND—continued.

2.
I ask thee for a thoughtful love,
Through constant watching wise,
To meet the glad with joyful smiles,
And to wipe the weeping eyes;
And a heart at leisure from itself
To soothe and sympathize.

3.
  would not have the restless will
That hurries to and fro,
Seeking for some great thing to do
Or secret thing to know;
I would be treated as a child,
And guided where I go.

4.
Wherever in this world I am,
In whatsoe'er estate,
I have a fellowship with hearts
To keep and cultivate;
And a work of lowly love to do
For the Lord, on whom I wait.

5.
So I ask thee for the daily strength,
To none that ask denied,
And a mind to blend with outward life,
While keeping at thy side;
Content to fill a little space,
If thou be glorified.

6.
And if some things I do not ask
In my cup of blessing be,
I would have my spirit filled the more
With grateful love to thee;
And careful—less to serve thee *much*
Than please thee *perfectly.*

7.
There are briers besetting every path,
That call for patient care;
There is a cross in every lot,
And an earnest need of prayer;
But a lowly heart that leans on thee
Is happy anywhere.

8.
In a service that thy love appoints
There are no bonds for me,
For my secret heart is taught the truth
That makes thy people free,
And a life of self-renouncing love
Is a life of liberty.

♩ = 80.

21.—Holy Bible!

2.
Mine, to chide me when I rove;
Mine, to show a Saviour's love;
Mine art thou, to guide my feet;
Mine, to judge, condemn, acquit;
　　Holy Bible, &c.

3.
Mine, to comfort in distress,
If the Holy Spirit bless;

Mine, to show, by living faith,
How to triumph over death;
　　Holy Bible, &c.

4.
Mine, to tell of joys to come,
And the rebel sinner's doom:
O, thou precious book divine!
Precious treasure, thou art mine!
　　Holy Bible, &c.

♩ = 68. **22.—The Bible the Light of the World.**

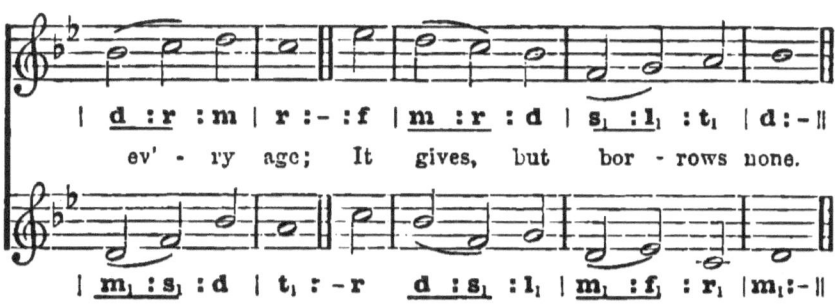

2.
The Spirit breathes upon the word,
And brings the truth to sight:
Precepts and promises afford
A sanctifying light.

3.
Let everlasting thanks be thine
For such a bright display,
As makes a world of darkness shine
With beams of heavenly day.

NEW YEAR'S HYMN—continued.

hid from view, With-in the si-lent grave.

Ah! not a few who seem'd life's toil to brave, Are

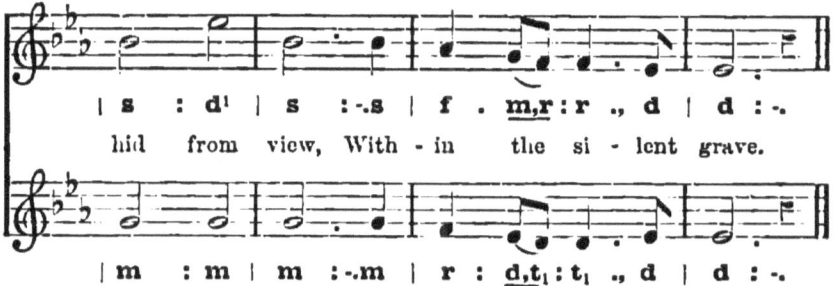

hid from view, With-in the si-lent grave.

2.
Why am I spared
  To see another year?
Why have I shared
  So many mercies here?
From God alone
  My mercies I receive;
To him alone
  I would for ever live.

3.
Then aid my tongue,
  Companions on the road,
To raise a song
  Of gratitude to God.
Hallelujah!
  Let *all* their voices raise;
Hallelujah!
  To God be all the praise.

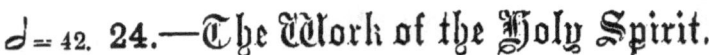

24.—The Work of the Holy Spirit.

2.
Convince us of our sin;
Then lead to Jesus' blood;
And to our wond'ring view reveal
The secret love of God.

3.
Revive our drooping faith;
Our doubts and fears remove;
And kindle in our breasts the flame
Of never-dying love.

4.
'Tis thine to cleanse the heart,
To sanctify the soul,
To pour fresh life in ev'ry part,
And new-create the whole.

5.
Dwell, Spirit, in our hearts;
Our minds from bondage free;—
Then shall we know, and praise, and love
The Father, Son, and Thee.

25.—The Worth of Prayer.

♩ = 66.

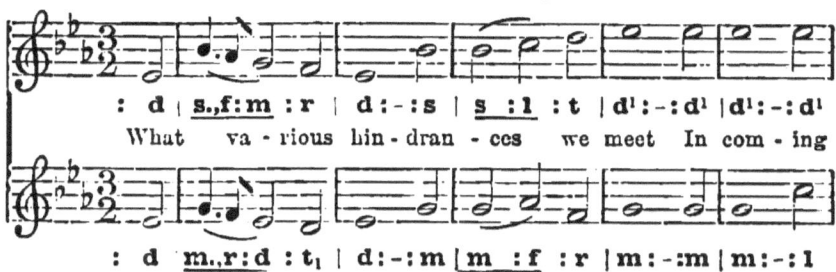

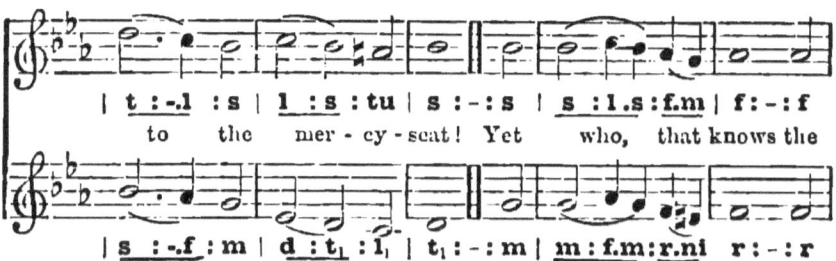

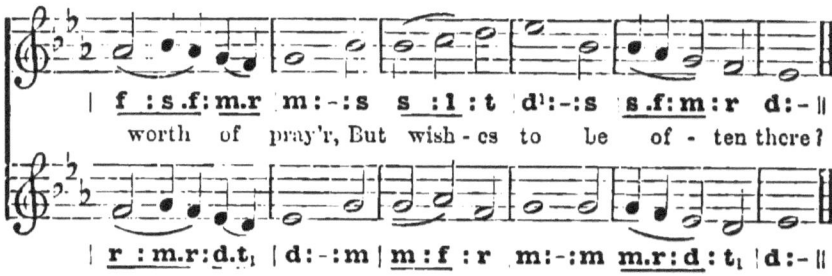

2.
Pray'r makes the darken'd cloud with-
Pray'r climbs the ladder Jacob saw, [draw;
Gives exercise to faith and love,—
Brings ev'ry blessing from above

3.
Restraining pray'r, we cease to fight;
Pray'r makes the Christian's armour
And Satan trembles when he sees [bright;
The weakest saint upon his knees.

4.
Have you no words? ah! think again;
Words flow apace when we complain,
And fill our fellow-creature's ear
With the sad tale of all our care.

5.
Were half the breath thus vainly spent,
To heav'n in supplication sent,
Our cheerful song would oft'ner be,
" Hear what the Lord has done for me! "

2.
If thou should'st call me to resign
What most I prize,—it ne'er was mine;
I only yield thee what was thine,—
　　"Thy will be done!"

3.
Though dark my path and sad my lot,
Let me be still and murmur not, [taught—
But breathe the pray'r Thyself hast
　　"Thy will be done!"

4.
What though in lonely grief I sigh
For friends beloved, no longer nigh;
Submissive still I would reply—
　　"Thy will be done!"

5.
Should pining sickness waste away
My life in premature decay,
"My Father," still I'll strive to say,—
　　"Thy will be done!"

6.
Renew my will from day to day,
Blend it with thine, and take away
All that now makes it hard to say,—
　　"Thy will be done!"

7.
Then when on earth I breathe no more
The pray'r oft mix'd with tears before,
I'll sing upon a happier shore—
　　"Thy will be done!"

27.—The Gospel Invitation.

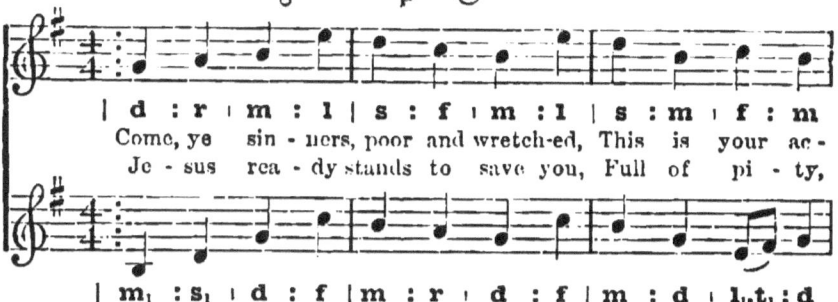

2.
Come, ye weary, heavy laden,
Lost and ruin'd by the fall;
If you tarry till you're better,
You will never come at all:
Not the righteous—
Sinners, Jesus came to call.

3.
Lo! th' incarnate God ascended,
Pleads the merit of his blood;
Venture on him, venture wholly,
Let no other trust intrude:
None but Jesus
Can do helpless sinners good.

28.—Deeds of Kindness.

♩ = 63

```
:s₁  | m:-m  | r:d  :r  | d:-:- | s₁:-:s₁
Sup- pose  the  lit- tle  cow- slip Should

:m₁  | s₁:-:s₁ | f₁:m₁:f₁ | m₁:-:- | m₁:-:m₁

| l₁:-:l₁ | l₁:t₁:d | s₁:-:- | :m
  hang   its  gold- en cup,        And

| f₁:-:f₁ | f₁:s₁:l₁ | m₁:-:- | :d

| f:-:f | r:-:r | m:-:m | d:-:d
  say,  "I'm such a  ti- ny flow'r, I'd

| r:-:r | t₁:-:t₁ | d:-:s₁ | m₁:-:m₁

| r:-:r | t₁:-:t₁ | d:-:- | :s₁
  bet- ter not grow  up!"       How

| f₁:-:f₁ | r₁:-:r₁ | m₁:-:- | :m₁
```

DEEDS OF KINDNESS—continued.

2.
Suppose the glist'ning dew-drop
　Upon the grass should say,
"What can a little dew-drop do?
　I'd better roll away!"
The blade on which it rested,
　Before the day was done,
Without a drop to moisten it,
　Would wither in the sun.

3.
Suppose the little breezes
　Upon a summer's day, [cool
Should think themselves too small to
　The trav'ller on his way:

Who would not miss the smallest
　And softest ones that blow,
And think they made a great mistake,
　If they were talking so?

4.
How many deeds of kindness
　A little child can do,
Although it has so little strength
　And little wisdom too!
It wants a loving spirit
　Much more than strength, to prove
How many things a child may do
　For others, by its love.

THE HARVEST PAST—continued.

3.
When the holy have gone to the region of peace,
To dwell in the mansions above;
When their harmony wakes, in the fulness of bliss,
Their song to the Saviour they love:

4.
Say, O sinner that livest at rest and secure,
Who fearest no trouble to come,
Can thy spirit the swellings of sorrow endure,
Or bear the impenitent's doom?

30.—Just as I am.*

2.
Just as I am—and waiting not
To rid my soul of one dark blot—
To thee whose blood can cleanse each spot,
    O Lamb of God, I come!

3.
Just as I am—though toss'd about
With many a conflict, many a doubt,
Fightings within, and fears without,
    O Lamb of God, I come!

4.
Just as I am—poor, wretched, blind,
Sight, riches, healing of the mind,
Yea, all I need in thee to find—
    O Lamb of God, I come!

5.
Just as I am—thou wilt receive,
Wilt welcome, pardon, cleanse, relieve,
Because thy promise I believe,—
    O Lamb of God, I come!

6.
Just as I am—thy love, I own,
Has broken every barrier down,
Now, to be thine, yes, thine alone,
    O Lamb of God, I come!

* This piece with pianoforte accompaniment by Mad. Delcour, can be had from CRAMER, BEALE, and Co., 201 Regent Street, London.

31.—The Great Sacrifice.

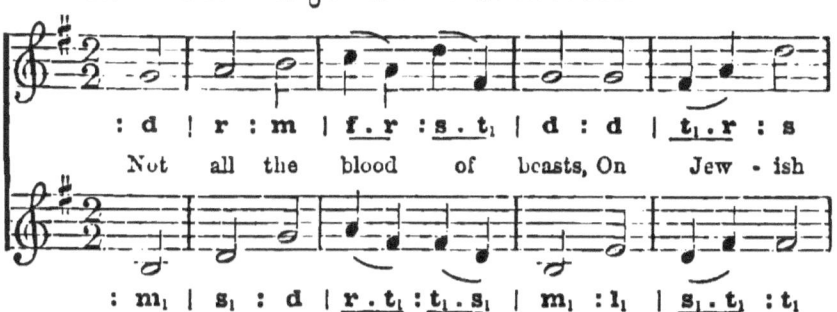
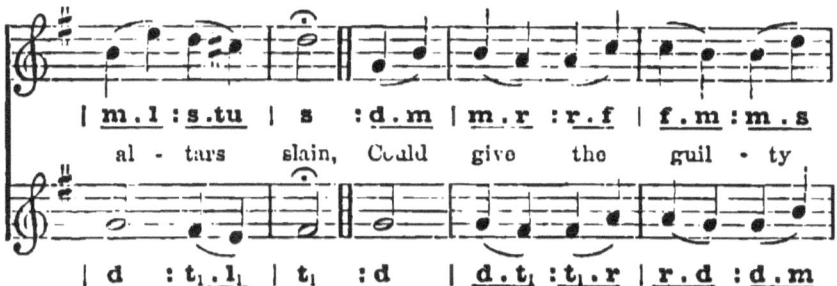

2.
But Christ, the heavenly Lamb,
Takes all our sins away;
A sacrifice of nobler name
And richer blood than they.

3.
My faith would lay her hand
On that dear head of thine,
While as a penitent I stand,
And there confess my sin.

4.
Believing, we rejoice
To see the curse remove;
We bless the Lamb with cheerful voice,
And sing his bleeding love.

MISSIONARY HYMN—continued.

2.

What though the spicy breezes
  Blow soft o'er Ceylon's isle;
Though ev'ry prospect pleases,
  And only man is vile;
In vain with lavish kindness
  The gifts of God are strewn;
The heathen, in his blindness,
  Bows down to wood and stone.

3.

Can we, whose souls are lighted
  With wisdom from on high;
Can we to men benighted
  The lamp of life deny?

Salvation! O Salvation!
  The joyful sound proclaim.
Till each remotest nation
  Has learn'd Messiah's name.

4.

Waft, waft, ye winds, his story,
  And you, ye waters, roll,
Till like a sea of glory,
  It spreads from pole to pole:
Till, o'er our ransom'd nature,
  The Lamb for sinners slain,
Redeemer, King, Creator,
  In bliss returns to reign.

34.—The Jubilee.

THE JUBILEE—continued.

2.
Exalt the Lamb of God,
The sin-atoning Lamb;
Redemption by his blood
Through all the lands proclaim:
          The year, &c.

3.
Ye who have sold for nought
Your heritage above,
Shall have it back unbought,
The gift of Jesus' love.
          The year, &c.

4.
Ye slaves of sin and hell,
Your liberty receive;
And safe in Jesus dwell,
And blest in Jesus live.
          The year, &c.

5.
The gospel trumpet hear,
The news of pard'ning grace;
Ye happy souls, draw near,
Behold your Saviour's face.
          The year, &c.

6.
Jesus, our great High Priest,
Hath full atonement made;
Ye weary spirits, rest;
Ye mourning souls, be glad.
          The year, &c.

| m.,f : s | l : f.l | s : f.r | d : t₁.r | d : ||
Je - sus— 'Tis the voice of mer - cy calls.

| d.,r : m | f : r.f | m : r.t₁ | d : s₁.f₁ | m₁ : ||

2.

Haste, O sinner! to the Saviour,
Seek his mercy while you may;
Soon the day of grace is over—
Soon your life will pass away!
Haste to Jesus—
You must perish if you stay.

♩ = 60.

36.—Jesus passing by.

Y.
By permission.

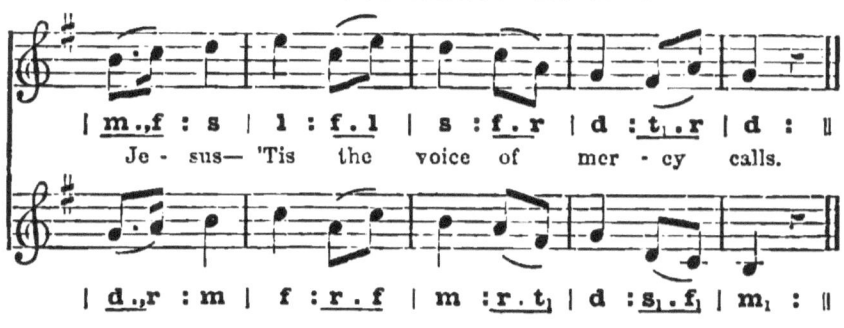

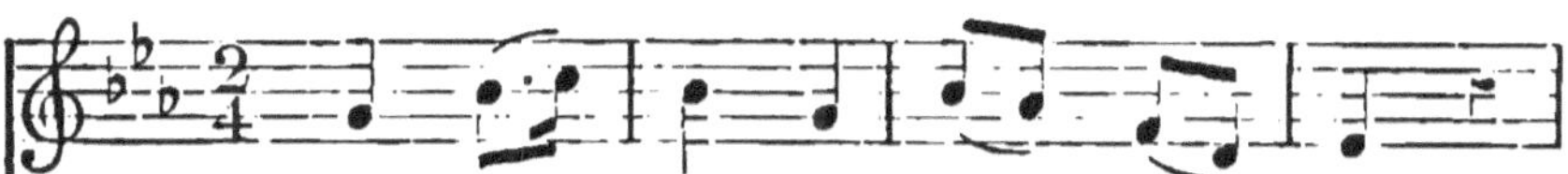

| m : s.,l | s : m | s.f : r.t₁ | d :
Je - sus Christ is pass - ing by,

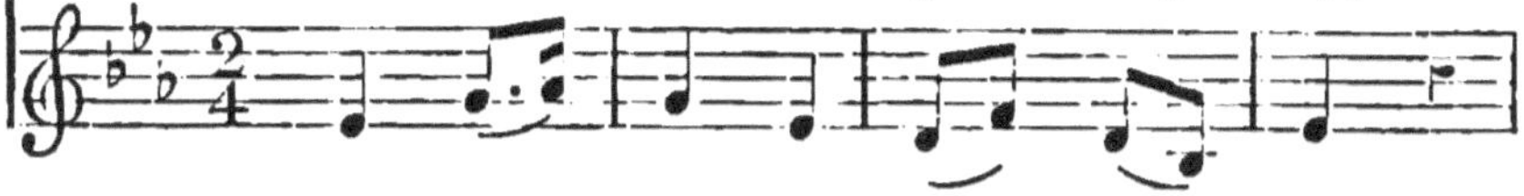

| d : m.,f | m : d | t₁.r : t₁.s₁ | d :

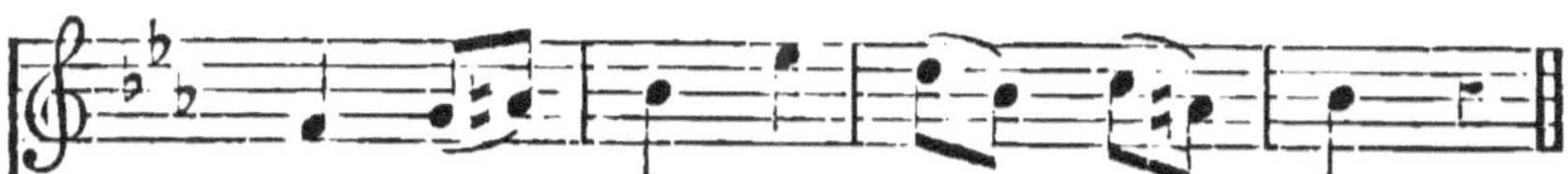

| r : m.tu | s : d' | t.s : l.tu | s :
Sin - ner, lift to him thine eye;

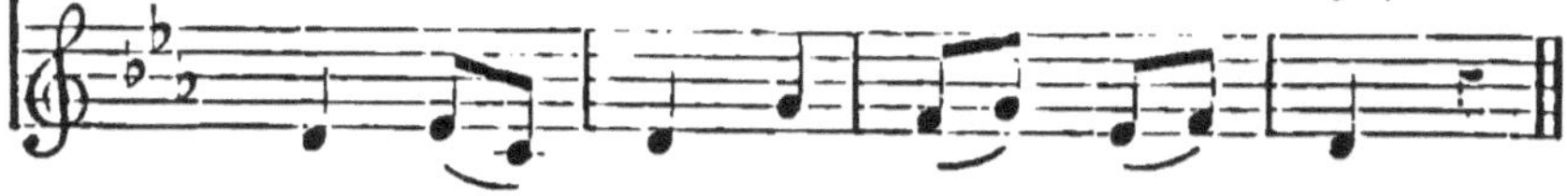

| t₁ : d.l₁ | t₁ : m | r.m : d.r | t₁ :

JESUS PASSING BY—continued.

2.
Jesus Christ is passing by,
Will he always be so nigh?
Now is the accepted day,
Seek for healing while you may.

3.
Fearest thou he will not hear?
Art thou bidden to forbear?
Let no obstacle defeat,—
Yet more earnestly entreat.

4.
Lo! he stands and calls to thee,
"What wilt thou then have of me?"
Rise, and tell him all thy need;
Rise, he calleth thee indeed.

5.
"Lord, I would thy mercy see!
Lord, reveal thy love to me!
Let it penetrate my soul,—
All my heart and life control."

6.
Oh, how sweet! the touch of power
Comes—it is salvation's hour;
Jesus gives from guilt release,—
"Faith has saved thee, go in peace."

7.
Glory to the Saviour's name!
He is ever still the same;
To his matchless honour raise
Never-ending songs of praise.

37.—Talents.

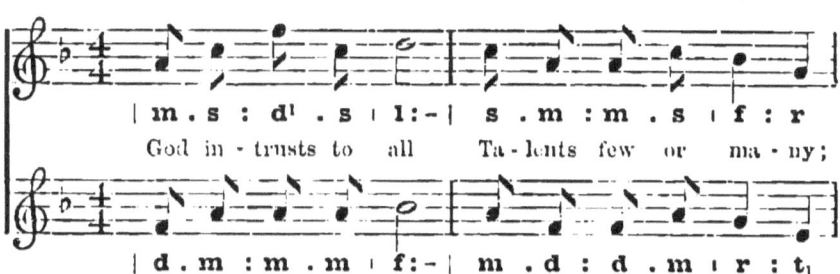

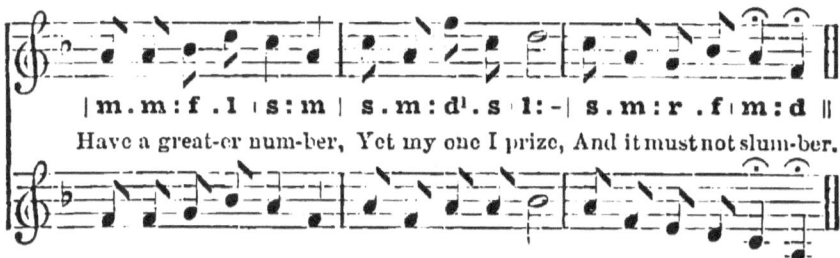

2.
Ev'ry little mite,
　Ev'ry little measure,
Helps to spread the light,
　Helps to swell the treasure.
Little drops of rain
　Bring the springing flowers;
And I may attain
　Much by little powers.

3.
God intrusts to all
　Talents few or many;
None so young and small
　That they have not any.
God will surely ask,
　Ere I enter heaven,
Have I done the task
　Which to me was given

♩= 74. **38.—The Mighty Trumpet.***

```
:s₁  | d .r  :m  :d  | r .m  :f  :f
The    blast  of  the   trum- pet,  so

:s₁  | m₁.s₁ :d  :m₁ | s₁.d  :r  :t₁

| m .r  :d  :t₁ | d :- :s₁ | d .r  :m  d
  loud   and  so  shrill, Will  short- ly  re-

| d .s₁ :m₁ :r₁ | m₁:- :s₁ | m₁.s₁ :d  :m₁

| r .m  :f  :f | m .r  :d  :t₁ | d :-
  e-  cho   o'er    o-  cean  and   hill.

| s₁.d  :r  :t₁ | d .s₁ :m₁ :r₁ | m₁:-

:m .f  | s :- .f :m .r | m .f  :s  :s
When the might-y, might-y, might-y  trump sounds,

:d .r  | m :- .r :d .t₁ | d .r  :m  :m
```

* From "Revival Tune-Book," by permission of the publishers, MORGAN & CHASE, Holborn, London.

THE MIGHTY TRUMPET—continued.

2.
The earth and the waters will yield up the dead,
The righteous with joy will awake from their bed,
　　When the mighty, &c.

3.
The chorus of angels will burst from the skies,
And blend with the shouts of the saints as they rise,
　　When the mighty, &c.

4.
The cry of the lost ones—the yell of despair,
And loud hallelujahs will meet in the air,
　　When the mighty, &c.

5.
The throne of Messiah in clouds will descend,
And voices like thunder the heavens will rend,
　　When the mighty, &c.

6.
The cry of "The Bridegroom!" will echo around,
And the Bride in her beauty go forth at the sound,
　　When the mighty, &c.

7.
Acknowledged by Jesus—confessed as his own—
Transported to glory, we'll sit on his throne,
　　When the mighty, &c.

8.
O land of the holy, the happy, the free,
In Jesus thy portals are open to me.
　　When the mighty, &c.

PRAY WITHOUT CEASING—continued.

2.

Remember all who love thee—
All who are loved by thee;
Pray, too, for those who hate thee,
If any such there be;
Then for thyself, in meekness,
A blessing humbly claim:
And link with each petition
Thy great Redeemer's name.

3.

Or, if 'tis e'er denied thee
In solitude to pray,
Should holy thoughts come o'er thee
When friends are round thy way;
Ev'n then the silent breathing
Thy spirit lifts above,
Will reach His throne of glory,
Who is Mercy, Truth, and Love.

4.

Oh, not a joy or blessing
With this can we compare—
The grace our Father gives us
To pour our souls in prayer!
Whene'er thou pin'st in sadness,
On Him who saveth call;
And ever in thy gladness
Thank Him who gave thee all.

♩ = 74. 40.—The Eden above.

```
:d .r   | m  :m  :m    | m :- :f ., l
We're    bound for the   land of  the
Ye       wand'-rers from God  in  the

:d .t₁  | d  :d  :d    | d :- :r ., f

| s : r : f | m : d : s | d¹ :- .t : d¹ ., t
pure  and the  ho - ly, The  home of  the
broad road of fol- ly,  O    say, will you

| m : t₁ : r | d : d : m | m :- .r : m ., s

| l : f : l | s : s .f : r | d :-
hap-py,  the  king - dom  of   love:
go   to   the   E  -  den  a - bove?

| f : r : f | m : t₁ : t₁ | d :-

:s ., f | m :- :m ., f | s :- :f ., m
Will you   go,  will you   go,  will you

:m ., r | d :- :d ., r | m :- :r ., d
```

THE EDEN ABOVE—continued.

2.
Each saint has a mansion prepared and all furnish'd,
　Ere from this clay house he is summon'd to move;
Its gates and its towers with glory are burnish'd:
　O say, will you go to the Eden above?
　　　Will you go, Will you go,—
　O say, will you go to the Eden above?

3.
March on, happy pilgrims! that land is before you,
　And soon its ten thousand delights we shall prove:
Yes, soon we shall walk o'er the bright hills of glory,
　And drink the pure joys of the Eden above.
　　　Will you go, Will you go?
　O yes, we will go to the Eden above.

4.
And yet, guilty sinner, we would not forsake thee,
　We halt yet a moment as onward we move;
O come to thy Lord—in his arms he will take thee,
　And bear thee along to the Eden above.
　　　Will you go, Will you go,—
　O say, will you go to the Eden above?

5.
Methinks thou art now in thy wretchedness saying,
　O who can this guilt from my conscience remove?
No other but Jesus; then come to him praying,
　Prepare me, O Lord, for the Eden above.
　　　Will you go, Will you go,—
　At last, will you go to the Eden above?

41.—Longing after Holiness

♩ = 76

LONGING AFTER HOLINESS—continued.

3.
A humble, lowly, contrite heart,
Believing, true, and clean!
Which neither life nor death can part,
From Him that dwells within.

4.
A heart in ev'ry thought renew'd,
And fill'd with love divine;
Perfect and right, and pure and good,—
A copy, Lord, of thine.

42.—Truthfulness.

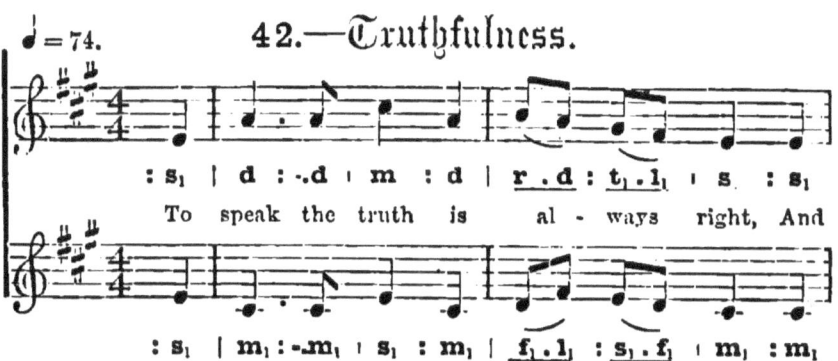

TRUTHFULNESS—continued.

TRUTHFULNESS—continued.

| d .r | :m .f | s | :.l | s :.f | m :r | d :- ||
be de- nied, What-e'er the con- se- quence.

| m₁.s₁ | :d .r | m | :.f | m :.r | d :s₁.f₁ | m₁ :- ||

3.
Falsehood can never prosper long,
Its triumph soon is past;
But Truth, howe'er opposed, is strong,
And will for ever last.

4.
There's One above doth all things know
And a strict reck'ning keep;
God is not mock'd; and as we sow
So shall we surely reap.

𝅗𝅥 = 60. **43.—How Much I Owe!**

| d :t₁.l₁ | s₁ :m₁ | l₁ :d | s₁ :m₁
When this pass-ing world is done,

| m₁ :s₁.f₁ | m₁ :d₁ | f₁ :l₁ | m₁ :d₁

| m :r.d | l₁ :r | d :t₁ | d :- | m :m.f
When has sunk yon glar-ing sun, When we

| s₁ :f₁.m₁ | f₁ :f₁ | m₁ :r₁ | m₁ :- | s₁ : .r

HOW MUCH I OWE—continued.

2.
When I stand before the throne,
Dress'd in beauty not my own;
When I see thee as thou art,
Love thee with unsinning heart;
Then, Lord, shall I fully know—
Not till then—how much I owe.

3.
When the praise of heav'n I hear,
Loud as thunders to the ear,
Loud as many waters' noise,
Sweet as harp's melodious voice;
Then, Lord, shall I fully know—
Not till then—how much I owe.

4.
Ev'n on earth, as through a glass,
Darkly let thy glory pass;
Make forgiveness feel so sweet,
Make thy Spirit's help so meet;
Ev'n on earth, Lord, make me know
Something of how much I owe.

5.
Chosen not for good in me,
Waken'd up from wrath to flee;
Hidden in the Saviour's side,
By the Spirit sanctified:
Teach me, Lord, on earth, to show,
By my love, how much I owe.

6.
Oft the nights of sorrow reign—
Weeping, sickness, sighing, pain;
But a night thine anger burns—
Morning comes, and joy returns:
God of comforts! bid me show
To thy poor how much I owe.

44.—The Best Friend.

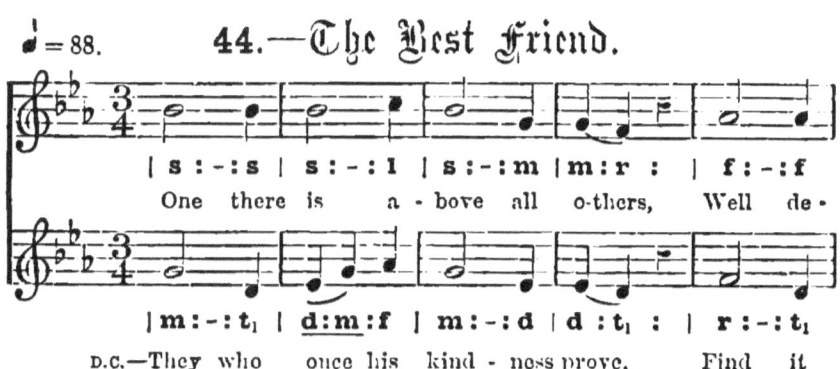

2.
Which of all our friends to save us,
　Could, or would have shed his blood?
But our Jesus died to have us
　Reconciled in him to God.
　　His was boundless love indeed!
　　Jesus is a friend in need.

3.
Oh! for grace our hearts to soften!
　Teach us, Lord, at length to love;
We, alas! forget too often
　What a friend we have above.
　　But when home our souls are brought,
　　We shall love thee as we ought.

CONSCIENCE—continued.

In the morning, when we rise,
　And would fain omit to pray,
"Child! consider!" Conscience cries;
　"Should not God be sought to-day?"

2.

But if we should disregard,
　While those friendly voices call,
Conscience soon will grow so hard
　That it will not speak at all.

46.—The Realms of the Blest.

♩ = 70

:s₁ | m :r :d | s :f :m | r : :r | l :s :f
We sing of the realms of the blest, That coun-try so

:s₁ | d :t₁ :d | m :r :d | t₁ : :s₁ | f :m :r

|f :m :r | m :- :s₁ | m :r :d | t₁ :l₁ :ne₁ | l₁ :- :l₁
bright and so fair; And oft are its glo-ries con-fess'd, But

| r :d :t₁ | d :- :s₁ | d :t₁ :l₁ | ne₁ :l₁ :m₁ | f₁ :- :f₁

|s₁ :d :r | m :.f :r | d :- : | s :- :- | l :- :-
what must it be to be there? There! there!

|m₁ :m₁ :s₁ | d :- .r :t₁ | d :- : | m :- :- | f :- :-

|s :- :d .r | m :.f :m | m .r :d :r | d :- ‖
there! Oh, what must it be to be there!

|m :- :d .t₁ | d :- .r :d | s₁ .f₁ :m₁ :f₁ | m₁ :- ‖

THE REALMS OF THE BLEST—continued.

2.
We speak of its freedom from sin,
From sorrow, temptation, and care,
From trials without and within—
But what must it be to be there?
    There! there! there! Oh, what, &c.

3.
We speak of its service of love,
The robes which the glorified wear,
The Church of the First-born above—
But what must it be to be there?
    There! there! there! Oh, what, &c.

4.
Do thou, Lord, 'midst pleasure or woe,
For heaven our spirits prepare;
Then soon shall we joyfully know
And feel what it is to be there.
    There! there! there! Oh, what, &c.

47.—Joyfully, Joyfully.

JOYFULLY, JOYFULLY—continued.

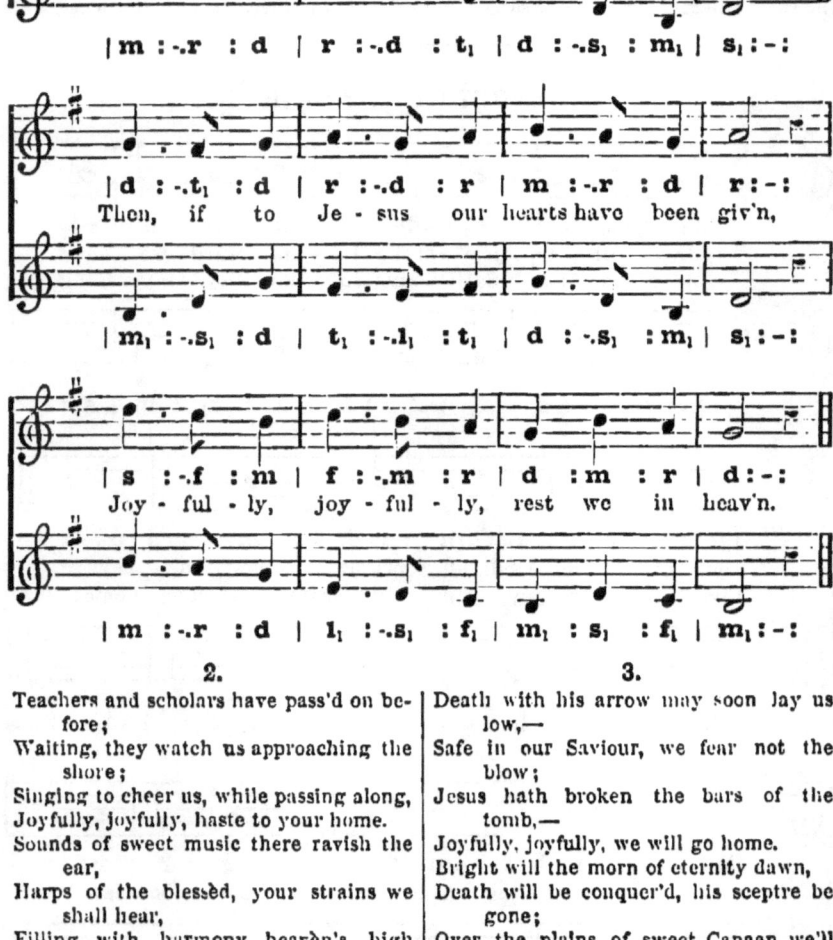

2.
Teachers and scholars have pass'd on before;
Waiting, they watch us approaching the shore;
Singing to cheer us, while passing along,
Joyfully, joyfully, haste to your home.
Sounds of sweet music there ravish the ear,
Harps of the blessèd, your strains we shall hear,
Filling with harmony heaven's high dome,—
Joyfully, joyfully, Jesus, we come.

3.
Death with his arrow may soon lay us low,—
Safe in our Saviour, we fear not the blow;
Jesus hath broken the bars of the tomb,—
Joyfully, joyfully, we will go home.
Bright will the morn of eternity dawn,
Death will be conquer'd, his sceptre be gone;
Over the plains of sweet Canaan we'll roam,
Joyfully, joyfully, safely at home.

48.—I'm a Pilgrim.

♩ = 64.

| :d .r | m .d :d | .d :r .m |

I'm a pil-grim, and I'm a

| :d .t₁ | d .m₁ :m₁ | .m₁ :s₁ .d |

D.C.—I'm a pil-grim, and I'm a

| s .f :r | s .f :m .m | m .m :s .f | r .m |

strang-er; I can tar-ry, I can tar-ry but a

| t₁ :t₁ :t₁ .r | d .d :d .d | t₁ .r :t₁ .s₁ |

strang-er; I can tar-ry, I can tar-ry but a

Fine.

| d :- | .d :t₁ .d | r :s .f | m .r |

night. Do not de-tain me, for I am

| m₁ :- | .m₁ :s₁ .l₁ | t₁ :t₁ .r | d .t₁ |

night.

D.C.

| d .r :m | d :t₁ .d | r :s .l :s .t,u | s .l :s ‖

go-ing To where the foun-tains are ev-er flow-ing:

| d .,t₁ :d | m₁ :s₁ .l₁ | t₁ :t₁ .d :t₁ .l₁ | t₁,d :t₁ ‖

I'M A STRANGER—continued.

2.
There the glory is ever shining!
Oh, my longing heart, my longing heart is there!
Here in this country, so dark and dreary,
I long have wander'd, forlorn and weary.
I'm a pilgrim, &c.

3.
There is the city to which I journey:
My Redeemer, my Redeemer is its light!
There is no sorrow nor any sighing,
Nor any tears there,—nor any dying.
I'm a pilgrim, &c.

4.
Father, mother, and sister, brother!
If you will not journey with me, I must go!
Now since your vain hopes you will thus cherish,
Should I, too, linger, and with you perish?
I'm a pilgrim, &c.

5.
Farewell, dreary earth, by sin so blighted;
In immortal beauty soon thou'lt be array'd!
He who has form'd thee will soon restore thee,
And then thy dread curse shall never more be.
I'm a pilgrim, and I'm a stranger,
Till thy rest shall end the weary pilgrim's night.

49.—Onward, Christian!

ONWARD, CHRISTIAN—continued.

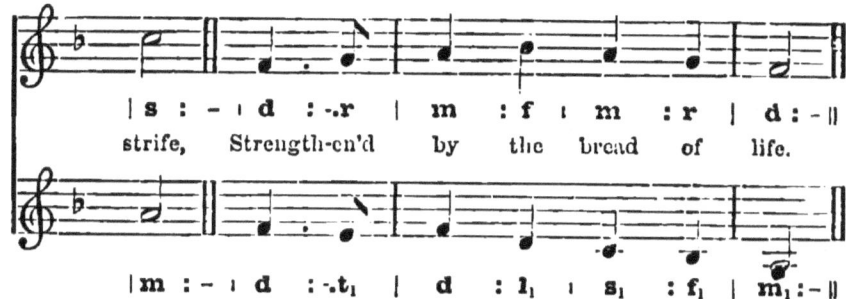

s : -	d : -.r	m :f	m :r	d :-	

strife, Strength-en'd by the bread of life.

| m : - | d : -.t₁ | d :l₁ | s₁ :f₁ | m₁ :- ||

2.
Let your drooping heart be glad,
March in heavenly armour clad;
In your very weakness strong,
Fight! nor think the battle long.
3.
Let not sorrow dim your eye,—
Soon shall ev'ry tear be dry;

Let not fears your course impede,—
Great your strength, if great your need.
4.
Onward, then, to battle move!
More than conq'ror you shall prove;
Though opposed by many a foe,
Christian soldier, onward go!

50.—The Little Pilgrims.

To be sung to the Music on opposite page.

1.
Little trav'llers, Zionward,
  Each one ent'ring into rest
In the kingdom of your Lord,
  In the mansions of the blest!
There to welcome, Jesus waits,
  Gives the crowns his foll'wers win:
Lift your heads, ye golden gates!
  Let the little trav'llers in!
2.
Who are they whose little feet
  Pacing life's dark journey through,
Now have reach'd that heavenly seat
  They had ever kept in view?

"I from Greenland's frozen land;"
  "I from India's sultry plain;"
"I from Afric's barren sand;"
  "I from islands of the main."
3.
"All our earthly journey past,
  Ev'ry tear and pain gone by,
We're together met at last,
  At the portal of the sky."
Each the welcome "Come" awaits,
  Conq'rors over death and sin:
Lift your heads, ye golden gates!
  Let the little trav'llers in!

HOMEWARD BOUND—continued.

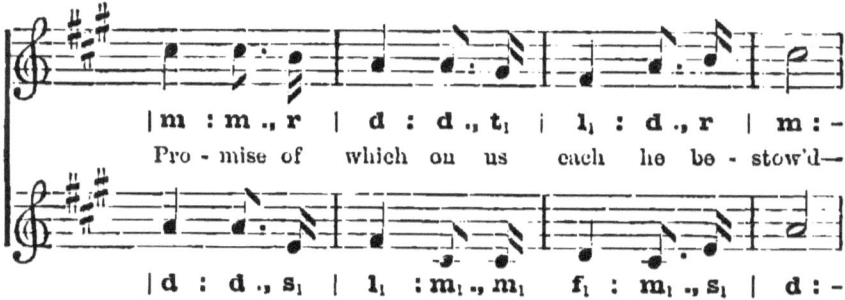

2.
Wildly the storm sweeps us on as it roars—
    We're homeward bound;
Look! yonder lie the bright heavenly shores—
    We're homeward bound.
Steady, O pilot! stand firm at the wheel,
Steady! we soon shall outweather the gale;
O how we fly 'neath the loud creaking sail—
    We're homeward bound.

3.
We'll tell the world as we journey along,
    We're homeward bound;
Try to persuade them to enter our throng—
    We're homeward bound;
Come, trembling sinner, forlorn and oppress'd,
Join in our number, O come and be blest!
Journey with us to the mansions of rest—
    We're homeward bound.

4.
Into the harbour of heav'n now we glide—
    We're home at last;
Softly we drift o'er its bright silver tide—
    We're home at last.
Glory to God! all our dangers are o'er,
We stand secure on the glorified shore;
Glory to God! we will shout evermore—
    We're home at last.

THE SHINING SHORE—continued.

2.
Our absent King the watchword gave,
"Let ev'ry lamp be burning;"
We look afar, across the wave,
Our distant home discerning.
　　　　For now we stand, &c.

3.
Should coming days be dark and cold,
We will not yield to sorrow;
For hope will sing, with courage bold,
"There's glory on the morrow."
　　　　For now we stand, &c.

4.
Let storms of woe in whirlwinds rise,
Each cord on earth to sever,
There, bright and joyous in the skies—
There is our home for ever!
　　　　For now we stand, &c.

53.—Breast the Wave.

By permission of H. BURNETT, Esq.

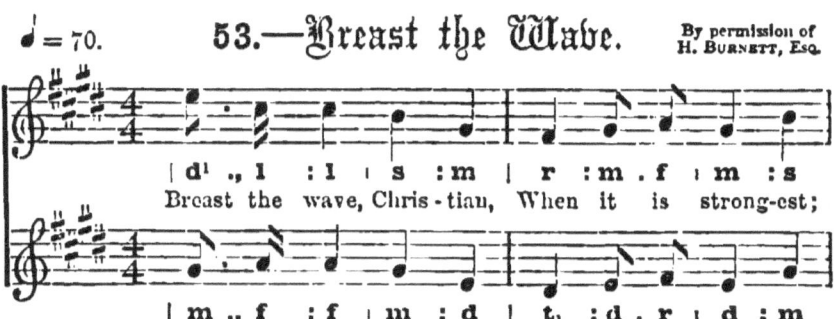

BREAST THE WAVE—continued.

(To be sung after last verse.)

* Fight the fight, Christian, Jesus is o'er thee;

BREAST THE WAVE—continued.

2.
Fight the fight, Christian,
Jesus is o'er thee;
Run the race, Christian,
Heav'n is before thee.
He who hath promised
Faltereth never;
The love of eternity
Flows on for ever.

3.
Raise the eye, Christian,
Just as it closeth;

Lift the heart, Christian,
Ere it reposeth.
Thee from the love of Christ
Nothing shall sever;
Mount when the work is done,
Praise him for ever!

* Fight the fight, Christian,
Jesus is o'er thee;
Run the race, Christian,
Heav'n is before thee.

54.—No Parting There.

Here we meet to part a-gain, Here we meet to part a-gain, But when we meet on Ca-naan's plain, There'll

NO PARTING THERE—continued.

2.
Here we meet to part again,
But when a seat in heaven we gain
There'll be no parting there,
In that bright world above.
　　　Shout! shout, &c.

3.
Here we meet to part again,
But there we shall with Jesus reign;
There'll be no parting there,
In that bright world above.
　　　Shout! shout, &c.

4.
Here we meet to part again,
But when we join the heavenly train,
There'll be no parting there,
In that bright world above.
　　　Shout! shout, &c.

55.—Ashamed of Jesus.

♩ = 76.

Je-sus, and shall it e-ver be, A mor-tal man a-shamed of thee! A-shamed of thee whom an-gels praise, Whose glo-ries shine thro' end-less days. A-shamed of Je-sus! soon-er far Let eve-ning blush to own a star; He

ASHAMED OF JESUS—continued.

| s₁ :-.s₁ | s₁ :d.t₁ | l₁ :-.l₁ | l₁ : .d | t₁ :-.d | r :t₁ | d :-.d | d ||
shed the beams of light di-vine O'er this be-night-ed soul of mine.

| m₁ :-.m₁ | d₁:m₁.s₁ | f₁ :-.f₁ | f₁ : .m₁ | r₁ :-.m₁ | f₁ :r₁ | m₁ :-.m₁ | m₁ ||

3.
Ashamed of Jesus! just as soon
Let midnight be ashamed of noon;
'Tis midnight with my soul, till He,
Bright Morning Star, bids darkness flee.

4.
Ashamed of Jesus! that dear Friend
On whom my hopes of heaven depend!
No; when I blush, be this my shame,—
That I no more revere his name.

5.
Ashamed of Jesus! yes, I may,
When I've no guilt to wash away
No tear to wipe, no good to crave,
No fears to quell, no soul to save.

6.
Till then—nor is my boasting vain—
Till then, I boast a Saviour slain!
And, O may this my glory be,—
That Christ is not ashamed of me!

♩ = 76.   **56.—Jehovah Tsidkenu.**   By permission.
"THE LORD OUR RIGHTEOUSNESS."

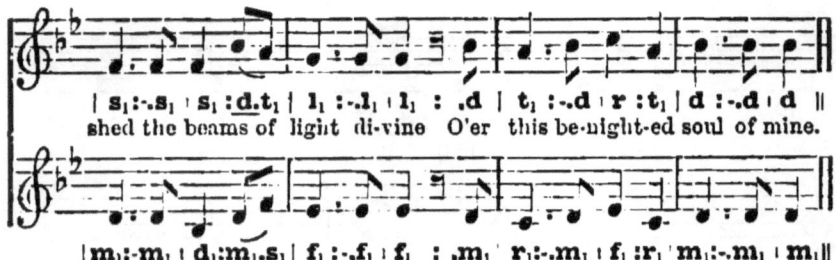

| :s₁ | d :-.r | m.f | m :r :m | r :d :t₁ |
I once was a stran - ger to grace and to

| :s₁ | m₁ :-.s₁ | d .r | d :t₁ :d | s₁ :l₁ :s₁.f₁ |

| d :-:t₁ | l₁ :t₁ :d | m :r :-.d | t₁ :d :l₁ | s₁ :- |
God; I knew not my dan - ger, and felt not my load;

| m₁ :-:s₁ | f₁ :s₁.f₁ :m₁ | d :t₁ :-.l₁ | s₁ :l₁ :tu₁ | s₁ :- |

JEHOVAH TSIDKENU—continued.

2.
I oft read with pleasure, to soothe or engage,
Isaiah's wild measure and John's simple page;
But e'en when they pictured the blood-sprinkled tree,
Jehovah Tsidkēnu seem'd nothing to me.

3.
Like tears from the daughters of Zion that roll,
I wept when the waters went over his soul;
Yet thought not that *my* sins had nail'd to the tree
Jehovah Tsidkēnu — 'twas nothing to me.

4.
When free grace awoke me, by light from on high,
Then legal fears shook me—I trembled to die;
No refuge, no safety in self could I see,—
Jehovah Tsidkēnu my Saviour must be.

5.
My terrors all vanish'd before the sweet name;
My guilty fears banish'd, with boldness I came
To drink at the fountain, life-giving and free, —
Jehovah Tsidkēnu is all things to me.

6.
Jehovah Tsidkēnu! my treasure and boast;
Jehovah Tsidkēnu! I ne'er can be lost;
In Thee I shall conquer by flood and by field,—
My cable, my anchor, my breast-plate and shield!

7.
Even treading the valley, the shadow of death,
This "watchword" shall rally my faltering breath;
For while from life's fever my God sets me free,
Jehovah Tsidkēnu, my death-song shall be.

♩ = 88.

57.—Who hath Believed?

```
|d :- |m  r | d :- | d :- | l₁ :- | d  :l₁
 Who    hath be- liev-ed?   who    hath  be-

|m₁:- |s₁ :f₁ | m₁:- |m₁:- | f₁:- | l₁ : f₁
```

```
|s₁:- |s₁ :m | s :- |s  :f | m :- |m :.r
 liev-ed?  To  whom  is  thine arm, Lord, re-

|m₁:- |m₁ :d | m :- |m  :r | d :- |s₁ :-.f₁
```

```
|d :- |d  :r | m :-.r m :f | s :- |f  :m
 veal'd?  The Mes-si-ah came to earth, But  so

|m₁:- |m₁ :s₁ | d :-.t₁ |d  :r | m :- |r  :d
```

```
|f :  m  :  r  :d | l₁:- |d  :l₁ | s₁:-.l₁ |d  :r
 low-ly   was  his birth, That his ma-jes-ty  from

|r : d | s₁ :m₁ | f₁:- |l₁ : f₁ | m₁:-.f₁ |m₁ : s₁
```

WHO HATH BELIEVED—continued.

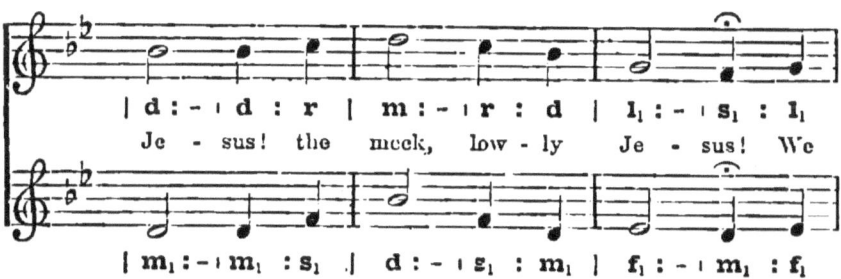

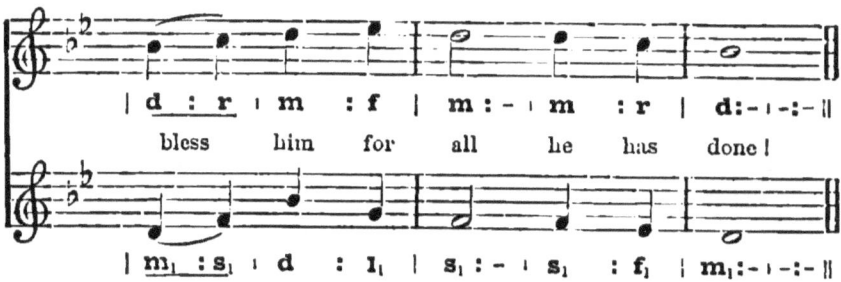

2.
He was afflicted—He was afflicted;
On him lay the sins of us all:
   As a lamb to slaughter led,
   So the lowly Saviour bled,
To redeem us from the curse of the fall.
        Blessed Jesus, &c.

3.
He has ascended—He has ascended,
And now sits enthroned in the sky
   But he'll come again to bear
   All his lowly people there,
And they'll reign as kings with Jesus on high.
   Blessed Jesus! kind Jesus! the meek, lowly Jesus
   They'll reign as kings with Jesus on high.

♩. = 46.   58.—Praise to Immanuel.

| m :- :s | m:-.f:m r:- :m | d:- :t₁
'Tis the   light of gos - pel sto - ry

| d :- :m | d:-.r:d | t₁:- :ne₁ | l₁:- :ne₁

| d:- :r m:- :s.f | m:- :r d:- : | m:- :s m:-.f:m
That at-tunes our hearts to sing Prais-es to the

| l₁:- :t₁ | d:- :m.r | d:- :s₁ | m₁:- : | d:- :m d:-.r:d

| r:- :m d:- :t₁ | d:- :r m:- :s.f | m:- :r d:- :
Lord of glo - ry, Prais-es to   our gra-cious King.

| t₁:- :ne₁ | l₁:- :ne₁ | l₁:- :t₁ | d:- :m.r d:- :s₁ m₁:- :

| d :- :d | d:- :r :d | m:- :m | m:- :r
O - ther sounds may e - cho round us,

| m₁:- :m₁ | m₁:-.f₁ :m₁ | s₁:- :d | d:- :t₁

PRAISE TO IMMANUEL—continued.

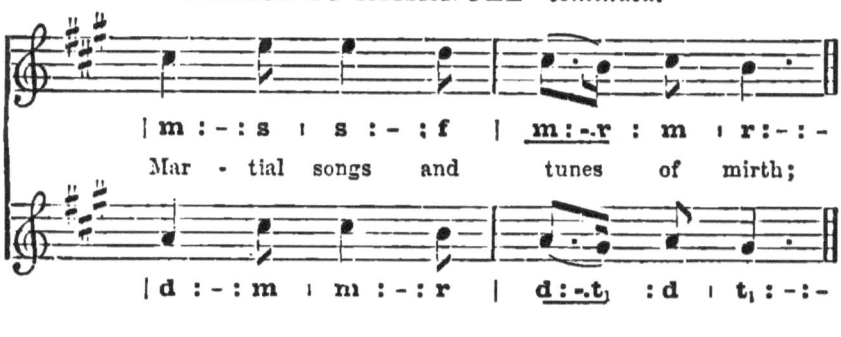

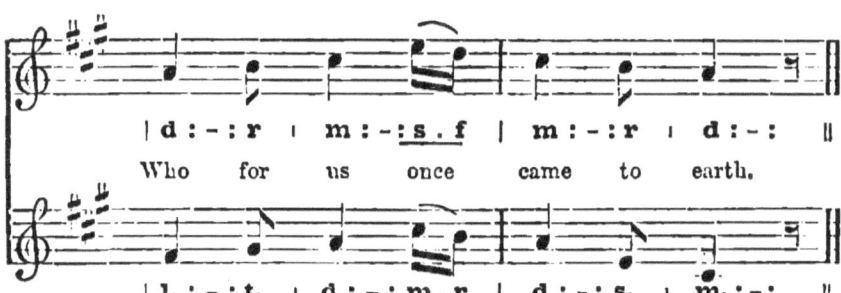

2.
He alone form'd all creation,
  By his word of mighty pow'r;
In his presence angels worship,—
  Him the hosts of heaven adore:
Yet his throne for us he quitted,—
  Came to earth a feeble child;
What a lesson thus he taught us—
  To be lowly, meek, and mild!

3.
He took on our human nature,
  Yielding to his Father's will;
He fulfill'd the law for sinners,—
  Holy, harmless, lovely still.
Give your heart—'tis all he seeketh,
  Better gift you cannot bring:
Let us sing Immanuel's glory,
  Praises to the Lord our King.

♩ = 76.   59.—I will Arise.
ANTHEM.

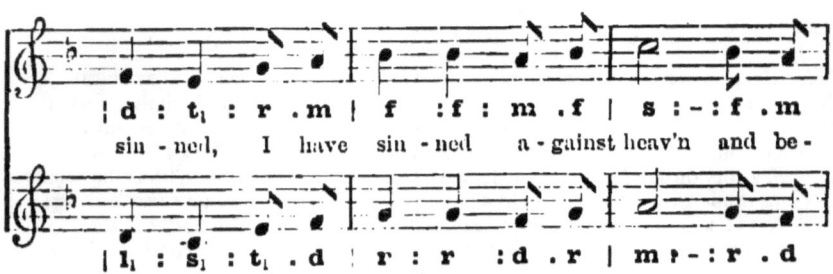

♩. = 51. 60.—The Fountain Opened.

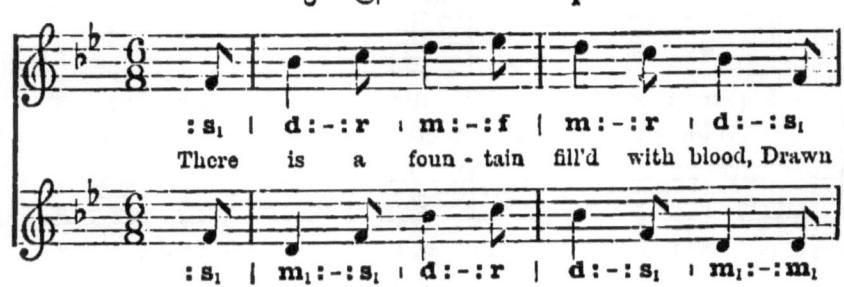

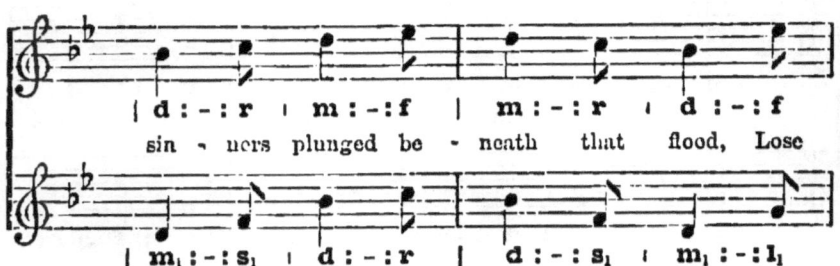

THE FOUNTAIN OPENED—continued.

3.
Dear dying Lamb, thy precious blood
Shall never lose its power,
Till all the ransom'd Church of God
Be saved, to sin no more.

4.
E'er since by faith I saw the stream
Thy flowing wounds supply,
Redeeming love has been my theme,—
And shall be till I die.

5.
Then in a nobler, sweeter song,
I'll sing thy power to save;
When this poor, lisping, stammering tongue,
Lies silent in the grave.

61.—Worthy the Lamb!

♩ = 69.

{ d : m : s | d¹ : -.r¹ : d¹ | r¹ : l : r¹
Come, all ye saints of God, Wide through the

| d : m : s | m : -.f : m | f : f : fe

| t : -.l : s | d¹ : r¹ : t | d¹ : - :
earth a-broad, Spread Je-sus' fame:

| s : -.tu : s | m : f : r | m : - :

| m : l : d¹ | t : -.ne : l | l : d¹ : m¹
Tell what his love hath done; Trust in his

| d : d : m | r : -.t₁ : d | f : m : s

| r¹ : -.d¹ : t | s : d¹ : r¹ | m¹ : -.r¹ : d¹
name a-lone; Shout to his lof-ty throne,

| tu : -.l : s | m : m : s | d¹ : -.s : m

WORTHY THE LAMB—continued.

2.
Hence, gloomy doubts and fears!
Dry up your mournful tears;
  Swell the glad theme:
To Christ, our heavenly King,
Strike each melodious string,
Join heart and voice to sing,
  "Worthy the Lamb!"

3.
Hark! how the choirs above,
Fill'd with the Saviour's love,
  Dwell on his name!
There, too, shall we be found,
With light and glory crown'd,
While all the heavens resound,
  "Worthy the Lamb!"

62.—Prayer.

PRAYER—continued.

3.
That Eye is fix'd on seraph throngs;
That Arm upholds the sky;
That Ear is fill'd with angel songs;
That Love is throned on high.

4.
But there's a power which man can yield
When mortal aid is vain,

That Eye, that Arm, that Love to reach,
That list'ning Ear to gain.

5.
That power is PRAYER, which soars on high
Through Jesus to the throne:
And moves the Hand which moves the world,
To bring salvation down!

63.—Evening Hymn.

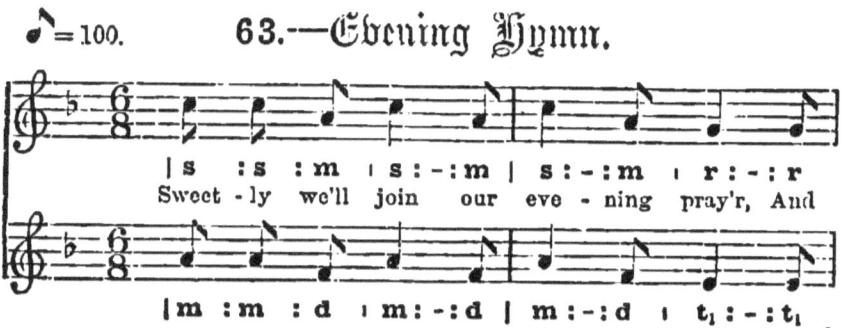

EVENING HYMN—*continued.*

EVENING HYMN—continued.

2.
Though dark the night in which we sail,
Our Pilot's on board,—we cannot fail;
The winds and waves his voice obey'd,
And the great deep by him was made.
  Blow, breezes, blow, &c.

3.
Faintly at times we pull the oar,
Yet ev'ry stroke brings nearer shore:
Cross winds, rough waves are in the way;
Pull strong the oar, and humbly pray.
  Blow, breezes, blow, &c.

4.
Make, make the port, the tide runs high!
Unfurl the white sails, the haven's nigh!
The hills and dales of earth grow dim,—
We'll sing to our friends the farewell hymn.
  Blow, breezes, blow, &c.

5.
And when the port of Glory's gain'd,
And full redemption we've obtain'd;
With saints and angels we will sing
The praises of our Saviour-King.
  Blow, breezes, blow, &c.

64.—The Rest Above.

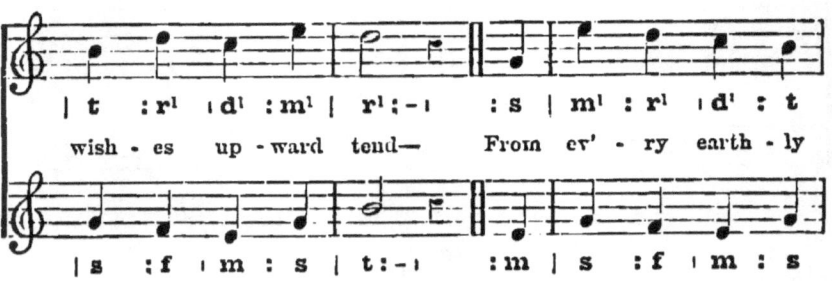

2.
On wings of faith ascending,
We view the land of light,
And see our sorrows ending
In infinite delight.

3.
'Tis true, we are but strangers
And pilgrims here below;

And countless snares and dangers
Surround the path we go.

4.
Though painful and distressing,
Yet there's a rest above;
And onward still we're pressing,
To reach that land of love.

65.—Children called to Christ.

To be sung to the Music of No. 56.

1.
Like mist on the mountain, like ships on the sea,
So swiftly the years of our pilgrimage flee;
In the grave of our fathers how soon we shall lie!—
Dear children, to-day to a Saviour fly.

2.
How sweet are the flow'rets in April and May!
But often the frost makes them wither away.
Like flow'rs you may fade;—are you ready to die?—
While "yet there is room," to a Saviour fly.

3.
When Samuel was young, he first knew the Lord,—
He slept in his smile, and rejoiced in his word;
So most of God's children are early brought nigh;—
Oh, seek him in youth!—to a Saviour fly.

4.
Do you ask me for pleasure? then lean on his breast,
For there the sin-laden and weary find rest;
In the valley of death you will triumphing cry,—
"If this be called dying, 'tis pleasant to die!"

66.—The Heavenly Canaan.

To be sung to the Music of No. 16.

1.
There is a land of pure delight,
Where saints immortal reign;
Infinite day excludes the night,
And pleasures banish pain.

2.
There everlasting spring abides,
And never-with'ring flow'rs;
Death, like a narrow sea, divides
This heavenly land from ours.

3.
Sweet fields beyond that swelling flood
Stand dress'd in living green;—
So to the Jews old Canaan stood,
While Jordan roll'd between.

4.
Yet tim'rous mortals start and shrink
To cross the narrow sea,
And linger, shiv'ring on the brink,
And fear to launch away.

5.
Oh, could we make our doubts remove,
These gloomy doubts that rise,
And see the Canaan that we love,
With faith's illumined eyes,—

6.
Could we but climb where Moses stood,
And view the landscape o'er,
Not Jordan's stream nor death's cold flood
Should fright us from the shore!

Index.

The Words of those marked * are inserted by Permission.

Title	No.
The Bible the Light of the World. A glory gilds the sacred page,......... *Cowper.*	22
The All-seeing God. Among the deepest shades of night, *Jane Taylor.*	14
New Year's Hymn. Another year has told,...................	23
Beautiful Zion. Beautiful Zion, built above,............	32
Jubilee. Blow ye the trumpet, blow,............ *Toplady.*	34
Breast the Wave Breast the wave, Christian,.............	53
Worthy the Lamb. Come, all ye saints of God,..............	61
The Work of the Holy Spirit. Come, Holy Spirit, come,................ *Hart.*	24
The Gospel Invitation. Come, ye sinners, poor and wretched, *Hart.*	27
My Times are in thy Hand. Father, I know that all my life,...... *Anna L. Waring.*	20
Delight in the Scriptures. Father of mercies, in thy word,....... *Mrs. Steele.*	16
The Rest Above. From every mortal treasure,...........	64
Missionary Hymn. From Greenland's icy mountains,.... *Heber.*	33
Pray without Ceasing. Go, when the morning shineth........	39
Talents. God intrusts to all,....................... *Edmeston.*	37
Luther's Hymn. Great God! what do I see and hear? *Luther.*	6
Far, Far Away. Had I the wings of a dove,..............	2
The Call of Mercy. Hear, O sinner! mercy hails you,.....	35
No Parting There. Here we meet to part again,...........	54
The Bible. Holy Bible, book divine,.................. *Burton.*	21
My All in All. I am a poor sinner and nothing at all	10
I'm a Pilgrim. I'm a pilgrim, and I'm a stranger,...	48
Jehovah-tsidkēnu. I once was a stranger,.................... *M'Cheyne.*	56
I Want to be Like Jesus. I want to be like Jesus,................. *H. Bonar.*	1
Lost, but Found. I was a wandering sheep,............... *H. Bonar.*	15
I will Arise. I will arise and go to my Father,.....	59
Rest for the Weary In the Christian's home in glory,.....	7
Jesus Passing by. Jesus Christ is passing by,............. *Revival Hymn Book.**	36
Ashamed of Jesus. Jesus, and shall it ever be,............ *Gregg.*	55
The Best Robe. Jesus, thy blood and righteousness, *Zinzendorf.*	13
Joyfully, Joyfully. Joyfully, joyfully onward we move,..	47

INDEX.

Title / First line	No.
Just as I am.	
Just as I am, without one plea, *Charlotte Elliott.*	30
Children Called to Christ.	
Like mist on the mountain, *M'Cheyne.*	65
Little Things.	
Little drops of water,	4
The Little Pilgrims.	
Little travellers, Zionward, *Edmeston.*	50
The Shining Shore.	
My days are gliding swiftly by,	52
Thy Will be Done.	
My God, my Father, while I stray, *Charlotte Elliott.*	26
The Great Sacrifice.	
Not all the blood of beasts, *Watts.*	31
Onward, Christian.	
Oft in sorrow, oft in woe, *Kirke White.*	49
Longing after Holiness.	
Oh, for a heart to praise my God, *C. Wesley.*	41
The Best Friend.	
One there is above all others, *Newton.*	44
Homeward Bound.	
Out on an ocean all boundless,	51
Jesus is Mine.	
Pass away, earthly joy, *H. Bonar.*	17
What is Prayer?	
Prayer is the soul's sincere desire, *Montgomery.*	18
Return, O Holy Dove.	
Return, O holy Dove, return, *Cowper.*	11
Return, O Wanderer.	
Return, O wanderer, to thy home, *Hastings.*	12
Rock of Ages.	
Rock of Ages, cleft for me, *Toplady.*	5
Not Lost, but Gone Before.	
Say, why should friendship grieve,	9
Prayer to the Holy Spirit.	
Spirit divine! attend our prayer, *Reed.*	8
Sun of my Soul.	
Sun of my soul, thou Saviour dear, *Keble.*	19
Deeds of Kindness.	
Suppose the little Cowslip *Songs and Hymns by "Uncle John."*	28
Evening Hymn.	
Sweetly we'll join our evening prayer	63
The Mighty Trumpet.	
The blast of the trumpet, so loud, *Revival Hymn Book.*	38
The Fountain Opened.	
There is a fountain filled with blood, *Cowper.*	60
The Heavenly Canaan.	
There is a land of pure delight, *Watts.*	66
Prayer.	
There is an Eye that never sleeps,	62
Praise to Immanuel.	
'Tis the light of gospel story,	58
Truthfulness.	
To speak the truth is always right, *Curwen's "Child's Own Hymn Book."*	42
The Eden Above.	
We're bound for the land of the pure	40
The Realms of the Blest.	
We sing of the realms of the blest,	46
The Worth of Prayer.	
What various hindrances we meet, *Cowper.*	25
Conscience.	
When a foolish thought within, *Taylor.*	45
Mothers of Salem.	
When mothers of Salem,	3
The Harvest Past.	
When the harvest is past,	29
How Much I Owe!	
When this passing world is done, *M'Cheyne.*	43
Who hath Believed?	
Who hath believed?	57

www.ingramcontent.com/pod-product-compliance
Lightning Source LLC
Chambersburg PA
CBHW030549300426
44111CB00009B/912